Worldwords

Global Reflections to Awaken the Spirit

Victor La Cerva, MD

HEAL Foundation Press
Cordova, Tennessee

Published by: **HEAL Foundation Press**
1770 North Germantown Parkway
Cordova, TN 38018

Copyright © 1999 by Victor La Cerva, MD

Printed in the United States of America on acid-free recycled paper

Publisher's Cataloging-in-Publication
(Provided by Quality Books, Inc.)

La Cerva, Victor.
  Worldwords : global reflections to awaken the
spirit / Victor La Cerva. — 1st ed.
   p. cm.
  Includes bibliographic references and index.
  ISBN: 0-9661575-9-1

  1. Peace—Literary collections. 2. Peace—
meditations. 3. Multiculturalism—Literary
collections. 4. Multiculturalism—Meditations.
I. Title.

PN6071 P34L33 1999   808.8'0358
        QB199—477

This book is dedicated to my dear gramps and grandma who gave so much of their love, time, and energy to start me on a good path. They lived their lives with kindness and compassion and taught me to respect, accept, and appreciate everyone I encountered, especially those whose ethnic origins were very different from ours.

Notes of Gratitude

Deepest thanks for my two daughters, Gina and Rosa, who light up my life and keep on teaching me, even when I am a stubborn pupil. May their lives be filled with the gifts of many cultures.

Mille grazie to the circle of men in my life, who enrich my being and generously share their diverse ethnic heritage: Barry, Gaylon, Hank, Harold, John G, John L, Len, Michael, Mitch, Rick and Tim; Juan, a wise and generous amigo; and Steven, the brother I never had. They are always there when I need them most.

I am grateful for the joy and privilege of friendship with Steve, Cori and Madeleine. May the work of HEAL continue to blossom!

Special gracias to Tim Burns for his elegant, glorious line drawings, and for an ongoing, deep, enriching friendship.

Thanks to my friends at Hazelden: Caryn Pernu for her encouragement, and Domenica di Piazzi for her fine editorial work.

Much appreciation to Elisa Troiani of Toward Inc. for her tireless work in researching some complicated word concepts, and for creating the pronunciation guide, so favorite words can more easily enter everyday usage.

Kudos to Pat Patterson, Patterson-Graham Design Group, for cover design and art. Brian Milne, Milne Advertising Design, also assisted with this aspect of the project.

Thanks to Ellen Kleiner for a superb book proposal, and Richard Harris for book layout, and to both for their general wonderfulness.

Heartfelt thanks to Aiko for deepening my understanding of appreciation and compassion, and for the gift of so many beautiful Native American and Japanese word concepts.

Thanks to all those marvelous beings from diverse cultures who offered words for this book: especially Rita, Jan, Helen, Ruth, Estrellita, Evelyn & Mike; Ssu, Dubhaigh, Juan, Harold, Claudia, Susan, Bertrand, Qaiser, and many many more, from the Albanian waiter in a NYC restaurant, to a Yoruba social worker at a conference, to a Korean fellow passenger on an airline flight, to lots of different cab drivers along the way!

Mitakuye Oyasin to my wider circle of friends. You know who you are, and I am honored and blessed by your love and support.

No one writes a book alone. May the voices of all those who contributed to this endeavor fill your heart and mind with peace and wisdom. Enjoy dear reader. Gule gule!

Opening Thoughts

Worldwords is a celebration of language as a vehicle for peacemaking. Amid the extinction of numerous plant and animal species, we tend to overlook the profound silence of disappearing languages, whose gifts we may never harvest. The Americas alone have witnessed a decline from nearly 2,000 native dialects to less than 200 in merely 500 years. As an ancient Hawaiian proverb states, "I ka'olelo no ke ola a me ka make" ("In the language is life and death"). It is the "life" aspect that this book strives to preserve, breathing vitality into words used in hundreds of cultures, keeping a flickering fire growing in the darkness of a long moonless night.

In our search for answers to enigmatic questions about tensions and conflict, we often turn to tribal anecdotes, ancestral lore, lines voiced by gurus- in short, shards of insight from other times and places. These kernels of sagacity attune us to the wisdom already hidden deep within us. They awaken an understanding of who we are as a people engaged in a struggle for social justice, eager to move our communities beyond prejudice and poverty. They create a sacred space, summoning us to fall in love with life again and again, to sail down the river of our imagination as we play the edge.

As we enter this next century, it is imperative for each of us to reclaim the spiritual depth of our lives, and to strengthen our connection with the natural world. Huge portions of our brains are devoted to communication and social interaction. Worldwords are the vessels, the seeds that can carry and disperse collective awareness. When we enlarge the language banquet available to us, we fortify and enhance those values we hold dearest. We begin to appreciate the panoply of concepts that support our relationship with the sacred. We deepen our humanistic impulses, our natural sense of compassion. When words express experiences we have never paid attention to, they become invitations for growth and personal evolution. Our horizon of possibility expands. The vision blossoms, as daily contemplation of multilingual words encourages covenants of understanding across borders, on school playgrounds, at the dinner table and, where it all begins, deep within the heart.

JANUARY

It's all so simple
I'm just too complicated
To figure it out.

nasha hozho (nah-SHAH ho-ZHOW)   Navajo
To walk in the beauty way in one's life and actions.

Our lives are a great gift. We can move, play, eat, make love and work to sustain ourselves. Everyone of us makes a unique contribution to the patterns of creation in the world. When we appreciate the need to find our place in relation to all that is good around us, we begin to comprehend the depth of the worldview known as *nasha hozho*. In this Navajo concept, all life is viewed from the lens of relationships with natural and supernatural forces as well as other human beings. Generosity, affectionate duty to one's kin, pleasant manners, humor and self control are not abstract values but rather essentials of daily existence. Prosperity is not defined by the accumulation of material objects, but by the peace of standing in relation to all of life in a nurturing way that promotes mutual survival through cooperation. Prestige lies in the knowledge one has of songs, dances, stories and practical skills. These are what create harmony and beauty as one moves through the day. When one lives with such balance, then mind body and spirit mingle together in wondrous interplay with all that is.

To walk in beauty is to explore the goodness of all of creation.

January 2

kairos (ky-ROHS)   Greek
Right timing.

How easy to get attached to those days when the flow of life seems seamless. The rhapsody of perfect timing is intoxicating. When we experience *kairos*, everything falls into place effortlessly. It is as if we are tapping into some universal wisdom, being guided by unseen forces. Whether we are engaged in cooking or sports, building a business or a relationship, having good timing enhances our effectiveness. Is it possible to invite such beneficial synchronicity into our lives? It seems to be beyond good luck. Perhaps it is based on being fully present and paying attention. Grounded and centered in our own being, with clear intentions. Another leg on the stool is committed surrender. To stop thinking and to start acting intuitively with trust in whatever technique or training we have developed over time. To know when to act and when to wait, and honor that knowing. When we can apply it to our entire lives, rather than specific circumstances, then we will understand big *kairos*.

I trust that part of me always knows when to act, and when to wait.

**mitakuye oyasin (mee-tah-KOO-yay o-YAH-sheen)   Lakota
We are all related to everyone and everything around us, above
us, below us.**

To walk through the world with new eyes is a desire born in the
depths of our yearning to be one with all that is. The pattern of
rabbit feet in newly fallen snow, the quiet song of an evening bird
before it settles into its nest, harken to all who are observant that
we dance in a fine web of each other's creation. We are patterns
in a tapestry that constantly enriches, rather than confines. When
we utter *mitakuye oyasin*, we are simply acknowledging in a
sacred way that which we know to be true. It is often spoken as
one enters a Lakota sweat lodge on hands and knees. To bring
forth such words is to profoundly accept our humble place in this
vast creation. When we honor our relationship with all the life
with which we share our little planet and fragile existence, we
pray for the wisdom to continue in a good way. We can carry such
awareness through our day, like a sacred candle of understanding,
and allow it to light our path. Just as the life force of all creation
moves in its varied splendor and magnificent bounty, we can live
knowing that all of that existence is in us, and we are part of its
great unfolding.

I honor that I am related to all the life around me, above me and below me.

January 4

mushin (MOO-shin)   Japanese
Empty mind, free of worldly thought.

The calm and silent mind is like the crystal clear sparkle of a mountain lake, or the enveloping embrace of midnight snowfall. There is enormous power to both reflect and absorb. Because such a state is concentrated in present moment, truth is easily discerned. In a world of jet planes and electronic communication, such a mindset seems extraordinary and elusive. When we do achieve *mushin,* things can be perceived exactly as they are, without illusion or emotion. We can grasp life's significance, for intuitively we appreciate the grandeur of clarity. If such conditions as pleasure and pain, gain and loss, like and dislike, are creations of our own mind, then the state of awake and aware inactivity is the doorway to a more expansive universe. A confused mind is its own enemy. It is limiting and narrowing. When the mind is cleansed of all thought movements, our actions are pure and aligned with our deepest purpose. We become like the soaring Zen arrow, at one with its target. We invite the universal to be a part of our own bodymind.

Emptying and calming the mind allows me to touch universal truth.

utang na loob (OO-tahng nah LOW-ob)　　Tagalog
A debt of the heart.

At times the strands of love that connect us to each other are so delicate. Certain friendships fade away as individuals move away or our work together is completed. Somewhere along our journey we realize that certain people will remain in our circle of caring until death calls. In the hurry of our modern world, they may be acquaintances with whom we share only occasional conversation, picking up where we last left off. They are always welcome in our hearts, and there is comfort in just knowing they still walk the planet. Others, with whom we have more frequent contact, reveal more of their lives, and often our bonds deepen through shared experiences. There is another special group of people that hold for us an *utang na loob*. These are the people who were truly there for us at a time of crisis and there is no way to ever fully repay that largesse. Perhaps they were a life-affirming companion when a mate or parent or child died; maybe they took us in when we needed shelter, lent us money, or helped us through the worst of an addiction or illness. It is possible they saved our lives or those of a loved one.. Whatever the action they took, it is etched forever within the deepest recesses of our being.

I honor and acknowledge that which has been given to me that can never be repaid.

January 6

perchten (PERKH-ten)   German
Old masks passed from generation to generation.

Everyone of us desires to communicate our varied identities.
People relate to us in the same old ways, even though we may
have just undergone a significant transformation. In ritual and
theater, opportunity abounds for wearing a face covering which
by virtue of its disguise allows freer expression. Masks contain
great power. The wearer is frequently believed to be possessed by
the spirit inhabiting or represented by the mask. The wood, bas-
ketry, bark, cloth, leather, or papier-mache of a mask is a living
and breathing dwelling for beings that wield influence over
humanity. In Austria the *perchten* are often fearsome animals
called upon to make as much noise as possible in order to scare
winter away. The accompanying dancing, singing, drum beating
and bell ringing complete the ancient custom of attempting to
drive out the cold and darkness of the season. Try wearing a
mask and see who or what emerges as your face is covered and
your unconscious exposed.

I can use a mask to symbolically and playfully initiate a life change.

vade mecum (VAH-deh MAY-koom)   Latin
Go with me; a book for ready reference.

It is always interesting to observe what we pack for vacation. There are so many possible conditions to prepare for; climatic realities and ever-shifting personal desires are usually the most important variables. You have been cultivating a vision of this time, images of desired relaxation, and want to bring what is necessary for such manifestation. You'd prefer to carry only what is most essential for your body-mind-spirit during this interlude. One of the requisite objects on such a list might be a small notebook or journal. With this indispensable *vade mecum*, we can capture random insights, create bits of poetry or songs, draw, jot down new addresses, phone numbers or websites, or reflect on the meaning of life. There is new possibility with every sheet; carrying pen and paper is an act of faith that something worthwhile will eventually fill the pages. Once established as a personal habit, this process becomes a life affirming perspective. Glorious intuitive pearls and synchronistic information begin to flow. This simple tool becomes a conduit for the universe to respond to our intentions. We alter our reality with thoughts, and recording the most useful of them for reflection and later action feeds our future.

I am receptive to whatever insights the universe is offering.

January 8

abigezunt (ah-BEE-guh-zint)   Yiddish
As long as one is healthy nothing else matters.

So often we fail to appreciate something until it is lost. Its place in our lives is taken for granted, sewn into the fabric of our comfort and expectations. When we encounter difficulties we may find it challenging to view what is occurring from a more positive position. It is liberating to reframe an arduous experience so that we truly see its gift. Often we prefer to just whine and complain. As we recite the litany of our current hardships to friends or family, you might be tempted to utter *abigezunt*! This phrase reminds you that when your body is strong and fit you have the energy needed to overcome obstacles, and to enjoy the richness of your vitality. You are capable and can positively influence what happens to you. From this new vantage point you are able to perceive the larger life lessons that are available within any dilemma. When we hear this reminder, we are also aware that our bodies require ongoing conscious attention and care in order to remain salubrious. We can do what is necessary today to assure a healthy tomorrow, engaging in behaviors that honor and nurture the temple of our well-being.

I continue to appreciate and celebrate my non-toothache.

wana (WAH-nah)   Yekuana
Twin ceremonial flutes.

The shrill sound dances just below the canopy, blending with the rainforest like a chameleon changing colors. The resonant sounds renew life, as the emptiness is dispelled by the repetitive rhythms. Awareness is sharpened, harmony is restored and balance reinvigorated. The community is grateful, as the *wana* stabilize their lives. These sacred instruments are kept hidden from anyone not yet initiated into tribal adulthood. Played as much as possible, the flutes demonstrate that there is always an occasion for celebration. Have you forgotten to rejoice at all the goodness in your life? You can discover a way to call forth the remembrance of what is good and wholesome in your daily existence. Perhaps it is a song, a phrase, or even a special instrument that lifts its voice in gleeful recognition, just for the sake of sanctification, a message of thanks to the spirit world.

I play a song of simple joy.

January 10

Ekeko (ay-KAY-ko)   **Aymara**
God of prosperity.

Many people confuse comfort with happiness or wealth with success. It is easy to get caught in a trap of working more and enjoying the job less, constantly striving for the next level which we are convinced will bring the delight we so desperately seek. Meanwhile there is little energy and time left for relationships, the true source of fulfilling nourishment. This is the time to honor *Ekeko*, whose wisdom is clear and compelling. Prosperity is having enough of what sustains our lives, in balanced relation to others getting what they need. For many of us the definition of enough is the sticking point. Enough often translates as just a little more, sowing the seeds of discontent. The best way to get what we want is to help others get what they want. If we seek attention and affection, then we can strive to give away more of it; abundance increases when we help others expand their own plenitude. Guilt fear and insecurity are demons easily cast out when we hold fast to a renewed vision of bounty in our lives.

I invite abundance and judge my success by the amount of peace joy and health I experience.

dephase (day-fah-ZAY)   French
To feel out of it.

We all have those days when enthusiasm for life seems elusive.
The dominant energy is somewhat depressed and we want to
crawl under the sheets and disappear, or not get out of bed at all.
If you manage to muster enough energy to get about the business
of daily engagement with the world, there is a definite mood of
being *dephase*. Every aspect of your being seems affected and out
of synch; the body protests any demonstration of liveliness, concentration is difficult, and we may feel disconnected. Whether the
stars are the cause or just mid-season blues, understanding why
is less essential than accepting and gently redirecting whatever is
occurring. Since productivity is out of the question, try to yield
your sense of control, and initiate some small action that allows
you to get a bit more centered. Observe the flow of this frag-
mented space, and be a witness to your own confusion.
Gradually you will emerge from this fog, and rediscover that the
pulse of life continues strong and steady.

Temporary loss of focus sometimes brings new insights.

January 12

angiqsarait (ahn-jeeq-SAH-rah-eet)   **Inuktitut**
Ready to accommodate.

Blaming others is a form of resistance to life. When we refuse to accept the imperfect perfection of here and now, we often look for someone to scapegoat. When we force a situation we often feed resistance. Both blaming and forcing waste energy. Better to rest in being **angiqsarait**. No defense is needed, no fight required to maintain a certain point of view. Only acceptance is cultivated. When someone realizes they do not have to force their ideas, opinions or desires upon you, a different relational quality is experienced. We become a neutral container that can hold whatever needs to be expressed. Many women in our culture have been trained to practice this acceptance, and have also experienced the abuse of male power and privilege. We incorrectly view accomodation and abuse as cause and effect. The ability to adapt is a powerful attribute; abuse must not be tolerated. To be willing to surrender like a willow in the wind, to be egoless like a leaf on a stream, is a position of strength. Such non-attachment in a potential confrontation does not indicate a lack of healthy boundaries; rather it reinforces the reality that lighthearted cooperation is a skill worth mastering.

Without experiencing abuse, I can embrace the freedom in allowing others to have their way.

qawwali (kaw-WAH-lee)   Urdu
Improvisational singer whose goal is to induce devotional ecstasy.

There is often a song in our hearts crying out to be sung. We learn early in life that unless we are particularly gifted, we should refrain from such expression except when alone in the proverbial shower. Singing along with the radio in a car might pass social muster; campfire collective melodies and carolling often fall in the realm of accepted public vocal utterances. The voice of the *qawwali* links intense passion to spiritual communication. Listening to such artistry evokes the bliss of contacting the divine. To find your true voice and raise it in song is to praise creation. To burst into spontaneous scat is to invite others to discover the depth of sacred feelings within themselves. The sacred chamber of our body is meant to hold song. Our whole beings yearn to reverberate with the tones of life, the rhythms of the universe.

Today I will feel the power of my own singing.

January 14

granzevolk (GRAAHN-tsay-folk)   German
Visionary people who live on the fringes of society.

We tend to have contact mostly with people who are just like us. When we share common styles of living, basic values, and interests, we feel comfortable and our perspectives are reaffirmed. The diversity of life on our planet is overwhelming and while we enjoy new experiences, there is something reassuring about the safety and reliability of the known. Yet we can be grateful that there are always some *granzevolk* among us, who are eager to explore the new and uncertain. Many individuals who contributed much to the advancement of humanity were rejected by their own peers. Considered weird or simply foolish, they were relegated to the margins of their societies. When you discover the internal aspects you share with remarkable persons, you touch your own dynamic idealism. Why not begin a conversation with an inner guide who resides beyond the limited realm of the acceptable? Perhaps you will uncover something remarkable.

Exploring my fixed boundaries brings surprise.

favela (fah-VEH-lah)   Portuguese
Impoverished sprawling hillside town.

Poverty cripples the human spirit and becomes more destructive over time. The poor often are afflicted with terrible health and suffer disproportionately from the twin scourges of violence and substance abuse. Self defining and self defeating, the impoverished mind folds in upon itself, severely limiting perceived options. The *favela* is there for all to see. In any ghetto the lack of basic services and financial resources leads to a declining spiral of misery and hopelessness. Racist policies contribute to the economic oppression. Children who come from such circumstances yet succeed usually benefitted from the ongoing support of at least one caring healthy adult in their lives. Such a presence expands practical opportunities and functions as a psychic mirror, reflecting a different image of what is possible. Perhaps the time has come for you to be a caring person for a youngster living in poverty.

I will extend my hand to someone in need through scouting, mentoring, being a big brother or sister, or involvement with my faith community.

January 16

pampero (pahm-PAY-roh)   Spanish
A wind that makes all the noises of man in various states of excitement.

The range of human vocal expression is enormous. We grunt, sigh, moan and ululate our way through life. This medley of emotional release originates within a primitive brain section and is often unconscious. How wonderful it is to find yet another region of ourselves that is mostly unknown territory! Like the wild and explosive *pampero*, the diversity of internal voices waiting to be unleashed is astounding. Generated within every nook of our emotional closets, such sounds emerge in dramatic bursts of turmoil and pleasure. Evocative utterances are your inner thunder; they herald sweet release and the dissipation of tension. Dynamic instability predominates as these fervent forces permeate your surroundings. It is as if your body is being wiped clean from inside, the way a swirling wind removes and scatters debris.

I listen to the wind and hear within it my own murmurings.

rasa (RAH-sah)   Sanskrit
The essential flavor of deep artistic experience.

The thrill of aesthetic pleasure cannot be adequately described by words. There is an intoxicating quality that invites us to seek further and return for more. We are inspired to expand our perspective and allow new impressions to evolve within us. Such exhilaration is transmitted by the *rasa* of the painting, poem or musical composition. What manifests is the delicious aroma and sensual taste of art, love and eroticism. The feelings elicited by such blessed passion are sacred. These exciting emotions are not just temporarily evoked; they often persist in a body memory one can savor again. Like being reunited with a lover from whom you have been separated, there is a mixture of powerful sentiments, a sense of resonance with what is most important. Whenever they do arise, these experiences strengthen the inner ground of peace and satisfaction. They are an offering of joyous light for darkened inner landscapes. Let them shine in all their magnificence, and drink deeply of their transformative fragrance.

In all its glorious manifestations, art carries me to higher consciousness.

January 18

susu (soo-soo)   **English Creole**
Be quiet; often said to a child in a soft way.

A culture can be judged by how it treats its children. When children are the recipients of consistent love and respect they gradually appreciate how to nurture others. Our offspring do as we do and not as we say. *Susu* evokes a gentle image of relating to a child. The word itself embodies a quality and value we are seeking to transmit intergenerationally. It declares that the role of adults is to provide direction and guidance while inviting cooperation. Compassion and understanding are more important than power and control. Almost a whisper, one can feel the tone of caring and caressing implicit in the request for silence. Tender words teach more effectively than shouts and lectures. They can be a soothing balm of affection and acceptance that open the heart to the path of peace.

I approach children today with the kindness and gentle touch I seek for myself.

aubade (OH-bad)   **French**
Morning music.

Soft colors gently rise as the dawn of a new day stretches across the eastern sky. Birds warm themselves and sing the praises of another unfolding symphony of light. There is a sweet stillness in the air, before human busyness takes control. The memories of the daily din are still distant as the world slowly wakes up. Such is the time of *aubade*. Serene, calm and uplifting tones of simple elegant delight transition us from the dreamtime into activity. Those who discover the beauty of this early morning time find a richness that nourishes the soul. Starting your day with meditation, the sunrise, a brisk run, or a poem sets a joyous beginning tempo. It can be a special time just for you, an occasion for prayer in whatever form appeals to your sense of enchantment. The very idea of commencing the day with an act that nourishes our deepest self is a powerful statement of intent. By embracing yourself at the onset, you issue an invitation for the rest of the day to move with beauty and benevolence.

I start each day with a song of joy and a form of prayer.

January 20

talanoa (tah-lah-NO-uh)   **Hindi**
Small talk as social glue.

Huge parts of our brain are devoted to social interaction. As babies we are capable of uttering sounds from every known language. As we learn to make our needs known verbally in our own tongue, we enter the realm of *talanoa*. Chitchat becomes a key ingredient for building community. Frivolous conversation acquires an elevated status when we appreciate its bonding nature. In giving such a small gift of our time and attention, you let another know that they are valued and needed. You get a snapshot of their lives to place in your heart. Maybe they speak of some details about the current weather or a favorite TV show; perhaps they reveal what they enjoy eating or offer rambled opinion about an item in the news. Given the opportunity many begin to share more significant aspects of their lives. As the protective onion skin peels, layers of their reality unfold in little stories of their children or passions. The mutual exchange of such vignettes, while framed in the context of idle talk, is really a revelation of the resilience of the human spirit.

The act of talking shapes and maintains relationships.

Awoojoh (ah-WOOH-joj)   Yoruba
Thanksgiving feast honoring the spirits of the dead in which all family disputes are settled.

Some of the most painful situations in your life occur within your extended families. Instead of a rich network of support and assistance, you may be faced with hatred and resentment. Grudges can go on for a lifetime, even after the original participants have passed on. Like a fossilized judgement set in stone, such disagreements can significantly alter the course of your personal history. In Sierra Leone, *Awoojoh* is a solution to such destructive patterns. Because the spirits of the dead are believed to have influence over the fortunes of the living, honoring the dead and inviting their participation is part of everyday consciousness. Feasting begins after a visit to the cemetery and a divination practice to receive a message from the departed. As a prelude to this celebration all quarrels must be settled. Both family members and invited guests, which in a small community may include the entire village, strive to discuss and peacefully resolve their differences. Settling controversies in this way acknowledges the value of cooperation. It sanctifies the peacekeeping work of our ancestors which provided the foundation for the life that presently sustains us.

I will use the occasion of a deceased relative's birthday to release resentments toward another family member.

January 22

kopiec (ko-PE-ts)   Polish
Earthen mounds erected in honor of great people.

People mould and shape our journey. Individuals whose vision and actions combined to benefit the greater good of many live on through their speeches and books; their ideas have universal relevance despite the changing of the times. Sometimes their contributions are appreciated only in the country which nurtured and sustained them. Larger than life, they represent the best of human creative expression. The *kopiec* is a symbol of both reverence and humility. Simple and elegant, these large structures memorialize those who made a difference. It seems right and fitting to also pay homage to those less well-known yet influential people in your own life. There were those beings who extended a hand to you when it was most needed. How they lived reminded you of your own psychic gold, the inner light found by engaging in what one loves. They will always be great in your eyes, and deserve an eternal monument in your heart.

Through some symbolic gesture I honor today those who have inspired me.

Nyambutan (nyahm-BOO-tahn)   Balinese
Ceremony when a baby is first allowed to touch the ground.

Babies trigger in us many instinctual responses. Caretakers will often unconsciously speak in a higher pitched voice, and hold the infant on the left side of their chest where they might hear the adult's heartbeat. With their constant demands, young ones offer more opportunities to deepen our patience, understanding, and giving. The Balinese culture truly honors infants as spiritual teachers with the special occasion of *Nyambutan*. Because they are considered to still be part of the spirit world for a few months, and not fully in human form, infants must never touch the ground. Balinese parents carry their babies continuously during the day, and reassure the infants by their presence in the family bed at night. Such constant touch and ready comfort early in life makes for highly secure and generous people. What was the mindset of the culture during your first few months of life?

Contact with babies reminds me of both the gifts and the wounds I received during that critical time in my development.

January 24

**inallaaduwi (ee-nah-LLAH-du-wee) Palaihnihan
Seemingly not connected to anything, meaning the destructive
aspects of the white man.**

For millennia humans cooperated and shared in a more harmonious balance with their planetary home. Sacred places, rituals, pilgrimages, and animal spirit relationships continually forged and strengthened a spiritual relationship with the natural world. Waste was not an option in the shifting cycles of abundance and scarcity of life-giving plants, water, and animals. Look around at your daily life and notice how much careless misuse of resources is present. To the extent that your existence is *inallaaduwi*, you will persist in an empty cycle of accumulating more material goods and enjoying them less. Fear and insecurity will continue to fuel the constant desire to fill up the inner void with power and possessions. By creating a simpler lifestyle, more of you is available for experiences that bond you to what is most important and essential. Time stretches out and suddenly the wooded walk or time by the ocean is not just something else on your list; it becomes the north star of your personal values, guiding you to a richer existence.

I am paying attention to and deepening my attachment to nature.

ama sua, ama llula, ama qella (AH-mah SOO-ah, AH-mah LYOO-lah, AH-mah QUE-lyah)   Quechua
Do not be a thief, do not be a liar, do not be lazy.

Our perception of what is most important to us is changeable. Yet the stable principles that guide our daily behaviors act as a rudder steering us through varying conditions. Values have to do with ways of being that foster giving rather than receiving. Standards of our actions and attitudes of our hearts, they shape who we are, how we live, and how we treat other people. *Ama sua, ama llula, ama qella*! The Incas used this phrase to say "good day". The appropriate response was "I wish you the same." Thus a compact would be formed through simple social exchange that reinforced socially desirable tenets. Have respect for property, for nature, and for the beliefs and rights of others. Develop the inner strength and confidence that is bred by exacting truthfulness, trustworthiness, and integrity. Maintain reliability and consistency in doing what you say you will do, with an awareness of natural consequences and the law of the harvest: what we sow is what we shall reap.

My daily greetings remind me of the fundamental truths that orient my life.

January 26

sabsung (SOB-soong)   **Thai**
To satisfy an emotional or spiritual thirst.

How attached we can be to what we beg to be released from! The haze of irritation and annoyance is thick. You may know that something is wrong with your life, yet be unable to identify exactly what it is. An emotional storm of human weather has us firmly in its fury. We spread our stress and anger all over the living room, oblivious to whomever might be in its path. Time out! Take just the first little step to make yourself feel better. Immerse your spirit in something wonderful and feel the rejuvenation and light permeate and release the tension and upset. To *sabsung* is to allow sacred refreshment. Like winter snows that deeply nourish thirsty mountain meadows, it is a process of gradually allowing contentment into our lives. When we quench our innermost longings, we celebrate our capacity for renewal. Music, art, food, people, contact with nature can all alter our immediate consciousness for the better. We choose to move beyond our uptight constricted worldview. We let in whatever is needed right now.

I acknowledge I have spiritual and emotional needs that can be satisfied.

tasadimos (tah-sah-DEE-mos)   **Romany**
Pregnant with tears.

We all recognize those first moans of sadness that come from depths untouched for so long. There is the catching of the breath as painful groans begin to emerge in spurts from a shaking body. The urge to surrender, to embrace being *tasadimos* is compelling. We feel a choking, suffocating, stifling sense of strangulation or drowning because of being so full of tears. The only choice is to cry! The waves of wailing sorrow drown attempts to speak, sentences are broken by the storm's fury, the body simply collapses into the moment. A good cry helps us remain open and vulnerable to life. It is through such cleansing that you are renewed, able to go on. When you are unable or unwilling to cry, then your grief will transform into anger and fears that will only cause tears in another. Tears flow from a well of inner strength, not weakness. There is also the sweet joy in those soft snifflings as the face relaxes, and the deep sighs and palpable calm of release signal that another part of another wound is healed. It is such gentle human rain that washes away the violence within and around us.

I welcome the delicious abandon of a good cry.

January 28

Windigos (WEEN-dee-go)   Cree
Monsters or demons.

There are many things to be genuinely afraid of; they include being physically hurt, mentally incompetent, emotionally wounded or spiritually lost. But fear often constricts or distorts energy, producing confusion. Fear can also be the mindtalk that prevents you from hearing your intuition. Its walls of protection become your self imposed prison. Most of us react by attempting to control these scary feelings, which produces more fear, since life is essentially uncontrollable. Fear produces dangerous *Windigos*, those that live inside, lurking in the recesses of one's shadow side, those negative aspects of the self we prefer to keep hidden, even from ourselves. These internal ogres can be important teachers, marshalling resources you did not know existed, reminding you to stay awake and alert. Develop a curiosity about your inner beasts. Walk their edge. Have a conversation with them. What you don't speak to, you don't understand. What you don't understand, you fear. What you fear, you often destroy. Courage is the willingness to act in spite of our fears. It is accepting your demons, your reluctance, your instinct to flee, and starting from there.

I can face my inner fears whenever they arise.

eneenin'kujit (ay-naa-nin-'koo-jeet)   Masai
A cathedral of seven old trees where the grass sheaves are tied.

Developing sacred space is an intimate and creative process. The preparation of the self and the space alters consciousness. Once we enter it, a threshold is crossed that allows access to our archetypal wisdom. Magical places can be mythic and legendary sites, such as lookouts in Hawaii, or rock art caves in Australia or the American Southwest. They can be vision questing and dreaming places, fertility sites, historical locales, sunrise ceremonial points. They are found everywhere, and are not limited to those that are well known. The *eneenin'kujit* is a special gathering place for the Masai people of eastern Africa, used over years for essential work and communal sharing. Have you created a place of healing, purification and divine renewal? It might be a favorite spot in the woods, a private shrine or altar in your home, a sacred plant or animal location near the ocean to which certain creatures or flowers seasonally return. Each specific space becomes alive with its own special qualities as you use it, feeding what is most essential for your growth and continued spiritual evolution.

I will spend time soon at a personally consecrated site.

January 30

melmastia (mell-MAHS-tee-ah)   Pashto
Hospitality to all visitors without expectation of reward.

To live the complex concept of *melmastia*, we need to understand rather than confront. Other important ingredients include the ability to make and keep friends, helpfulness, cheerfulness and gentleness, particularly toward those who are younger or weaker. Finally we must have generosity of both mind and spirit manifested in the willingness to share material goods. This magnanimous mixture is grounded in the realization that the entire universe is generous and expansive. Perhaps these giving attributes are rooted in the memory of hardship, of cold nights in mountain passes or hungry times for wandering nomadic tribes. When your benevolent actions are motivated by love, abundance multiplies and accumulates. Having an openhanded spirit as the reference point, rather than power over others or approval from them, allows you to harness energy for continued right action. A dynamic uplifting spiral is established which generates and expands goodness for all.

I give freely and openly out of love.

per cento anni (payr CHEN-toh AHN-nee)   Italian
A toast; may you live your bliss for a hundred years.

One hundred people gather to celebrate human interaction. Men are caring, nurturing, open, communicative, gentle, strong and kind. Women are capable, assertive, powerful, creative, compassionate and loving. Everyone has access to each of these qualities, and we can learn to be a healing presence for each other. Both young and old are honored for their unique gifts. A community of open arms greets those who have just arrived. Blessings are exchanged and a toast is proposed. *Per cento anni!* May you experience everything you desire, and grow into the fullness of who you are. There is such a rich tapestry of human emotion and possibility, and every experience contains its own indescribable sweetness. Life-centered present-moment awareness can immerse you in the eternity of here and now. By using your imagination and intentionality, each stage of the journey offers its own delights. Passion and serenity find they share the same home, companions on the quest for a long healthy life. This salute invites you to discard more of the shoulds and ought tos that weigh you down, and to reclaim the joy of living fully and with gusto.

I celebrate the marvelous gift of just being alive.

FEBRUARY

Morning light whispers
All your answers lie inside
Welcome mystery

bihtere gelechtr (ah-BIT-ter-in guh-LEJ-ter)   **Yiddish**
Laughter through tears; bitter laughter.

Human feelings are an interconnected complex emotional ecosystem. Many people are confused when trying to sort out the basics of intense and transient emotions such as mad sad glad and afraid. Sometimes there is no dominant chord; rather a free floating symphony of sensations rules. People may cry when they are happy because the predominant sentiment is one of relief. A loved one has come through a difficult time, or arrived safely after an arduous journey. *Bihtere gelechtr* reflects the opposite end of the spectrum, where life's difficulties seem so overwhelming that one comprehends the absurdity of trying to maintain control. In the midst of sinking deeper into despair, one sees the humor in the situation and appreciates any small impulse that briefly lightens the load. A joke is made or a light hearted statement about what will go wrong next, and suddenly there is the surprise of laughter. Current hardships remind you of the great resiliency residing in the human spirit.

Crying is a natural and easy way of releasing strong feelings.

February 2

bith'haa (peet-h 'hah)   Tohono O'odham
Making decisions as if cooking with a clay pot.

Our hopelessness is often less challenging to others than to ourselves. There are those periods when confusion is the dominant chord. Whenever there seem to be only two apparent choices, try to wait for the third to emerge! If a decision affects an entire community, the process is likely to be even more complex. Time to remember *bith'haa*. As when cooking beans over a fire, the large clay cooking pot holds many ingredients—beans, water, salt spices. The simmering takes a long time with lots of slow percolating. The beans are ready not when the clock says they are, but when it is time for them to be done. This nonlinear approach applies to resolving conflicts or making important determinations. Many people are involved in the mix and ideas need to be slowly stirred and stimulated. The final judgment, in order to be harmonious and reasonable, comes after time, but only by consensus and when sufficient blending of viewpoints has taken place. The process cannot be rushed, for if it is, the results are inedible.

I have all the time I need to make up my mind about something of consequence.

wu wei (woo way)   Chinese
Continuous letting go of expectations.

Why do we have to give it up to get it? Detachment from a specific expectation allows the universe free play in assisting you. It declares that any intention must be held lightly so there are many possibilities to create the energy needed for it to manifest. The wisdom of uncertainty is honored. In order to experience the flow of *wu wei*, enormous trust is required. Life does provide. Simply acknowledge that your power is always in the present moment. The past is history, the future mystery and right now is where life is lived. Yet much of daily life seems to conspire against such a worldview. Planning out our week or weekend consumes our attention and suspends spontaneity. Paying the monthly bills uses up our life energy, and this special quality of just reveling in the present moment seems elusive. Perhaps the cosmic plan has designs for you more expansive than the ones you have spawned. By remaining alert but not tense, non active but not passive, and relaxed yet intensely concentrated, the way is cleared for your strongest desires to be fulfilled.

Today I expect nothing but am ready for anything.

February 4

pi say (pee say)   Burmese
Traditional protective tattooing.

From the time of the remotest antiquity, cultures worldwide have engaged in various practices to enhance the beauty of the human form. Ancient peoples employed a large variety of jewelry, cosmetics, hairstyles, body painting or tattooing and scarification. Intricate patterns of hair braiding, beading, plaiting or elaborate skin designs indicated social rank or tribal affiliation. Sometimes such adornments were a sign of mourning, or achievement of new status. *Pi say* is a specific form of body decoration believed to magically guard against injuries from weapons. While getting a tattoo may not be a high priority for you, considering the notion can be a revealing exploration. If we think of a skin embellishment as the personal equivalent of a flag or family crest, then the statement a tatoo makes could represent an essential aspect of your core beliefs. What design might you choose, and what would it represent?

I can enjoy discovering what body enhancements are most appealing to me as external declarations of inner transformations.

meldado (mell-DAH-tho)   Ladino
A gathering that focuses on reading spiritual literature togeth-er.

Finding a community of kindred spirits is uplifting. We feel accepted and blessed. Shared interests can bind us together in healthy and productive ways. We examine new perspectives and learn from each other in a co-operative environment that potentially brings forth the best in each member. Whether it is a regular support group, a self-help meeting for ending addiction or abuse, or a flyfishing club, such gatherings enhance communication and forward human development. The existence of a *meldado* offers the possibility of sacred evolution. It actively demonstrates that reflection and contemplation are not limited to the personal realm. Much can be revealed through the communal traverse of spiritual terrain. Inspiring passages reveal their hidden mysteries in the light of minds and hearts meeting together. There are some truths that can only be discovered by collective concentration and analysis. Group insights expand and set free individual perceptions. Together the assemblage establishes an inquisitive force, which can be more powerful than private prayer, that reaps benefits for all.

I can find a spiritual community that animates my path.

February 6

kuden (KOO-den)   Japanese
Gems of secret guidance passed on orally by mentors.

There are no experts, only learners sharing the path of mastery. You are charged with the joys and responsibilities of teaching those who walk behind you, and learning from those whose steps have already passed your way. A mentor can guide a young person through various disciplines, facilitating the labyrinthian passage into adulthood. Serving as both parent and peer, such persons inspire dreams by who they are and how they live. A Buddhist concept of whispered transmission from teacher to student refers to the most vital aspects of oral tradition, the esoteric teachings that are never written down. Strict rendering of these certain elements of teaching is demanded, and a break in a single generation would mean their loss forever. The Japanese word for such teachings is *kuden*. They are gifts from a master who guides you, provides counsel in discouraging times, and offers new learning opportunities. These kernels of wisdom encourage you to play your edge, to consciously explore just beyond your limits.

I embrace the guidance of my teachers, and the responsibility of instructing others.

yah ah tay (yaj-aj-tay-EEJ)   Navajo
A form of greeting meaning it is good.

Language describes as well as shapes and controls events. Some cultures consider the initial words spoken to a newborn to be extraordinarily important, since this first communication must provide both blessings and protection. There is a time immediately post-partum when the average newborn is extremely quiet, alert and responsive, gazing for a long time at parents or caretakers. At such a moment in Navajo tradition, their little hand is grasped by a family member, and *yah ah tay* is murmured softly. Besides wishing the newcomer well on their journey, this salutation acknowledges the child as a separate being, worthy of respect and capable of having their own voice in the world. Every time this greeting is later used, it reinforces the basic tenet that only by treating each other with such esteem can life be good. Imagine how this simple salutation might consistently and cumulatively alter your relationships. You would hold another's hand as you greet them and in that instant of hello honor the other being as a separate and unique individual with their own place of beauty in the world. You openly communicate that because of such mutual acceptance all is in a good way.

I will use greeting another person as an opportunity for meaningful exchange.

isumaqsayuq (ee-sue-mahq-SAH-yooq)   Inuktitut
To cause thought; a conscious method of instruction.

We learn through socialization about our basic emotions, how to resolve conflict, and how to treat men and women. By modeling the behaviors of the human beings raising us we form perceptions about right and wrong. But if our first teachers are confused about these essentials, they pass on to us patterns of being in the world that contribute to turmoil or to unhappiness. In cultures that value the avoidance of conflict and aggression, to be angry with a child is considered demeaning, demonstrating one's own immaturity. *Isumaqsayuq* is a dramatic technique that instructs young children how to resolve conflict. Warm and tender interactions stimulated by questions and dramas create the safe context in which dangerous thoughts and attendant emotions can be recreated and explored in the young child. Envy, jealousy, possessiveness, humiliation, and doubts about being loved are dramatized. "Do you love your new baby sister? Why don't you kill her?" asks the parent. This process brings to conscious awareness feelings the child may already be experiencing, and creates the possibility of safely exploring deep concerns in a playful, affectionate way. The child begins to learn that there are many feelings that must not be acted upon for the sake of group harmony. Asking ourselves essential questions throughout our lives is an extension of this marvelous practice.

Today I can safely explore a disturbing question that has been troubling me.

shoshit (sho-sheet)   Albanian
To discuss a problem as if sifting flour.

The toddler's protests of "no" and "mine" herald a new stage of development. We rebel against those with power and control who force their will upon us. Because of early unpleasant experiences with disagreements, we may refuse to state our point of view for fear of retaliation or of causing hurt feelings. Blaming, emotional withdrawal, or angry venting are ineffective methods of relating. A more loving and peaceful method of resolving differences does not support revenge, aggression, or retaliation. When we encourage *shoshit*, we engage in productive communication, and seek first to understand the other's perspective. Like screening out impurities so only the purest ingredients are left, we see to the heart of the matter. Through active listening and respectful sharing the various nuances of the dilemma are gradually uncovered, and the range of possible solutions fully explored. What matters is not who is right and who is wrong, but rather what agreements will feel good to all involved. Disagreements are a sign of vitality: they catalyze our personal growth, deepen our relationships, and, when approached skillfully and sensitively, permit everyone to win.

When in conflict I focus on solutions rather than blame.

February 10

narahati (nah-rah-HAH-tee)   Farsi
Experiencing a wide range of negative emotions.

Each day we face many possibilities for irritation and annoyance. When we view the world from a clouded reference point, everything becomes tainted. Hearing news on the radio, waiting in line at the store, wearing shoes that are a bit too tight, an interaction with a relative can all can be vehicles for the generation of *narahati*, the mixed sensations of feeling depressed, disappointed, inconvenienced and restless at the same time. Silence or sulkiness may be ways of communicating your distress. One may feel powerless and vulnerable, or fearful of being exploited or permanently stuck in an undesirable situation. Breathe slowly and deeply, and start by doing something small and easy to make yourself feel just a bit better physically. In order to avoid continuing to generate such a complex emotional brew, it is important to speak kindly, softly and courteously to ourselves. Positive self talk is the key that unlocks this prison. "I choose peace this moment" or some other practiced phrase can reconnect us to a calm inner center. When you refuse to let go of these feelings they often pass on to others or convert to complaints about bodily discomfort. Be compassionate with yourself; an attitudinal shift rather than more struggle can help alter the course.

Whenever I enter a state of upset I treat myself with loving kindness.

oleg (OH-leng)   Bahasa Indonesia
The swaying of the dancer in a flirting dance.

Two bumblebees dance in early morning sunlight. Their flight is smooth and sensual, as each caresses the space around the other. The duet is subdued and seductive, mischievously filling the garden with magic. As the circle of flight grows smaller, their teasing increases. Such pleasing movements are typical of the artistry involved in *oleg*. One need not travel to Bali to witness the essence of such romantic interplay. Any cafe offers ample opportunity to observe the delicate flowing of love's blossoming. All the elements are there; a sensuous sweep of the hands, eyes that embrace briefly, body motions that woo while pretending to be unaffected by the other's presence. Any human mating dance contains the suggestive charm of conquest, haughtiness, and the temperamental push-pull of teasing and affectionate caresses. Whenever you encounter a person you find attractive the unconscious performance begins. Easy to see in others, it may remain hidden from your own awareness. Making it known to yourself not only entertains but teaches and reveals much about what you are yearning for.

I will reflect on how I use my alluring energy.

February 12

oc ye nechca (ok yea NAYCH-kah)   **Nahuatl**
This is a true story.

Stories are formed in the collective dark night of our psyche; that is why a legend told in one culture can often be shared by any people. Story means storehouse of knowledge, and tales draw their power from the archetypal world, with themes common to all humanity. Although told in a cultural context, each story contains universal wisdom. Every narrative speaks to us in literal, psychological and mythological ways. *Oc ye nechca* is a traditional opening for many well loved tales of indigenous Mexican peoples. In some traditions storytellers hold the young in the lap when stories are told, so that both body and mind of the listener receive the teachings. Tales can be gathered like sticks and shells and feathers, and then strung together. The Yombe people on the Congo River in central Africa string such objects together as memory devices for learning songs. As each object is touched, part of the yarn is recounted. You can create an epic with bits and pieces of your own memories. Such a process touches your mind and imagination, as well as the unconscious depths, where it may remain through many years, surfacing intermittently to yield new insights. Learn the old stories, create new ones, and become a storyteller yourself.

The art of learning and sharing an appealing story is life affirming.

roogoodoo (roo-goo-doo)   English Creole
Noisy disturbance.

Stillness and quiet penetrate deeply. They resonate at a frequency of peace and calm that the universe provides as a balm for the senses. The natural world offers an abundance of silence punctuated only by the sounds of wind and sea and animal life. Our existence in an intense age of technology sometimes assaults our faculties, contributing to stress and irritability. Many people seek the comfort of solitude in parks and other quiet enclaves. You are most likely to encounter a *roogoodoo* in a crowded city environment. Such onomatopoeic intrusions have their own timing and rhythms. Each is disruptive in a distinct fashion: a loud party, an altercation between intimates, the piercing screeches of emergency vehicles on their way to a scene, the intrusion of motorized hubbub on a trail. The appropriate response also varies, yet is both assertive and compassionate. You may not be able to control disruptions as they unfold, but there is always opportunity to creatively shape and shift your responses to them.

I can manage intrusions into my sense of peace.

February 14

priya (PREE-yuh)   **Sanskrit**
The beloved.

We have been with each other all along. It is as if our whole lives have been a journey to bring us to this moment of finding the beloved at last. Whispering, we speak each other's names with reverence, and the sound of the other's voice is uplifting to our spirit. To gaze into their eyes, and see there an old friend, a companion of many lifetimes, a unique being, is to embrace our *priya*, in a form of prayer. Relationship can be a devotional, spiritual, practice of awakening. When we are really able to see with the heart, and appreciate that our most intimate partner is only a universal breath away, we are filled with gratitude for the truth and beauty of what is present, now in this moment together. Walls of fear come down, and this beloved person is appreciated for the mirror they are to our own true nature. Beyond the old ideas of our self, we guide each other to new realities. Most of us can taste and savor such moments of connection, but rarely can we bring such light into permanent focus. A glimpse is enough to remind us that it is possible to be fully accepted as we are, and to experience the intimacy we long to create.

I am bringing conscious awareness and reverence to my relationship with my beloved.

teleios (TEH-lay-ohs)   Greek
Fully complete.

There is a restlessness inherent in human nature. Perhaps it is a drive unique to a species intent on rapid evolution and growth. Though difficult to define, whatever is missing seems important. Like happiness, satisfaction seems elusive, a transient state experienced intensely but all too briefly. We experience a vague sense of being unfulfilled in some way, of facing obstacles still to be surpassed before real life begins. Many spend their whole lives searching outside of themselves for a completeness that is already present within. The concept of being *teleios* describes the opposite sentiment. It speaks of contentment and acceptance, consummation and wholeness. You may encounter its serenity in a sunset walk, a theatrical performance, a conversation, or a child's imaginative play. Like beads strung into a necklace, individual life experiences have a cohesion and pattern obvious only as they accumulate. Unless each is appreciated for the individual gift it is, then accumulating more is an endless and meaningless pursuit. The more you allow the sensation of being replete to permeate your daily life, the more it becomes descriptive of your entire existence.

I welcome the joy of feeling satisfied.

February 16

muatupu (MWAH-tu-pu)   Uto-Aztecan
An elder.

Old people don't protect you with their bodies, but with their
spirit. Keepers of cultural and family history, the elderly are
repositories of lessons learned through generations. They have
learned to acknowledge, listen to, and act upon their own inner
wisdom. *Muatupu* represents knowledge, reflection, insight, and
cleverness on the one hand, and moral strengths such as goodwill
and readiness to help on the other hand. In tribal cultures the
aged are almost always the guardians of the community's mysteries and laws. An essential task of elders is to affirm young
people by asking them the important questions of who, why,
whence and whither to stimulate self reflection, and to help
mobilize a concentration of powers. The questions themselves
cultivate seeds of awareness, and the ongoing dialogue brings
assurance and increased possibility of success. Only the young
can walk through the door of their own future. But the elder is the
one who can present an opportunity for awareness that helps in
the preparation for the challenge.

*As I move toward elderhood I become more aware of the gifts I have to
share.*

ben detto (bayn DAYt-toh)   Italian
Well said!

Many people are trapped in the belief that it is better to swallow their own truth than create conflict by discussing it. Over time, withholding emotionally produces an erosion of trust, and an eventual pouring forth of repressed hostility. Collective lightening of an invisible load occurs when the truth is spoken. Heads nod in agreement as a palpable stillness embraces all who are present. The relief is particularly cleansing when the issue has been a difficult and uncomfortable one to raise. The impact for the listening hearts is enormous. One might be tempted to exclaim *"ben detto!"* whenever someone has handled a difficult situation with honesty and tact, verbally righted a wrong, or skillfully praised another for their contribution. This phrase is testimony that words can be truthful and can mend rather than hurt. Sometimes the clarity and passion with which a statement has been delivered demands this utterance of forceful agreement. With this phrase we stand up to be counted, and affirm what has just been revealed. It is verbal applause, a recognition of the care and sensitivity with which an insight has been articulated.

I openly respond when truth is clearly expressed.

February 18

Kumbh Mela (koomb MAY-luh)   Hindi
Festival to wash away sins of past lives.

Kumbh Mela is the largest periodic gathering of human beings on the planet. Every twelve years millions of Hindu pilgrims gather at the confluence of the Ganges and Jumna Rivers in north central India. Bathers pray to escape the endless suffering of cycles of reincarnation. Purification by bathing at such a sacred site is a ritualized discharge of whatever is holding you back from spiritual growth. It opens and exposes the secrets of the psyche, providing a safe container for their unbinding. Like the twelve step process, there is a deep recognition that forgiveness is letting go of the past, dropping the baggage of an earlier experience, releasing judgments about yourself and others, while accepting responsibility for your actions. We all have similar desires and wants to increase happiness and avoid suffering. Making peace with the enemies within occurs when you examine your past actions and realize that you can never fully live up to your values. Your personal integrity, in the end, is always imperfect. Forgiveness of self, others, and life's unfairness softens you, dissolving bitterness and illusion. It is the beginning of compassion, which cannot be, until you have opened the doors to your own emotional life.

I forgive myself again and again for my hurtful choices.

oloiboni (aw-loy-BOH-nee)   Masai
Ritual expert.

Ceremonies have been used throughout history to invoke change, mark transitions, celebrate, heal, commemorate, initiate, transform and facilitate grieving. Time to engage the services of an *oloiboni*, someone to serve as a knowledgeable guide and resource. To demystify the essential elements involved in creating a ritual, think back to a funeral you helped to arrange. The purpose of the event is defined, supportive witnesses gather, and a symbolic point of transition occurs framed by opening and closing events. Your survival through this passage in your life exposes you to hardship and pain, and gives you a sense of your own power, which is so small in relation to the larger forces of the planet and the universe. You will emerge humble, as well as more powerful and less afraid. Your success in any transition is dependent not so much on outcome, but rather on your ability to fully embrace the difficult questions.

I honor those who create healing observances which serve as markers on my journey.

February 20

pega (PEH-gah)   Portuguese
Display of bravery when confronting a tired and enraged bull.

Courage is the strength of mind that is capable of conquering whatever threatens the attainment of highest good. When united with wisdom it fosters self discipline as well as justice in relation to others. Valor is self affirmation in spite of anxiety or fear, the willingness to act and move beyond what feels comfortable. A unique form of this value is *pega*, an elaborate demonstration of confidence and ability in the face of great physical danger, wherein a choice is made to spare the animal from demise, despite the increased threat to oneself. There is an intense awareness of the interdependence of the fear of death and the fear of life. It takes heroism both to live and to die well. In order to truly understand the suffering of other living beings, one must become aware of one's own destructiveness, lived through their own weakness, and explored their own shadows. Only then can empathy and compassion emerge. Do you dare to attempt difficult things that are good? Do you have the capacity to say NO, and mean it? Being true to convictions and following good impulses even when they are unpopular or inconvenient inspires others, even as you stand before your own beastly fears.

I am capable of generating compassion, even under fearful conditions.

nowa ochiamou (No-wah O-chee-AH-moo)   Yanomami
To ask to be invited in times of scarcity.

We have little tolerance for the idea of scarcity and the notion that scarcity can be shared. In our money driven world, the bonds of community seem fragile. Living in abundance, many of us have forgotten how difficult it is to ask for help in providing the basics of food, clothing, and shelter. Massive upheavals such as floods, wildfires, and earthquakes may unexpectedly destroy our sense of security. It is then that we might come to understand the humility, shame, and risk required in uttering *nowa ochiamou*. Our dominant cultural myth is that you must make it on your own; to fail is a form of moral weakness for which we are blamed. Yet each of us has moved forward in life by standing on the shoulders and relying on the toil of those who came before us. Not one of us has survived without a helping hand along the way. It is illuminating to consider how different the world might be if each of us made direct individual contact with only one of the billion people who don't have the basics of survival, and responded to their simple unassuming request for assistance.

Asking for help in times of need is a sign of strength.

February 22

piropo (pee-ROH-poh)   Spanish
Flowery spoken compliment.

Rarely do people exclaim: "Stop! I'm suffering from too many compliments. Please, I cannot take even one more." And yet, we believe that the more positive feedback we give to others, the more we'll fill their heads with harmful illusions of grandeur, or contribute to them becoming approval junkies. Looking for opportunities to validate those around us creates a positive flow of energy that transforms families, workplaces and friendships. When we embellish praise with poetic language we beget a *piropo*. Not restricted to just seductive encounters, these words can open and free beings to appreciate their own beauty. Such adornment adds additional value and esteem to the acclaim, and can be wonderful fun. Imagine telling your children that their eyes sparkle like early morning sunlight glistening on snow clad treetops. Metaphor and simile abound in these delicious phrases that roll sweetly from the tongue and are greeted eagerly by listening ears and hearts. Free license is given to be wildly ingenious as the gracious lightness and good cheer become infectious.

Poetic praise enlivens my world.

tiwalla (tee-WAH-lah)   Tagalog
Deep sense of trust.

Self doubt is spiritual suicide. When we cannot find shelter at the core of our being, then we are exposed to all the destructive elements of the universe. Honesty is the lifeblood of developing inner strength and confidence. It is first discovered within the vast landscape of our own hearts, rooted in being truthful with other individuals, with institutions, with society, with self. Its confidence is bred by consistently manifesting trustworthiness and integrity. We hide from truth because of the perception that it creates conflict. Yet its absence ultimately produces only more discord, as faith withers from a lack of nurturing open communication. When another speaks and acts in a straightforward manner, you learn to value their dependability. Especially in matters of the heart, a willingness to share openly promotes *tiwalla*, a special quality usually afforded only to those closest to you. Betrayal is not an option. Because you have moved through conflict and difficulty in the past, there is the confidence and commitment to do so again if necessary.

I watch trust develop as honesty increases.

February 24

pregierz (PREN-gesh)   Polish
Punishment post; site of Medieval flogging.

Where did we ever get the crazy idea that for people to do better, we first had to make them feel worse? Humiliating and shaming someone, especially a small child, fosters resentment and defiance. Hitting them for what they did wrong does not instruct them in what to do right; it also delivers the message that if you are bigger and stronger, force is an acceptable way to get what you want. The existence of the *pregierz* reminds us that we have made advances in decreasing wanton cruelty. We have become more willing to face the widespread existence of child abuse, domestic violence, sexual assault and elder abuse. We have at last admitted that most violence occurs between people who know each other. We know there is a clear relationship between a history of abuse and subsequent violent behaviors. Ending family violence is a clear path toward creating a more peaceful society. Choosing to not use corporal punishment, and avoiding emotional abuse with our children is an important beginning.

I am grateful for the part I play in decreasing violence in my world.

salat (sal-LAAT)   Arabic
Repeated prostrations as part of the call to prayer.

The Prophet Muhammad often journeyed to a desert cave named Hira, just outside Mecca. It was there that he was first inspired by Allah to set forth the revelations of the Qur'an. At dawn, noon, afternoon, sunset and night, Muslims everywhere are called to *salat*. Knowing that these offerings of prayer are shared by the community of the faithful consolidates the vision of collective cohesive surrender to the will of God. As they say these prayers they face in the direction of Mecca. They kneel and place their foreheads on the ground, symbolizing the equality of all men, the need for humility, and a reminder that from the earth we come, and to it we return. Touching the earth in this way can bring you closer to the true dwelling of your inward village. It is a form of permission, rather than prescriptions or restrictions. Allow yourself to seek truths beyond your perception. Though prayer and prostrations may leave you with many questions, offering them creates a path of awakening.

I share my prayers with all of humanity and touch the earth in humility.

February 26

sisu (SEE-soo)   **Finnish**
Self-reliance.

Responsibility, self-discipline and competence are often portrayed as burdens rather than the bedrock of our survival. This triumvirate rules the substance of the complex notion of *sisu*. Taking responsibility for our actions means overcoming the tendency to blame ourself or others when things go wrong; it is to focus instead on the seeds of opportunity that may be present in apparent failure. The practice of self-discipline is not a "should" or a "have to" imposed from outside; it means consistently doing what we know is good for us. It is a self enlarging process by which small conscious acts of embracing nurturing activities naturally let you avoid the dangers of extreme, unbalanced viewpoints. Gradually one stabilizes awareness of our uniqueness and successfully develops inherent gifts and capabilities. Strengthening each of these core facets through a commitment to personal competence and excellence leads to the discovery of a dependable deep inner well. Spontaneity and creativity can be marshalled in any situation because the foundation is strong and healthy. What you make of your life is up to you, and there are many resources available to assist you on the path.

I can depend on internal forces to guide me.

elke (EL-keh)   Algonquin
An expression of joy; great! wonderful!

Joy is a gift you can give yourself, and then scatter all around you. Just as one candle lights another and in that moment of contact sparks a brighter glow, so joy multiplies as it spreads. In the giving is a receiving. Joy insists on celebration, dissolving boundaries, opening wide the gates of passion and enthusiasm, and enhancing our connectedness to all of life. It invites passion and nurtures our natural expansiveness. It arises from delight in the world, from the beauty and bounty of our senses, and from the great dance in which simplicity joins with infinite diversity. When we witness this happiness in others, exclaiming *elke!* is a way to partake of and increase the excitement. We become part of the rising tide of gladness. Sharing the good news or blessings has a direct uplifting effect. Joy asks us to affirm our essential being. It invites us to light up our little corner of the world.

I allow the emotional alchemy of joy to radiate upon me.

February 28

birkie (BEER-kee)   Gaelic
Lively intelligent clean cut person.

Sometimes we meet people and wonder if they are for real. They seem to have it all together. Perhaps they are not only bright, talented and sensitive but also wealthy and healthy. How can we deal with such beings when they seem such a contrast to our own deficiencies? Usually they have spent time with their own demons and are quite aware of their own shadows. They have gradually come to embody the best aspects of their truest self. Their presence helps you to remember that you do not dislike or admire anything about anyone else that is not a reflection of a similar quality in yourself. Others are simply mirrors of you. In Scotland, encountering a genuine *birkie* also reminds you to let your own light shine. We do not serve life by playing small; allowing our own brilliance to develop and manifest is an inspiration for others to do the same. It is not the endless analysis of the dark that brings us closer to what we ardently desire. It is moving towards the beauty in ourselves and others.

I can appreciate the light others create on their journey.

affectus (ah-FECK-toos)   Latin
Openness in which we are vulnerable to the world around us.

It is paradoxically both scary and exhilarating to freely allow life to touch us. When we are closed off in fear and withdrawal, there is an illusory safety and protection. To greet whatever is arising at the moment with compassion and generosity is to expose ourselves to pain. So much easier to remain concealed than to risk exposure. Yet when we are in a state of *affectus*, we enter into a new realm of possibility; we stretch the edge of our comfort zone, tasting the border where all growth takes place. By renouncing whatever holds you back from full engagement with existence, you welcome both danger and blessings. That conscious release of fear allows a magical doorway to appear, leading to our dreams, extending the energy of unimpeded awareness into the details of living. You become less self-centered, learning to feel with and for others. Empathy, tolerance, and love are deepened because of your greater comprehension of your own susceptibility to pain and pleasure. A delicate sensitivity develops to every aspect of the world around and within you.

I usher in today with uncovered hands and heart.

MARCH

Your destiny waits
On the road you have taken
To avoid its grasp.

aji (AH-gee)   Japanese
An energy imparted over time through the loving handling or wearing of an object.

At some point we fall in love with the tools we use each day. The fabric of our lives weaves within that favorite pair of earrings or scissors, grandmother's serving dish, a musical instrument we have embraced for many years, the small statue that "spoke" to us at a yard sale. We make contact with hundreds of physical objects over the course of a day. Yet only a few hold a constant place of reverence in our hearts. These have become imbued with *aji*. The energy of our caretaking, the natural oils of our hands, and the pleasure we exude while using these special possessions create changes in the object itself. It is almost as if over time, certain belongings respond to our touch with gratitude. We create a loving relationship with them that honors their significance in our lives. Such realization can fill us with awe. These objects designed, made, and used by human hands reflect to us the remarkable technological distance our species has traveled among the eons. Such objects, having embodied part of our essence, remind us of the profundity of the seemingly mundane moments of our lives. We give these material companions the gift of our attention and care; they respond with deepening elegance and more vibrant beauty.

I will consciously and lovingly touch some of my favorite things today, and give thanks.

March 2

goadnil (go-ahd-neel)   Saami
The quiet part of a river, free of current, near the bank or beside a rock.

Imagine living so close to nature that the words you used everyday reflected an intimate understanding of the myriad contours of Gaia's body, an endearing term used to define our planet as a living organism. How our consciousness would be transformed, if the majority of the words we used daily reflected terms describing terrain, weather, or seasonal changes, rather than technology. Spending less time in cyberspace, we might venture to a *goadnil*, and listen to secrets the flowing water has to share. There we are always welcome. The rock will not refuse us; the grass on the bank will not say it is inaccessible for the afternoon. We can simply drift along and contact inner knowings. When the warp and woof of our daily existence is rooted in natural phenomena, a certain clarity reveals itself. A cosmic perspective shines through, placing our problems and confusions in a larger context. We all know the healing power of a walk in the woods, or the deep chords struck within by a magnificent sunset. We need only respond to the call.

I honor the quiet place within, and nature's ability to lead me there.

zerrissenheit (tsay-REE-sen-height)   German
**A torn to pieces-hood, the state of being divided, fractured;
pulled in a dozen directions.**

We are all to some degree simultaneously falling apart and coming together. Each of us experiences tension and conflict among
various elements in our lives. The war within can pull body,
mind, and heart in different directions, both draining our energy,
and creating an endless battle of hide and seek within us. In order
to function, we begin walling off parts of who we really are. The
more estranged we become from our true nature, the more
opportunities there are for fear and depression to dominate our
inner landscape. When we are mired in *zerrissenheit*, the desire
to experience peace can lead us beyond the fear of facing our dark
side. Once we understand that by grappling with our internal
chaos we are actually reclaiming the wholeness that is our
birthright, then the inner struggles begin to ebb and healing
occurs. We come to accept the reality and indeed the necessity of
chaos, darkness, and suffering. What a joy it is to discover the
possibility of no longer feeling divided and homeless in the realm
of our own being. We can be released, if only temporarily, from
such pain.

I acknowledge that my brokenness is what allows me to become whole.

March 4

lila (LEE-luh)   Sanskrit
All of nature seen as the creative activity of the divine; the sportive, playful, free willing God.

Some observers of human nature have called us Homo ludens, the species that loves to play. It is part of our divine nature to marry raw, uninhibited energy with emerging skills, to bring forth a spark of our unique spiritual passion. To live with playful artistry is to dance between the conscious and unconscious, so that what takes form is uniquely mine, yet calls forth a deep memory in you. When we cook a good meal, dance spontaneously around the living room, make love under the stars, allow music to bring us to tears, we are immersed in the language of sacred play, the parlance of *lila*, cosmic vitality, the free play of the gods in creative expression. To relax and allow music, art, dance, poetry, theater, and literature, to transport us inward to the elemental energy of creativity, we must silence the inner critic—no easy task after so many years of training! Yet our innate craving to reach beyond ourselves and playfully explore often hides in the demands of adult life. How exquisite it is to be swept away by creative play and passionate living.

I welcome the magnificent sense of play that flows within me.

do do (doo-doo)   **English Creole**
To take a nap.

Ah, the sweet bliss of surrendering to fatigue, of escaping to a fetal dance with the unconscious while the world is still moving at its hectic pace. Blessed are those societies that appreciate the need for a siesta. There, where permission is given, any nook can be conducive: couch, hammock, park bench, beach blanket, bedroom, pillow by the fire. One can often feel the call for a nap before the time is fully ripe, a drowsy foreplay of sorts. The body's ability to communicate a need for rest is a wonderful gift. Yet many of us resist our physical desires. Work usually demands that we live on someone else's schedule. Even while at home, aroused by the phone, we are fearful of being caught being "unproductive", and may deny that a delicious nap was in progress. Listening to your body deepens your relationship with it. Honor its wisdom and go *do do*, while the sun is up, even if only for a few exquisite moments.

I listen well to the messages my body gives me about weariness.

March 6

peras (PEH-rahs)   Greek
A space cleared out and made free; a boundary from which something begins its essence.

When we create boundaries, and then move beyond, we expand our freedom. To establish a defined space in which to explore, we establish a boundary. Then in an effort to enlarge the self imposed limits we have constructed, we bounce up against it. How exhilarating it is to break out of ourselves. As we repeat this process over and over again, we begin to grasp the notion of *peras*, a boundary that helps establish our identity, forming a space in which our essence can be free and safe. The edge is where possibilities emerge; the center is where we can feel safe. Both are needed in the course of growth. We experience vulnerability when our boundaries are broken, yet we survive, and even thrive. Personal borders allow us to feel at home in ourselves, to know that there is a place of healing and wholeness that is always available. Our private sanctuary sustains us, the nurturing womb from which we can then emerge into a new way of being in the world.

I appreciate my ability to create and expand boundaries in my life.

ma ta la shol (mah tah lah shohl)   Mayan
How is your heart ?

Being fully present with another is a profound experience. Normally when we exchange brief social amenities, our eyes meet momentarily, we offer a few words, then our energy drifts elsewhere, along with the deepest parts of ourselves. These casual contacts take on a different tenor when our initial greeting invites a transformative response. Rather than "How's it going?", or "Hello" or "What's up?" we might try "Blessings on you, friend. Are you awake to the glory of this moment?" or perhaps "There is a special reason we are sharing this moment. Let us discover it!" The Mayan **ma ta la shol** will certainly generate some interesting responses. With such an opening, we acknowledge the seat of the soul, and the source of well-being. Hearts nurture love as the earth nourishes corn—a crop sacred to the Maya— hence greeting another with this form of social embrace, we gently clear the way to a seedbed of affectionate support. We then join in a special bond of meaningful, generative exchange.

With each being I meet I acknowledge that it is safe to let my heart lead my mind.

March 8

**jam karet (jahm KAH-reht)   Bahasa Indonesia
Rubber time.**

If we could bottle time, or package it like a nutritional supplement, the demand for it would be overwhelming. We are a time-conscious society, juggling commitments against the ruthless flash of a digital monster. Is it time to go, eat, sleep, work, make love? Bowing before the clockmaker god we've become swept up in a superphysiologic pace, a hurry sickness that is destructive. What's more, time is constantly perceived in terms of not enough. Enter *jam karet*! Consciously, if only for a brief interlude, let time be stretched to accommodate the natural rhythms of your day. Expand the window you usually allow for an activity. Perhaps invite lunch to evolve into an all-afternoon affair. Or permit a visit with friends to take as long as it needs to go on until you feel complete. Give yourself the gift of an unstructured day. The purpose of singing, or dancing, or living itself, is not to get to the end of the "piece," so that we can move on to something else, but rather to be suspended in the moment, to experience the joy of timelessness.

Today I will live as if time were a blank canvas, rather than a prison wall.

uffda (OOF-dah)   Swedish
A word of sympathy used when someone else is struggling in pain.

There is pain and struggle in being human. Because we have loved, grief walks by our side. Relationships, physical breakdowns, and deep disappointments all lead to pain. We even create agony by doing what is expected rather than following inner guidance; to the extent that our inner and outer lives are incongruent, we may experience hopeless helpless futility and loss of the authentic self. Life sometimes seems a tragedy in endless acts. Pain, however, is stuck energy and once shared, can begin to dissipate. When we utter *uffda* to people, we simultaneously acknowledge their pain, and express sympathy, joining them in their suffering, if only for a moment. Grieving has its own rhythms, and often demands sharing. It is an occasion for healthy dependency, for not "going it alone". In fact, the "I want to get it over with" mindset is ultimately self-defeating. When we are there for another, despite the confusion and devastation, we become more of who we are.

In being present with another's pain, I expand my capacity for compassion.

March 10

t'aeguk (ta-GOOGK)   Korean
Yin Yang circle in the center of the Korean flag.

Nature is always moving toward balance. Just as day seeks night, and heat permeates cold, the flow of our beings surges toward homeostasis. Such a state is not deadened or static, but rather dynamic and evolving. Thousands of times in a day, our bodies adjust to maintain temperature, pulse, blood pressure, and hormonal activity. Our minds and emotions also seek a return to the comfort of the familiar and habitual. *T'aeguk* is an expression of the constancy of seeking equilibrium. It calls to us, fluttering in the breeze, asking to explore the great cosmic forces that oppose each other, to achieve perfect harmony and balance. As we play with the energies of active and passive, masculine and feminine, construction and destruction, we discover diverse ways of expressing our true nature. Balancing opposing forms gives us the strength to test the margins of the unknown.

I am both the sun that rises and the night that falls, light and dark, active and passive.

gunik (goo-neek)   Semai
Benevolent spirits that appear in a dream and teach the dreamer a song.

The Semai people of Malaysia have many ways of inviting the assistance of nonhuman allies to protect them against the forces of evil. First meeting them in dreams, one presents them with offerings such as drawings or music on a regular basis and learns to summon them in times of need. Most of us have at one time or another integrated into our lives the gifts of a powerful dream. It may have helped solve a dilemma or warned us of difficulties ahead. When we consciously incorporate material from our dreamscape into our waking lives, we build a bridge between the physical and spiritual worlds. Over this passage come *gunik*, at first to teach us a song. Later they can be summoned for spiritual guidance. As life goes on, you can sing the song to ask these allies to assist you and your kin with their difficulties. Can you imagine what a profound act it is to create a dream prayer? Welcome these spirit guides into your family, and into your world. By nurturing them, and acting on their guidance, you may enrich your life.

I am open to the wisdom and gifts of my dream travels.

March 12

dana (dah-nuh)   Pali
Generosity of giving, as in the form of Buddhist teachings, which are offered freely because they are considered priceless.

Cultivating generosity, we awaken an inner extravagance and sense of being fully alive. The size or value of the gift is of little importance; what matters is the act itself, which generates a moment filled with loving kindness. For just an instant, we diminish our self-absorption, and give over, with no thought of return. We are catapulted beyond greed and the narrow focus of our own desires. When we practice *dana*, we enter into the great circle of giving; we support others who are giving freely of themselves. Immediately we experience immeasurable benefits. An uplifting spiritual energy slowly permeates our being, and expands heartfelt compassion. Remembering how much you have received from others, enter humbly into this vast landscape of offerings.

Today I freely offer something of myself, seeking only to experience giving.

deptak (DEP-tak)   Polish
Central pedestrian promenade where the life of the town concentrates.

We all seek to go home to a place where open arms will receive us, hold us when we falter, and celebrate with us in success. Some of us spend our whole lives searching for a sense of community, catching only glimpses of it. Others have the gift of creating it wherever they go. As a species we are born with enormous capacity for social interaction. The fundamental unit of human survival is the clan. In our lives, which may be governed by isolating high-tech communications systems, we often feel primitive longings for human company, or we may have a feeling that something is missing in our daily existence. This is our cue to head for the *deptak*, the town square, which is today's psychological equivalent of early human campfires. It is the center which holds together our relationship with one another. When it is alive and vital, then everyone prospers. Support its existence by visiting it on your own, or by spending time there with neighbors and friends.

I choose to spend time at the community commons.

March 14

saka na (SAH-kah nah)   Tagalog
Anytime later, maybe next year.

The eyes of a toddler glisten with defiance. Like a puppy testing the limits of rough play, the edges of the parental "no" are explored, until a clear response is elicited. All our lives we can get trapped in the web of our wonderings about this simple concept of "no." Books have been written about how to find and use your "no," like some protective shield, a psychic line in the sand, that declares an emotional boundary. Yet there are other times, when our intentions are not clear. *Saka na* is a great way to respond in such situations. It is a more playful negation, open to interpretation. Rather than a harsh unacceptance, it honors possibility, and saves face. We often are balancing a "no" with being open and receptive to what might unfold. Is it really a maybe? Sometimes. Or it may be a "yes," just waiting to be discovered, playing hide and seek within.

I have my yes and my no, and also my "possibly."

miratio (mee-RAH-tee-o)   Latin
Amazement; miracle; the wonder of the unique.

Wonder and surprise are the voices of mystery. They infuse us with joyful awareness that we are but reeds in an infinite ocean of being. Immersed in our goal directed activities, we may fail to notice the gifts showered upon us each day. Then something of beauty captures our attention, moving us into a state of amazement, of prayer, of surrender to the moment. We then realize we are not in full control of our existence. Our ability to marvel and delight reminds us that the hows and whys of our existence are fundamentally unknown. To embrace the miracle of the extraordinary, and, in turn, the ordinary is to experience *miratio*. A sunset ablaze with the colors of the season, early morning light dancing on ocean spray, a baby's world-hugging smile, deer appearing in a clearing, are all invitations to the celebration of the wonder of the everyday. The more our relationship to mystery expands, the more connected we feel to the indescribable beauty that envelops our existence.

I seek and welcome mystery rather than mastery.

March 16

mai pen rai (my bpen! rye)   Thai
Let it go; not worth hassling about; get off it.

Some people confuse anger with vibrancy. They view it as a protective friend, bringing extra energy when needed. This energy, however, is blind, and as likely to be destructive as it is to be constructive. It often becomes an inner enemy that destroys peace of mind, an unwelcome guest that shows up in the living room. Transforming anger requires time and patience, tenderness and kindness, acceptance and a mending of the pain and fears that fuel it. As children we often were exposed to our parent's destructive temperment more than constructive teachings about this emotion. Anger is not good or bad; it simply is. How you express and channel anger is more important than the fact that you have it, or rather that it has you firmly in its grasp. *Mai pen rai* reminds us to let it go. Whatever the precipitating irritation or annoyance may be, let it roll off your back as soon as you become aware of it. Let it flow, let it go, keep it from getting trapped in your body, where it is apt to harm you or others.

I can easily let go of the minor irritations that trigger my anger.

craic (KRAHG)   Gaelic
The art of conversational banter.

Smiles and laughter flow freely. The atmosphere is friendly, palpable, and inviting. People seem open and receptive. An intentional community has been temporarily created for enjoying the company of friends and acquaintances. This is a training ground for the practice of *craic*, an Irish form of communication with universal appeal. While often associated with bars and sports, its arena extends beyond these realms. The slow, gentle, lilting quality of social exchange is evident in the verbal play of lovers and friends and in the jocular teasing parents engage in with their children. Like a wave of words crashing upon a shore, the interchange can also be quick and somewhat overwhelming. One must listen well, notice intensely, and respond with lightning speed. Nothing in this delicious verbiage is predictable; paradox and uncertainty lead directly into the unknown. The reciprocal joking generates an energy that is sweet and endearing for all who are present.

I will cultivate easygoing conversation and repartee.

March 18

mollo mollo (MOH-lo MOH-lo)　　　French
Easy does it; carefully, cautiously, sweetly.

You are trying to move a huge rock into the perfect spot in your garden; your attention is riveted on each little movement. You are removing a souffle from the oven; it has baked slowly to perfection and so far has not collapsed, as it waits to sacrifice itself to the hungry mouths of our guests. The trail you are on with your family edges along a precipice that is narrow and slippery with scree; a loved one is next to negotiate it. *"Mollo mollo!"* you say, aware of the energy you need to bring to such situations. What you're striving for is a combination of relaxed attention and a calm understanding of the possibility that things may not go well. Like a doctor shouting at his patient "Just relax!" we can wreak havoc by struggling too hard to get something right. In delicate situations the energy flows best when allowed to expand rather than constrict, and we embrace the task, rather than attempt to control it.

I can bring forth sweet and easy energy whenever it is needed today.

conscientizacao (cohn-sien-tee-zah-SOWN)   Portuguese
Learning to perceive social, political and economic inequities.

The air is filled with the sounds of protest, of betrayal mixed with healthy doses of self-pity. "But . . . it's not fair!" Hearing these words you remember using them yourself, perhaps in an attempt to alter a parental decision, or to muster up raw determination in the face of an unpleasant task. Unlike the impulse to roll with the punches or retreat from the fray, *conscientizacao* fuels an ongoing desire to create better conditions for oneself and others. Such a humanistic perspective demands that action be taken against oppressive forces. How easy it is to insulate ourselves from the poverty, prejudice and suffering that plague much of the planet. Each of us must find a way beyond the circle of our own comforts. Hearing the voices of the wounded, however, can propel us through our resistance. Forever changed by our exposure to injustice, we become compelled to make a difference within our own sphere of influence.

Because I am touched by the suffering of others, I work for change.

March 20

Nyambinyambi (nyah-mbee-NYAH-mbee)   Bantu
Rain calling ceremony in spring.

Our bodies respond to the changes occurring as the earth begins a new cycle of emergence. The sun bathes us, melting away memories of cold and snow. There is a pervasive sense of cleansing and renewal. In many cultures, spring is a time of prayers to ask for a prolific growing season, and requests for the life giving rain that will be required. The rituals of *Nyambinyambi* unfold as members of the Kwangali people of Namibia place seeds and tools at the entrance to their villages. Dancing and songs call the rains to wash away ill fortune before planting. What do you do to welcome spring? The first rains of spring call sweetly to our innermost hopes and dreams. They invite us to walk the land, and join in the regeneration. It is a time to bring forth the energy and commitment of creation. As we anticipate warmer days, exuberant buds and flowering bulbs, we can welcome the stirring within us. Now is the season to ask for what we really want. Let the rains wash away hesitation and uncertainty. All of nature is supporting us in yet another cycle of growth.

I honor my endless capacity for renewal, and welcome the spring rains as reminders.

Nyepi (nyeh-PEE)   **Balinese**
Day of silence.

The soothing tranquillity of a spring night's soft rainstorm enters unannounced. Alone and awake in the darkness, there are many questions. In this time of transition, the silence between the notes, the pause between the acts gives access to our hidden instincts. The vernal equinox is celebrated in Bali with *Nyepi,* an entire day when all activity on the island is suspended, filled only with stillness and quiet. It is the culmination of a time of purification in which devils are driven out from their hiding places in villages. We sometimes can feel heavy and uneasy with quietude, because we do not know how to just be, without something accompanying us. Radio, TV, a book or computer can become mindless distractions that prevent us from discovering the richness of silent solitude. Remain alert, for your impulse is always to fill up space with matter, and time with activity. Quiet time is a gift, like the first buddings of spring. Regular contemplative moments offer a liberty that allows new possibilities to rise into awareness. Such a process cannot be forced by a demanding ego. It is its own potentiality, unfolding in the serenity of being present.

I can enjoy a totally silent meal, walk or evening.

March 22

hyggelig (HEEG-gay-leeg)　　　**Danish**
Warm hospitality.

The imperceptible movement of a plant toward the light has its counterpart in human relations. We are drawn instinctively to people who radiate warmth and openness. These nurturing individuals, although perhaps not the predominant figures in our lives, are often the most stable, and can be counted upon for a cup of tea, some delicious home baked goods, and comforting conversation. Nearly everyone who meets them is touched by their *hyggelig*, and feels welcomed in their presence. It is this energy that invites us simply to be who we are. Met by sparkling eyes and an affectionate embrace we feel immediately at home. These are people with a genuine affection for human contact, evident in the continual opening of both hearth and heart. Perhaps their greatest gift is the reminder that such qualities reside in every one of us.

I bask in the light of warm hospitality and radiate it outward to others.

hoka hey (HO-kah hay)   Sioux
"Hold fast, there is more"- a phrase uttered in times of duress.

Like a great desert storm that buries everything in its path, life can at times do us in. We feel assaulted on all fronts, off balance, and lost. Confusion and fear blind us further until it seems impossible to find the happiness we seek. When this occurs, exclaim *hoka hey!* Know that although there is more to endure, you will find the strength to do so. Surrender to survival. Focus on how to get through the next few minutes. Call upon inner strengths and reserves of energy. There you will tap into pools of resilience you did not know existed. Psychological hardiness is based on commitment, control, and challenge. One commits by being fully involved in the present circumstances. Control is rooted in influencing the changing aspects of life, even if only in terms of developing a positive attitude. Challenge prompts one to discover the gifts contained within the difficulty. Accompanying all hardship is a purpose and meaning silently guiding the emergence of whatever new quality we need in our lives.

I can reach inside and discover what I need to survive my difficulties.

yong (young)   Chinese
Eternal; permanent; the oneness seen in water as it moves.

The life force within us is a seamless continuity uniquely expressed from infancy to adulthood. Looking closely into a mirror, we can see both the lights of childhood and of old age. The constancy of our being is so evident that we often exclaim as our bodies age, "but I feel like the same me inside!" Taking life a current at a time, as we are apt to do, cannot eradicate the essence of the whole stream. This is the message of *yong*, which in written form is composed of characters representing "oneness" and "water." How remarkable it is to be aware of the stillness in flowing water, of the sameness underlying all the changes we undergo. If you close your eyes and imagine this vitality stirring endlessly within you, it will generate a sense of calm and centering. Contacting this inner stillness will help you live eternally from the core of your being. It is a place of remembrance you can return to again and again.

Gently touching the calm center beneath the flow of my being strengthens my ability to remain true to it.

felt (felt)   Yiddish
Something wanting; that which is missing and thereby preventing a feeling of wholeness.

Do you tend to dwell more on what's not in your life than what is? Is this one of the lenses you bring to your relationships? Perhaps we don't experience the level of intimacy we want, or are filled with a vague awareness of "Is this all there is?" Usually something that seems to be missing from another person is something we desire for ourselves. Focusing on someone else being too serious is easier than acknowledging that we need more play in our lives. If we become more mindful of what we perceive as lacking, we begin to traverse the path of self-discovery. To enter deeply into our *felt* is to contact the essence of that which we most desire. This can result in a tender, somewhat melancholic reverie, particularly when the object of our desire can never be present. The death of a child, parent or dear friend, after all, creates a hole in our soul that can seemingly never be filled. Allowing the emptiness to arise clears the way to acceptance and fullness.

I can appreciate my emptiness as a means to define my deepest desires.

March 26

mammalucco (mahm-mah-LOOK-koh)   Italian
Dope, jerk.

Others are simply mirrors of you. In fact, there is nothing about another person that you like or dislike, that isn't a reflection of something you love or hate about yourself. Look in a real mirror sometime, and see if there isn't a total idiot living inside you. Some of us are too proud to acknowledge his existence; others spend too much time with him, constantly putting themselves down. But what if we lived in a world where we could let loose our raw energy, spontaneity, and unfettered gusto, and spend more time marveling at the untamed parts of ourselves, without fear of being judged a *mammalucco*? Each of us has moments of being the quintessential jerk. Mistakes are really friends that teach us what we most need to know. But the fear of messing up, of not being perfect, of embarrassment keeps us prisoners and stops us from taking risks. Learning to embrace our imperfections each day allows us to treat ourselves lightly, and to take any and all commentaries as compliments.

It is easy to forgive myself for my mistakes and to be thankful for their teachings.

sama (soh-moh)   Persian
Whirling dance as a conduit for abandoning oneself to god.

Delicious abandonment to spiritual ecstasy is not only possible but common. This can be achieved by surrendering to the form of prayer, trusting the passage, and letting go of struggle. Then off we go into a sacred vortex that carries us closer to Creator. That we are capable of such rapture is itself an indication of our connection to the universe. When we enter *sama*, we dance as if our only reason for being is to feel the movement of our spirit in devotional ecstasy. Abandoning our ordinary mortal self, we give expression to our deepest eternal nature and are reminded that we inhabit an exquisite temple of physical being. Is it possible to move through a day with this awareness? Indeed it is if we are open to the possibility, simply by caring for the body in a sacred way. Taking a walk, brushing your hair, preparing and eating a meal can be passages to the divine glory of existence. As is dancing naked around the living room, or gathering flowers from the garden at day's end.

As my body dances through the details of life, I appreciate the sacred.

March 28

ya'biiltiih (yuj-BEE-ISH-tee-ij)   Navajo
A dying person's words, which might not otherwise be spoken.

This very moment people around the world are dying. In our culture, many of us fear death. As Woody Allen says: "I'm not afraid of my death. I just don't want to be there when it happens." If these are your sentiments, you may want to begin befriending the dying process and to vow to be as pain free, awake and aware as possible at the final moment. Death is a part of life shared by all humans, and not a calamity directed at you alone. Perhaps, like birth, it is merely a place where you change horses for the next part of the adventure. The joy of death is that it poses the question, what am I living for? When we are willing to explore our own relationship to death, we can be of more help to those for whom it is more imminent. *Ya'biiltiih* reminds us of the sacredness of dying, and the importance of honoring the process of passing on. It gives us permission to be more open than we have ever been before. To say what needs to be spoken, so that secrets of the heart may fall like flower petals, beautifying the path to a greater unknown.

I honor those who are dying, and embrace their final teachings.

bricolage (bree-coh-lahz)   French
Making do with the material at hand; expanding apparent limits.

Through what sort of elegant alchemy are we capable of transforming the ordinary into the extraordinary? Out of the raw stuff of life that is available to us we fashion things of immediate usefulness. Like building sand castles on the beach, we make use of whatever is at hand. *Bricolag*e is testimony to the immense inventive spirit of humankind. Children are most adept at this undertaking, incorporating into their play anything and everything in their immediate environs. Adults, on the other hand, are pros at blocking off the creative muse by declaring that to fire up our imaginations we first need the studio space, or a better instrument, or newer tools, or intervals of silence. How quick we forget that the universe constantly supports us in the art of living. Anytime we construct a bridge of intention, it carries back a contribution to the new creation. We always have all the tools and resources we need to move forward on our journey; life provides. To expand your perceived limits, practice utilizing what is already available to you. Improvise!

Making do with what is expands my capacity for creative growth.

March 30

ziji (sih-jih)   Tibetan
The shining out and rejoicing that is attendant to confidence.

Confidence is the unwavering stable awareness of the fact that whatever is happening in my life, I can accept it and handle it, because I have all the resources needed to cope with it. It is to embody the notion that vast sky does not hinder white clouds coming and going. Doubt and fear, while they may arise, cannot diminish the glow of this vision. The more time we spend in this light, rather than in the endless analysis of darkness, the better able we are to live in our *ziji*. Here gentleness flows easily, and the need to compete or judge drops away. Even worries about our own state of mind dissipate. We see that our lives are rich and full; we begin to feel love in everything we do, and we yearn to share this discovery with others. Uplifted by our ever-present psychic sturdiness, we inspire others to uncover their own brilliance, and share the joy of resting fully in one's own basic strength.

My confidence shines forth in exuberant joy.

po (po)   Hawaiian
The finishing process of making a lei; the final details of an offering.

Life expresses itself in exquisite details. We appreciate most any work of value; the care taken in creating a meal, an arrangement of flowers, or a piece of art. What is intuitively appealing about such an experience is often the energy of concern and attention brought to various elements of form. *Po* accentuates the importance of continuing this thread of concentration to the very end of a creative act, even if the action is just an ordinary part of our day. To give this consummation appropriate homage, we might pause for a moment, feeling the fullness of finality, like the last embrace of a lover about to depart on a long journey. Good endings are gateways to assimilation, to bringing together—and taking in—all that has come before. This is a time for relishing rather than rushing! Attention to these moments of denouement brings the sacred circle to completion.

I will pay special attention to moments of completion, and appreciate their vitality.

APRIL

Does a bird not know
The quickest way to its nest?
Why do I delay?

koyaanisqatsi (coy-on-iss-COT-see)   Hopi
Life out of balance.

The fast paced harried world of heart pounding intensity that we inhabit often reflects a deep sense of loss and confusion. As individuals we can easily become distracted by the various roads or choices in our lives, simultaneously attached to wanting more, and fearful of losing what we have. There are times when each of us turns our back on our true self, and then frantically begins to search for clarity elsewhere. The greater disharmony we experience on a planetary scale lives in intimate relationship to personal imbalance. This vital connection is what the Hopi term *koyaanisqatsi*, and represents a whole species careening about in a maze of chaos and desire in direct proportion to the confusion of millions of individuals. Rather than depressing us, this notion creates a deeper understanding and sense of hope. By focusing upon the microcosm of our individual existence and living with as much balance and integrity as possible, we are contributing to a lessening, in a small way, of the greater confusion. To move toward harmony within ourselves is to help heal the greater whole.

The simple choices I make everyday bring me closer to my essential self.

April 2

maka (MAH-kah)   Lakota
The womb of mother earth, which nourishes all life.

Two thirds of the way from the center of the Milky Way galaxy, which spans 100,00 light years, lies our sun. Ninety three million miles from the sun our four and a half billion year old earth dances in space. On this self sustaining biosphere every organism is interconnected however tenuously to every other through a global exchange system that flows through ocean currents, climate patterns and winds, the travels of animals which spread seeds, and the endless cycles of feeding, growth and decay. *Maka* is a term which reflects this sacred sustaining linkage. Like a living organism our planet operates its own life support systems through natural feedback mechanisms, including temperature control and the respiratory exchange of gases. Like the earth, you have limited inner resources with which to nurture yourself, which must be used wisely. Maintaining your inner equilibrium and creating an intimate relationship with your immediate physical surroundings can shape a healthy inner ecology of mind.

I can appreciate the many ways in which I am supported by my home planet.

kubembeleza (koo-behm-beh-LEH-zah)   Kiswahili
To caress.

Touch is the earliest functioning sensory system for all mammals. It is an important form of stimulation and pleasure throughout life but especially for the young of a species. Parents tenderly embrace their infants for the first time in a consistently predictable sequence, starting with the limbs and moving towards the chest and finally the head. In many cultures, babies are "worn" by their mothers, carried close to their bodies constantly in a modified sling. Close physical contact is encouraged, whether by sleeping together or ritual bathing as a family. We learn through direct experience about healthy touch, as the hands softly transmit what is felt in the heart. When one is allowed *kubembeleza*, our most primitive calming responses are stimulated. It is a flowing union of two people relating, enjoying satisfying moments of closeness. Such intimate expression reveals gifts beyond words. The bliss of gentle touching is that time ceases for you and you become ego-less, a part of nature immersed into something greater, lost and found in something else.

I can give and receive touch in nourishing ways.

April 4

primum non nocere (PREE-moom noan NO-kay-rey)   Latin
First of all do no harm.

In our attempts to help we may sometimes do damage. Often in conversation we may get into "fix it" mode offering endless suggestions when all the other person really wants is someone to listen. Unkind words or a harsh tone of voice may do irreparable damage to a child's sense of self worth. The cure for an illness may be worse than the disease. *Primum non nocere!* In any interaction one can choose to remember this advice and keep at the forefront of awareness the basic notion of not making things worse. Being conscious of our words and actions takes diligence. Even with focused attention you cannot always predict an outcome; sometimes holding the intention to be helpful rather than hurtful is all that is possible. More than just a healer's credo, there is a universal truth contained in embracing right speech and right action. The more attuned you are to these qualities, the less likely that your involvement in a situation will produce untoward results. You speak and act in a manner congruent with your compassionate nature.

I am capable of paying attention so that I contribute rather than injure.

ocurrencia (oh-coo-REN-see-ah)   **Spanish**
Sudden bright idea.

The blinding flash of insight is sometimes more like a drip from a leaky faucet; many drops had to escape before the one that really made sense overflows the glass. Acute insightful perceptions often arise when the mind is quiet in the bed, bath or on the bus. The ensuing ripening of one of these imaginative notions occurs when our attention is elsewhere, evolving through stages of birth, blockage and final breakthrough before it ultimately bursts open as an *ocurrencia*. Brainstorming is a welcoming technique used to generate as many ideas as possible so that the creative flow will offer one or two exquisite concepts that fit just what is needed. It is a way to encourage "out of the box" original thinking, to find pathways of expression previously unexplored. Can we regularly invite such transforming concepts to emerge? Is it possible to make yourself more susceptible to receiving these gems of inner guidance? By following the path of mindfulness and regularly calming the internal chatter perhaps you allow what was hidden to be seen and that not yet created to be born.

New notions that show me the way arise easily.

April 6

ting ting (ting ting)   English Creole
Introductory phrase for a folktale.

Every good story has a message that will come and seek you out. Somehow a thread finds its way deep into our psyche, and does its work. We are inspired in some small way, as the hidden dimensions are slowly revealed. We get caught in the magical weave. The oldest stories tap into cultural roots that still deeply sustain and nurture us. Folktales are a splendid heritage of visions and dreams. They create intentional contact between our outer world struggles and inner being conflicts. Stories are bridge builders between the collective unconscious, and our own sphere of reality. They are designed to help us grasp what is most essential, entertaining as they teach. *Ting ting* means prepare yourself, get ready, a tale is about to unfold! Behold! Imagination flourishes and transports us to new dimensions. Our listening opens the door to a different way of perceiving. Timeless and powerful, stories invite us to visit unknown spaces within ourselves.

I will soon discover and enjoy a story that is meaningful to me.

malama (mah-LAH-mah)   **Hawaiian**
Mutual caring.

Relationship is the doorway to conscious healing. If our lives are full of vital open nourishing contact with others we are truly blessed. Even the healthiest relationships experience fluctuating levels of intimacy. People have different past experiences, temperaments, rhythms, likes, and dislikes. Creative tension always exists, and it is essential to a deepening partnership to sort out your own unfinished business. At various points in our lives, we are all longing to both contribute to and be supported by the strength of community. Just as one takes individual responsibility for his own life, each member contributes to the life of the group through their open hearted, generous involvement. *Malama* reminds us that we are here to learn together to let go of fear and hurt and to embody kindness and compassion. For many "support" feels like someone getting on your back, telling you what to do, and your reaction is LEAVE ME ALONE. Support is asking for assistance in the form we need, not blindly taking what others think is good for us. Creating a circle of loving exchange is some of the most vital handiwork you will ever engender.

I seek relationships that inspire mutual love.

April 8

pysanky (pee-SAHN-kee)   Ukrainian
Intricately designed Easter eggs.

The origin of communal celebration is lost in our mysterious past. Most ancient festivals arose in association with planting and harvest times, and were based on lunar and solar calendars. In addition to feasting and merrymaking, they also helped to preserve unique customs and skills. The celebration of Easter, the principal event of the Christian year, originated as a spring fertility observance. The art of *pysanky* reflects the resurrection of life. Abundant bright colors express the sunlight of spring after the long desolation of winter. The egg, an obvious symbol of generative bounty, represents the collective hopes for a generous supply of food. The layers of careful painting and attention to specific patterns is testimony to the sacred motifs of life and death that hold together our fragile existence. Such adornment speaks eloquently of the interconnectedness of all life that is evident as this season emerges. In this time of rebirth and new hope what are your own points of connection as the sun and moon shift?

I use my artistry in some way to celebrate this season.

Shiva (SHEE-vah)   Yiddish
Period of mourning between the death and burial of a relative.

Many of us now live our entire lives without the privilege of ever seeing anyone die. It is viewed as something unpleasant and messy, best confined in the closet behind hospital doors. Increased participation in the process may allow for a more conscious farewell, though there is always a state of shock at the finality involved. The whole spectrum of feelings may unfold in the dreamy days immediately following. Anger, grief, fear, and even joy commingle in a rich tapestry of sensitivity to everything and everyone around us. We pull inward at the same time that funeral and practical details draw us out. These transient experiences are the essence of *Shiva*, full of moments frozen in time that later become warm and comforting memories embracing a significant event. It is a time of acceptance and surrender that ripples throughout the rest of one's existence.

I am present to whatever feelings arise as I grieve.

April 10

Martenitzas (mahr-ten-EET-zahs)   Bulgarian
Two tassels of thread symbolizing health and happiness.

If one were to wish for two lifelong companions, health and happiness would surely be included. It is these guests that we most often call forth and celebrate when sending greetings, giving thanks or making a toast. We hold them close to our core, embracing them as we would familiar relations. While it is possible to experience them separately, they most often dance together. Their interrelationship is emphasized when one offers *Martenitzas*, acknowledging the sweetness of possessing both. In Bulgaria, families often throw out the tassels for the first robins of spring to use in their nests. Partaking in this ritual is a way of wishing fertility and abundance for all creatures. As light is valued more because of darkness, so we may appreciate our health and happiness most in contrast to past illness. We all need simple reminders to be grateful, and to stay aware of how these blessed threads weave their way through our lives. How wise to rejoice and celebrate the absence of toothache!

I embrace health and happiness as lifelong companions.

cosi cosi (coh-ZEE coh-ZEE)   **Italian**
Life is so-so.

Trying to convince ourselves that everything is terrific when it isn't is pointless. Pouring positive goo over pain does nothing to ameliorate it; indulging in your personal drama can also be self-destructive. The balance between admitting what is not going well and wallowing in self-pity does indeed seem elusive. How then to respond to concerned friends without whining about it all, yet communicating that it may be a difficult time? Simply respond to the proverbial "how are you?" with *cosi cosi*. This phrase cuts through the mendaciousness of a simple okay and allows enough nuance to suggest the current burden of angst. Said with a wry awareness that bragging about what is good might lead to something bad, it also doubles as a mild form of appreciation that things are not worse. Not at all seeped in the doldrums of resignation, there is often an accompanying twinkle of the eye designed to communicate that although a little pity and understanding is welcome, this too shall pass.

I accept those times that are difficult with equanimity.

April 12

nasim (nas-SEEM)   Arabic
Whispering wind across the desert at dusk.

Wind, spirit, breath and soul often have the same roots in words in many languages. Cultures around the world have hundreds of names for the winds that affect them. Change is one of the constant breezes of the universe, occurring everywhere all the time. Sometimes it comes slow and steady like a trade wind, or is unwelcome like some upsetting invasive hot dry currents. At other times you seem caught in a whirlwind not of your creation. The wind is invisible yet it has clear effects. So too the process of inner change is often unseen until its manifestations gradually become palpable in the outer world. Metamorphosis can be chaotic but usually is not random, since it follows certain universal principles. The gentle *nasim* speaks of mystery and subtlety, the vastness of possibility. Like the wind, awareness comes and goes. Be an observer to your own unfolding. By taking the time for self reflection and listening to the secrets spoken only at day's end, you enter into communion with the great breath of being, and liberate upon the breezes those habitual patterns that do not serve you.

The wind transmutes whatever I want to release.

**Kalevala (kah-lay-VAH-lah)   Finnish
A long narrative epic poem.**

Be an audience to your own theater. Examine the profundity of your own biography to date. When you stand outside the saga of your life as a loving witness you can strengthen your ability to process insights and learn from mistakes. One can explore and appreciate the stories of both light and shadow. Contemplating the effects of the choices we have made, both conscious and unconscious, can profoundly illuminate the path of further healing. In the tradition of the *Kalevala*, entire cultures synthesize and preserve significant portions of their oral history. Here are the adventures of heroes, fragments of wisdom buried within magical tales, episodes of struggles applicable to each of our lives. Keeping a monthly journal is the beginning of contacting our own epic stories of failure and success. The larger view becomes evident as our personal chronicles accumulate over years. We thus generate compassion for ourselves and realize that throughout all the cycles of joy and sorrow we have survived.

I cultivate awareness by writing and reflecting upon my life adventures.

April 14

allemansratt (AHL-lay-mahns-rahtt)   Swedish
A law guaranteeing public access to the countryside.

Imagine that for a time your entire purpose in life is to visit the most beautiful wild places on the planet. A wondrous exploration and pervasive sense of discovery arise just in researching the first few locales. Part of the special character of certain spaces is their very inaccessibility which preserves their uniqueness and unspoiled elemental character. Many of us recognize the healing power of a rambling beach walk or the expansive sense of coming home to a favorite mountain spot. In our desire to preserve the richness, parcels of land and even entire habitats have often been set aside as preserves. There is always the delicate balance of maintaining the wild and the desire of humans to experience its gifts. *Allemansratt* acknowledges the communal ownership of land and responsibility of society to both enjoy and care for our greatest natural treasures. This Swedish concept guarantees that we all share the wealth of open space and protected glade.

I contribute to the health of our planetary home.

bas bas (BUS-bus)   Urdu
Enough! Refers to crowds, tea, anything!

Oh to disappear beneath the sheets, head and body hidden from reality and the endless onslaught of "have to's" and "shoulds." The sweet relief of a huge NO tattooed on our aura, a desperate flight from all that overwhelms and demands more attention than we can muster. *Bas bas!* Leave me alone is the operative principle, and "no more lists" the mantra in residence. Time for an affair with yourself, a nurturing exploration into the kingdom of do less and be more. We all can get so wrapped up in what is seemingly urgent and important, that escape to mindless activities is very appealing. Why do we allow ourselves to get so stressed out? Like wearing too many pieces of clothing on a hot day, we accumulate layers of tension and blocked emotional expression. Building into your day ways to dance with the inevitable difficulties and pressures allows you to shed the tightness of anxiety as it arises. Sighing is always available: no special lycra outfit or gym membership is required. Summoning the gifts of the present can also bring you to that restful center within.

I choose peace and calm in this moment.

April 16

dukka (DUK-kuh)   Pali
Suffering, misery, unhappiness.

The vacant stare of knowing eyes crosses the room effortlessly, a bird in stormy flight. We cannot grieve what we do not allow ourselves to feel. Denial wears many masks: we minimize, analyze, trivialize, fantasize, narcotize and distract ourselves so we don't fully experience pain. Gazing in a mirror, we fly away from the generations of sadness in our eyes. Doing doing doing will never heal our being. Holding back to avoid pain often creates greater unhappiness. The only way out of the *dukka* which is the essential nature of this life is through awareness and understanding. Hurt always instructs, and your wounds can teach you compassion. You have to carry your own pain. Welcome it from the depths. Wallow around in it. Accept the deep soul suffering and be patient with it. Dance it and be grateful for the growth it brings. Feel the wounds fully, find the beauty of the hurt. Let those barriers of strength and holding tight dissolve in a cascade of tears. Enter the trail of tears which will guide you through your fears. Touch the deep loss, allow the grief.

I can cry today because my suffering and that of the world are the same.

wokowi (wo-KO-wee)   Huichol
Peyote.

Humans have an innate desire to alter their consciousness, to change the channels of perception and awareness. For most societies in the world, healer and priest are one, and the state of the body is connected to the condition of the spirit. Shamans, as technicians of ecstasy, enter esoteric states of consciousness at will. Through the inward focus of trance they contact other realities and bring back information useful to the community. Among the Huichol of Mexico, use of *wokowi* is an intimate part of the culture. Because of their exposure to the spiritual context and use of this hallucinogenic herb, tribal members are aware of how to interpret and remember the significance of the visions that come to them. Apparitions are often translated into works of art in a culture that richly rewards the development of an inner life. Western culture often denies and denigrates such exploration, condemning publicly those who suggest there may be inherent value in such pursuits. Even with the proper devotional setting, all drugs are inherently dangerous, and many of us have had negative and difficult experiences with them. Perhaps it is time to release that past suffering, and appreciate our ability to make wise choices concerning these substances.

I forgive myself for past destructive behaviors with mind altering substances.

April 18

blajini (blah-ZHEE-nee)   Romanian
Kind magical beings who live on the banks of a river.

Voices fill an apparently empty wind, as it moves upstream on a warm afternoon. Determined to travel well, the breeze sings as it explores all the textures and shapes of the riverbanks. Anyone who has spent time sitting on the edge of a stream or river has heard such confident joyous musings. The water and the land beside it seems alive with a mystical quality. The *blajini* always surprise and delight, and we emerge more peaceful from time spent in their company. Scientists will credit the concentration of negative ions near flowing water as the source of any beneficial effects. We each inhabit an electrical field. Negative ionization of the air we breath interacts in positive ways with our own electrical net. The profound relaxation and alteration of our senses is clearly a combination of factors. Why not include magical beings in the mix? Especially ones that are beloved because of their innocence, purity and kindness. These are qualities worthy of cultivating, that do indeed seem to arise whenever one spends time near a beautiful meandering stream.

Magic time by a river gently calls to me.

kirpan (kee-pahn)   Punjabi
A knife that is always carried to remind one that there are things worth defending.

A warrior's strength lies in the ability to be awake, aware and centered in the present moment. The shadow side of the warrior is destructive. It is the frightened wounded inner child-warrior lashing out at the world. It is being tough and aggressive on the outside, yet scared and weak on the inside. The constant presence of a *kirpan* reminds you to recognize both your protective and destructive capabilities. If it could speak it might say: You do not have to stop force, it is easier to redirect it. Focus on learning more ways to preserve rather than destroy, to avoid conflict rather than confront, to stand in strength rather than hurt, to hurt rather than maim or kill when protecting. It is useful to enquire what it means to live our inner life with a sheathed sword. Perhaps it means we can learn not to fight the enemy parts of ourself, the negative mindtalk or self defeating behaviors. We can discover our true strength by dropping all resistance to engaging in life affirming behaviors.

I honor the positive potential of my warrior spirit.

April 20

lagniappe (lah-NJAHP)   French Creole
An unexpected gift to a stranger or customer.

Someone gives you a flower while waiting in a supermarket line. The owner of a boutique throws in a scarf you were admiring with your regular purchases. A waiter brings an additional appetizer, or a stranger offers you some change for a parking meter. Each arrives without warning and is gladly received. There is no expectation of return: it is an unadorned gift simply given. One cannot help but feel a sparkle of the best of humanity when offered a *lagniappe*. Yet why is it so difficult for some of us to receive? We are more comfortable being on the giving end. There is a stubbornness about wanting always to be in helper mode, as a way to reinforce our own competence and sense of power in the world. Somehow you were given the message that to receive is to be frail, needy, weak. Perhaps you are afraid to ask for what you really want, to expose the secrets of your heart. When the giving is balanced with receiving you experience a completeness in the circle. To express appreciation of the favor with a simple "thank you", allows satisfaction and pleasure for both you and the giver.

When I begin to receive in small, seemingly insignificant ways, I allow a new intimacy to emerge.

ujamma (oo-JAHM-mah)   Kiswahili
A tree carving representing the story of a Makonde family.

The endless stream of time captures many memories, releasing them like seeds of awareness further downstream. Silent eyes and broken hearts watched as friends and lovers and even children suffered and died. The ancient ones celebrated and gathered in their joys, overcame fears, and died as they had lived. Whether young or old in death, the grandparents of your grandparents survived long enough to pass a part of their being on to you. An *ujamma* contains legends and tales preserved in wood, reflecting the world of the African jungle, and the epic lifeblood of Makonde tribal lineage. Memorials to respected ancestors, the tradition endures as both the stories and the techniques of making these commemorative markers are passed on from generation to generation. Perhaps you have some old photographs in the closet or some anecdotes in the recesses of a relative's memory. Collecting and preserving these often inspires a search for missing pieces. Weaving together the narrative of your past creates a tapestry of deeper understanding. Such activities speak eloquently to us, honoring the places where stories are told, the tales themselves, and the storytellers who carry on oral tradition.

I honor those who have gone before and contributed to who I am.

April 22

nona gathe (no-nuh gut-heh)   Sinhalese
The few hours between the old and astrologically determined new year.

A hallmark of human reaction to change is ambivalence, as we keep one foot here while placing the other there. Teetering or caving in at the middle is always possible, undermining our determination to move forward. *Nona gathe* is an amazing time of transition when uncertainty rules. Between the history of the past and the mystery of the future, we are confronted by the void of the now, a challenging time of many possibilities. We remember that life is a secret to be lived, not a problem to be solved. We can realize it is possible to break out of believing we know so much. Perhaps just let go of your current plan. Empty yourself, like a bowl or a basket, and welcome possibility. You might move from breakdown to breakthrough by spending more time with what you don't know. Enquire into what you have considered to be obvious. Guide yourself to experiencing new things in the old, and old in the new. A distinct sense of meaning and purpose will become evident.

I welcome ambivalence as another step on the path to clarity.

nallik (NAHL-leek)   Inuktitut
To be helpful obliging and considerate.

All of the world's major religions emphasize forgiveness, kindness and service to others. As our spirituality expands into more moments of daily life we strive to help wherever help is needed. Yet walking the streets of major cities and seeing the homeless staring with outstretched hands may make us want to withdraw from the magnitude of human suffering. To cultivate the qualities of *nallik* is to surrender instead to the call to service. The joy of volunteering is immense. You have many gifts to share, whether of heart, hand or mind. In our present rush-about culture, the challenge is often to discover the satisfaction of a simple kindness. In the market, at work, or in the car, you have only to hold this notion at the forefront of your awareness and the opportunities for being helpful will appear. When we each embrace the chance to support each other in little ways, we create a wave of goodness that benefits everyone of us.

I am helpful and kind in many small ways.

April 24

tjotjog (CHAWH-chuhk)   Javanese
Harmonious congruence in human affairs.

In the hierarchy of socially desirable values, many world cultures
hold cooperation and getting along far above individual success.
The "me first" mindset is viewed as offensive and childlike.
Within this overarching constellation of mutual assistance, there
are those sweet moments when, like a lock and a key, the marriage of events is exquisite. Social harmony emerges easily in
terms of opinions, surroundings, food, or the outcome of a business meeting. Timing, sensitivity and skill combine when you
tjotjog to ceate a magical sense of connectedness that supports
the needs of all parties. It feels good to be in synch in this way, to
dance in the flow of life so that all involved benefit and feel comfortable. The realm of human affairs resonates with cosmic cor-
rectness and there is an unmistakable flow of goodwill among
parties. You have already tasted this notion in sports or at family
gatherings or at a well run meeting. It is almost as if the intention
of all to experience harmony invites the universe to respond and
assist in ways previously unimagined.

I welcome a synchronistic dance of cooperation into my life.

ba whgii ya' (ba-whgee-ya')   Navajo
Being in a state of wisdom that requires us to act in new ways.

Authentic power emerges when we align the highest part of ourselves with our thoughts, emotions and actions. When life holds meaning and purpose, and we are fully engaged in it, we empower ourselves. Whenever we begin to walk in universal truths and feel the sands of wisdom on our path, we take on a new mantle of responsibility, a blending of human intelligence and heart. We are said to become *ba whgii ya'*, and our practice is to continue to uncover misery and work for social justice. The very act of seeing and understanding is transformative. With new awareness we act for the benefit of others. If knowledge is power, then wisdom is compassionate service. Just as every problem contains the gifts that we most need, so each kernel of sagacity carries the seeds of inspiration and vision of what we must give.

When heart, mind and actions are joined in compassion, the way is clear.

April 26

mulata (moo-LAH-tah)   Portuguese
Revered beautiful female of mixed blood.

Some racism is really just cross cultural ignorance. We get bad information about each other, and unless we spend time in each other's company, we never learn the intricacies of ethnic awareness. Many of us were raised on varying diets of racist bigotry and prejudice, and have not taken the time required to drop destructive stereotypic perceptions. There is no doubt that both historical and ongoing institutional racism continue to traumatize deeply in our society. Cultural pain is an additional burden on the human suffering we all carry. It is rooted in a collective sense of shame about who we are, and in the distorted picture that history and the media continue to tell us we are. For minority mixed bloods in most cultures these wounds are even deeper, as they wander between ethnic homes. Yet the *mulata* sometimes seems to rise above this, and is appreciated not only for the striking diversity of her features, but also the expansive views of her heart. She is a bridge between cultures, striving to be accepted and acknowledged for this important role. There is a sense that only a unique mixture could produce such attractiveness, and that is a cause for celebration.

I will look at people in new ways today, grateful for their rich diversity.

gambaru (gam-BAH-ru)   Japanese
To strive against the odds.

Life would be quite perilous if we all had access to a magic wand. In the midst of the fray, we surely would wipe out difficult parts of our lives that we later came to cherish. Building our lives involves times of choosing, setting priorities and giving up other possibilities. Whenever we are willing to commit to an ideal that trancends our individual concerns, we open ourselves to enormous difficulties and suffering. Over time we each realize the potentials, bear the responsibilities and tolerate the costs of such commitments. We begin to fully comprehend the dynamics of *gambaru*. We learn to ignore any considerations we might have: I'm too tired, it's too cold out, I'll do it tomorrow, I don't feel like it today. The constant contact with your deep commitment sharpens and intensifies being alive. You touch it, taste it, smell it, hear it and see it, playing with possibilities in your mind. Sharpening such senses takes place within any discipline. Your deep desires will lead you to the path you must follow, as you finally realize that most obstacles ultimately issue from within.

I will keep on keeping on because I value the gifts of the struggle itself.

April 28

ketepepei (keh-te-peh-PAY-ee)   Xingu
Outgoing and sociable; aesthetically pleasing objects.

Delight is a unique form of human emotion. A mixture of joy, surprise and wonder, it is rooted in appreciation, and seems to flow over us like a wave upon a shore. Once caught in its intricate currents, our ability to notice and pay attention brings us the continual swirling of its gifts. Sometimes we find people delightful because of their special blend of interactive qualities; often it is the natural world or beautiful objects that transport us. In Brazil the concept of *ketepepei* encompasses much of the entire spectrum of such positive elements, and carries the additional notion of peacefulness. It embodies the aesthetics of both visually pleasing objects and the positive behaviors of well-dispositioned people. Beauty and balance together can lead us toward a shared cognitive understanding that nonviolence is expected and even inevitable. Spending enchanting time with pleasant companions in a sculpture garden hardly makes one want to wage war! When you regularly invite this mixture of serene qualities into your own daily reality, you profoundly influence your sense of calm and peace.

I feel peace when I interact with people and objects that are pleasing.

pomana (po-MAH-nah)   **Romany**
Death feast.

What did your dead friend or relative love? Imagine that you had an opportunity to celebrate whatever it was they most enjoyed one year after they had passed on. The scene is full of excitment and smiles as friends and relatives get together to cook fabulous food, and wear their best clothes. It is a three day party, staying up late into the night, exchanging gifts, burning incense, complete with dancing and music. Although there is lots of laughing and joy, the closest relatives wear no makeup, leave their hair down and look distraught, since this is the last goodbye. The *pomana* is intended to speed the loved one on their path to the next world, a goodbye done in their honor. For a year their spirit has wandered the earth, taking care of things, and still wanting to be with people. Now the cycle has been completed and the time has come for them to leave. There are shouts of joy indicating in various ways: "may your way be easy, may your path be beautiful, you're on your way to a better place".

I honor relatives who have passed on with some commemoration on the day of their departure.

April 30

pagdiwata (pahg-dee-WAH-tah)   **Tagbanua**
The feeling that one belongs to the land rather than owns it.

In the dim and ancient past beyond recall, human beings lived their lives close to the earth. They journeyed on it and felt its elemental power in their bodies as they struggled to keep a vision alive. They knew well the sweetness of early morning blossoms and the darkness of winter storms. There are those places on the planet that have captured pieces of our souls. We cannot imagine life without them: the sacred copse of trees, the favorite stretch of beach, the hilltop meadow or that special mountain stream. Each of these places harbors a part of our essence. We resonate with their energy and are caught in the web of their wonder and the nurturing of their teachings. *Pagdiwata* possesses us, and we can begin to conceive of such reverent connection existing between people and a vast expanse of land they know intimately because it is so much a part of their survival, both physically and spiritually. You can understand why people die rather than give up land that has been cared for by generations of their family. You can invoke this same principle to honor even land that is legally yours for temporary stewardship at this time.

I cherish the land that I am part of.

MAY

Peace like a river
Love like an ocean flowing
Deep within my soul.

ka'imi loa (kah-'ee-mee-lo-ah)   Hawaiian
The way culture helps in the personal search to find purpose and meaning.

Blessed are those who find a sense of purpose and meaning to guide their life. So many of us struggle for a long time with the essential questions. Who am I? What gifts do I have that might make the world a better place? How can I follow my heart and express myself creatively and still survive economically? Nothing we ever do is completely outside of the realm of our unique culture. It shapes and molds us slowly over time, like wind and water defining a rock formation. When you acknowledge *ka'imi loa,* you accept fully the richness of your heritage. The great yes! is spoken when you embrace all the guidance available through the nourishment of your cultural roots. Many aspects of culture extend and deepen one's appreciation of the beauty and bounty of the universe. Art, music, food, tools, and one's immediate environment are all significant and every dimension of life contributes to the fullness of being alive. In much the same way that people can exist within nature by drawing on its forces rather than disturbing them, we can lean on culture to support and strengthen all that is positive within us.

I allow my culture to contribute to my purpose.

May 2

kumsitz (kum-ZETST-uh)   Yiddish
Come sit, let's enjoy the cool of the evening after work.

Works consumes many of us. It saps our most vital energies, and demands so much of our time. Even when engaged in right livelihood, we may question why so much effort goes into this aspect of our lives. For many, a milieux of competition rather than cooperation adds to the stress. This sets up a dynamic within which you think you are better than everyone else, and at the same time you are afraid of everyone, simultaneously special and unworthy, superior and inferior, incessantly inflating or shaming yourself. Anxiety, tension, loneliness, rivalry and fear arise more easily. *Kumsitz* is a concept of the communal sense of identity and the understanding that we are all contributing to our collective success. In the end it is how we treat each other that is most important. The office potluck, holiday party or birthday cake are a taste of this community togetherness. Our workplaces can actually be more productive when we infuse this spirit into our day.

I embrace my fellow workers and celebrate our challenges and successes.

mano po lolo (MAH-no po LO-lo)   Tagalog
As a sign of respect for an old man or woman (lola), taking their right hand and touching it lightly to your forehead.

We often define aging as the absence of youth. We focus on what has been lost, ignoring the rich potential that is present throughout our lives. Elders have so many gifts to share. They are like mirrors, reflecting light into the dark places of the world, continually wiping the dust away so that our reflection may be bright. Their love is like misty rain, coming softly yet flooding rivers. Grandmothers and grandfathers embody not only wisdom, but also the transforming, stubborn energy of persistence and survival. When we practice *mano po lolo*, we consciously acknowledge such goodness, and ask for their blessings. Many elders know when to break the rules, and follow their heart. Some even experience the passion created by knowing that death is imminent, and that all life is vibrant. They remind us of the fleeting nature of youth, and the beauty of strong character that does not fade with age. They continue to explore both the near, and the far places of who they are, in the garden, on the streets, in the stores, with young ones. They have memorized the seasons of their lives, as they walk towards eternity.

Acknowledging the old ones, in some way, is part of my daily practice.

May 4

conte jondo (CAHN-tay hone-doh)   Spanish
Deep brooding fatalistic song.

You are an emotional time traveler, and your deepest self is always wanting to finish unfinished past business, to release what most craves healing. At times suffering is nothing more than the repetitious, compulsive complaints of the ego. It is bound up in denial, resistance and struggle. You blame others for the weight that is your own, and you are moody and full of self pity. Enter the penetrating mystique of *conte jondo*. Its tones enter the body and seek the soul. They speak compellingly to the deeper spirit suffering that occurs when grief and its attendant hopelessness and helplessness overtake you. Such music is an invitation to consciously experience the woe of the soul, and thrust open the doors of awareness and recovery. The singer whispers your suffering out loud, so that what was hidden need no longer be secret. The song draws all who are listening into the web, for each in their own hearts has experienced such agonizing aching.

Sad songs teach me to surrender to my current misery.

pacha kuti (PAH-chah KOO-tee)   Nahuatl
The rising and falling of a great event.

Humankind gazes out beyond the stars into the edges of the known universe. We also peer deeper into living cells with a technological lens that allows us to penetrate strands of DNA. Here we sit between the infinitely small and the indescribably large and try to understand the events that have brought us to this point in our evolution as a species. There are so many threads to unravel, more than one *pacha kuti* to comprehend. Climactic changes, wars, plagues, famines and technological breakthroughs have all shaped our destiny. Each occurrence possesses its own life cycle, its own rhythm of birth, being and receding. Just as these ripples in time tremendously affect our species, so in each individual life, there are those turning points, those periods of timeless awareness when we see the fork in the path and say farewell to the road not taken. Each encounter with fate prepares us for the next one. The choice is whether or not you pay attention to your own maturation, and learn the lessons required at each stage. Of one thing you can be certain. Your destiny awaits you on the road you have taken to avoid it.

I am awake and observing those forces shaping my lifepath.

May 6

mauvaise foi (moh-VAYZ fwah)   French
Deception.

How long does a lie live? The value of honesty is considered part of the foundation for an ethical life. Yet each of us dances with the interpretation of this priniciple in terms of our workplace institutions, intimate relationships, and even with ourselves. Making personal phone calls and xeroxing at work, maximizing possible IRS deductions, telling white lies or withholding information from lovers or spouses or children all lie within the gray zone of personal integrity. The most challenging aspect of a life of veracity is the tendency toward *mauvaise foi*. Such "bad faith" is especially destructive when we attempt to run away from ourselves. The sea of denial is dark and deep. Lying to yourself about your needs and wishes creates a veil of separation that cuts you off from your own nurturing radiance. While you may casually admit that you have some psychological blindspot, a feature shared with all of humanity, the refusal to see oneself clearly, in both shadow and light, is devastating. In the imperfection of the self we find not despair but joy. To speak the truth to yourself is to step on the road to serenity.

I embrace the truth of the paradox that within my imperfections lies inner peace.

mujo (moo-jo)   Japanese
A romantic sense of life's impermanence.

Cherry blossoms fall to the ground carried by a gentle spring breeze. The first fall frost steals the fragrance of the last garden roses. An exquisite sunset is swallowed quickly by a hungry dark night sky. We are constantly given the gift of predictable miracles. Yet so much of the beauty we feel in the world is transient. To see our experiences through such a lens is to appreciate *mujo*. There is a natural resonance between your body and the sensual apparition you have witnessed. As your sensitivity to the unfolding of nature is laid bare, there is a tenderness that develops toward all of existence. Rather than increasing your desire to cling to these moments, this notion enriches your spirit by accepting that for this brief period of existence, you were privileged to have perfection's temporary visit.

Fleeting beauty deepens my circle of compassion for all living things.

May 8

ng'ambo (ng-'AHM-bo)   Kiswahili
The opposite bank of the stream from where you are standing.

Just as the magnificence of an oak tree lies hidden in the acorn, so you contain vast storehouses of potential. We are always throwing ourselves into the future, gazing across the flowing water to the reachable yet distant potential that is *ng'ambo*. It is how we create and shape reality, this psychic boomerang game of intention and visioning. Seeds bloom internally before showing themselves to the world. Early on in life, you formed a dream which you secretly tended until it was ready for all to see. Perhaps as a young one, or during adolescence, you had a flash experience of your bliss, of what life might really be about. You couldn't get to that psychic gold then, only catch a glimpse of it to stir your passions and turn on the house lights. Since then these treasures have been allowed expression or been only buried deeper. As you pause now in your journey and look across to where you are headed, is that really where you want to go?

If I don't change direction I will end up where I am headed.

cuchument (koo-CHOO-ment)   **English Creole**
Odds and ends; paraphernalia.

Whatever the passion, there is a catalogue full of stuff to enhance
the development of one's avocation. We are immersed in a universe of highly specific goods designed to stimulate the pleasure
of exploration. Whether it is fly fishing, photography, gardening,
golf, guitar playing or in-line skating there is an abundance of
cuchument involved. We even have an endless array of containers
and sacks created to hold all of it. Imagine! Specialty cases to
carry and store all the particular essentials. Then we may even
need a garage or shed to hold all of the bags. At a more minimalist
level, each of us has at least one black hole of a junk drawer
where various collectibles and disposables mingle freely in chaotic
abandon. A select few may accompany us on a walk or be part of
a permanent traveling show in our handbag. Such delightful
devices are not limited to the utilitarian universe. Shelves at
home may display a variety of knick-knacks that have become an
indispensable aspect of our environment. Each of these objects
remind us daily not only of the complexity of our lives, but of
what is most essential and important to us.

I honor the bits and pieces of what holds my material world together.

May 10

Repotini (reh-po-TEE-nee)   Romanian
Festival in which the women are masters.

Women who seek to be equal to men lack ambition. The bumper-sticker takes a minute to fully comprehend, but the message is inevitably unmistakable. While men seem to have most of the power in the world, the way in which they wield it could be improved significantly by female involvement. This is acknowledged at least temporarily by the celebration of ***Repotini***, one day in the year when women are declared the masters. The women get together and traditionally make a shallow baking dish out of clay. Part of the day is always spent making bread and rolls and cakes. These are given to children and the poor as a symbolic offering to keep away war through sharing what is necessary for basic survival. The wisdom inherent in this practice lies in the clear statement that fulfillment is to be found in creating a cooperative community. There is reverence for the sacredness of mother earth in the use of clay and the baking of basic sustenance. It acknowledges social injustice as the root cause of wars, and the responsibility of the powerful to care for the most vulnerable. Finally it reminds us that the progress we have made in diminishing sexism is only the first baby step on a journey toward wholeness for all of us.

Today I honor the goodness in women and their ability to positively transform notions of power.

sanuk (sah-nook)   Thai
Healthy fun and enjoyment with friends.

Friendship is a long term dialogue that allows time to build the bonds. It is a mutual relationship based on equality. A friend invites you to be insecure, unsafe and vulnerable. Your connection allows each of you to be exactly where you are emotionally, without feeling wrong. You can be open about your interdependency, sharing areas of your separate selves that are difficult to reveal. Besides the enormous possibilities for emotional growth, we have the sweetness of *sanuk*. Some of our most pleasurable times in life are exchanged in a simple flow of well being with those we care about. Cooking, hiking, talking, playing music or sports together creates a synchronistic rhythm of mutual delight. There is nothing extraordinary to be accomplished and there is full permission to engage in the free play of the present moment. We connect in satisfying ways, matching postures of relaxation or alertness, as even the positions in which we hold our bodies and the pattern of our speech become more alike. We discover that time invested and spent in friendship enriches our being in unique ways.

I welcome the satisfaction of sharing time with friends.

May 12

ayuqnaq (ah-YUQ-nahq)   Inuktitut
Life is like that; it can't be helped.

The art of surrender involves a willingness to reframe circumstances, and reflects a mindset that trusts that conditions are exactly as they should be. It is not about listlessly giving in, but rather fully embracing what is actually happening. Surrendering to the flow is not passive. Rather it is an active yielding so that our energy can be channeled elsewhere. We can get in the habit of summoning this awareness when encountering difficult circumstances. *Ayuqnaq!* No point getting upset about it or taking it all so personally. The car won't start, the train has left already, the check didn't come in the mail, it is snowing on your outdoor party. Such unpleasantries are just like being caught in a rip tide. It is useless to resist their outward pull, and escape is possible by using your strength to swim across rather than against them. Like riding a wave, you can learn to harness the power of your inner knowings in harmony with what life brings. What are you most resisting at the present time? What reality don't you want to accept? Only when we blend seamlessly with what is, does peace have a chance to emerge.

Living without resistance empowers me.

geduld (geh-DULT)   Yiddish
Both patience and temper.

No one makes you angry. The feeling of anger is created in your body, and is your responsibility. It is based on the flight or fight reaction, a survival mechanism that supplies an instantaneous hormonal cocktail to prepare you for difficult circumstances. Since anger is dependent on physiology, everyone is more irritable when hungry, tired or in pain. The notion of *geduld* reveals the inherent complexity of this emotional state. Anger is as much the absence of compassion and understanding as it is the presence of judgmental righteous energy. Our normal kindness is displaced by the temporary insanity of this intense feeling. Anger always wants to blame, assign fault, and punish. It is often fueled by underlying fear or sadness. We may become angry when we have an expectation that does not get met, are trying to communicate something which is not being heard, or attempting an action which is blocked by circumstances or another person. Your anger is neither good nor bad. It simply is, and what you do with this energy is the important focus of attention.

All my feelings are okay. All my behaviors are not.

May 14

huskanaw (huus-KAH-naw)   Algonquin
Male rite of passage.

Initiation rituals in indigenous cultures usually contain three basic elements: separation, limen (transition), and return. In the first stage of *huskanaw* a boy is symbolically detached from his normal state and cultural standing. This may take the form of being physically separated from the tribe, removed to a selected sacred space, or hidden behind masks, costumes or body painting. In the liminal phase, the individual exists in an ambiguous state, like the snake whose skin is not fully shed, the bear in hibernation. He is naked, like a corpse and a newborn. This time is fertile ground for thinking about his life in society and the larger universe, and for contacting the inner powers that sustain and nurture him. Upon return his new status and standing is celebrated and acknowledged. The important work of such passages still continues in many diverse cultures. Whether formal or informal they signify a difference in how others perceive you. Some part of you dies during a passage, as you reappraise your life direction and dreams. Your success in any transition is dependent no so much on outcome, but rather on your ability to fully embrace the difficult questions.

I can participate in bringing young males into a nurturing positive experience of maleness.

p'ansori (phanhn-so-lee)   Korean
Narrative song contest.

Telling stories eye to eye without consulting a book evokes a unique excitement for both speaker and listener. A timeless magic is created that is capable of transporting us to new dimensions of consciousness. Even when the tale is familiar we still anticipate favorite elements and thrill to the remembrance of pieces that had been lost. There is also comfort in the predictable as well as new insights to be found in old legends. The tradition of *p'ansori* embellishes storytelling with a dramatic vocal flair. During the South Korean Ch'un-hyang Festival in May, epics are sung in fierce competition. A favorite recounting is that of a daughter of a commoner who secretly marries a nobleman. It is filled with romance and courage, love and fidelity and symbolizes the resistance of common people to the abuses of the privileged classes. As you enter the trance of a well told chronicle, your heart and mind dance in delight and primal memory. As we fill in the details with our imagination, we and the storyteller become co-creators of the drama. Who are the members of your tribe who know the stories and are willing to share their secrets?

In some way, I will resurrect the art of storytelling and listening.

May 16

samadhi (suh-MAHD-hee)   Sanskrit
Selfless absolute concentration.

The trance of meditative awareness is very inviting. Anyone who has developed even minimal meditation skills benefits from remarkable relaxation and sense of peace. We need only turn inward and seek the profound stillness. Initially a quiet environment and a comfortable body position are essential. Eventually only the two remaining elements, a passive attitude and a point of focus, are all that is required. Through this practice we are not forcing or trying to make things happen. By focusing on the breath, a sound, or a visual stimulus we invite tranquillity. When the mind is so deeply absorbed in the object of meditation that it loses itself in it and has no awareness of itself, one enters *samadhi*. Such a state of perfectly concentrated thought is a mystic ecstasy which transcends our normal sense of understanding, and is not limited to formal meditation. Babies exhibit this divine delight as they play and are happy, relaxed, unmindful of self, and fully concentrated and engaged in whatever they are doing. As an adult you may get a brief taste of this special quality while cooking, lovemaking, walking or playing music. All remind you of what has simply been forgotten.

I need only go home to myself to experience the bliss of the universe.

ffreg (FREHG) Welsh
Chatter or gossip.

The whole body of a baby moves in synchronized micro-rhythm with adult speech. Although the word infant is derived from the Latin infans, meaning "not speaking" there is quite a bit of vocalization as fussing and cooing evolve toward babbling and beyond. Baby talk is practiced universally and unconsciously by all human beings. The three year old phase of constantly verbalizing everything is a remarkable "no edit" state steeped in curiosity. Some aspect of that period never leaves us, and opens wide the door for *ffreg*. We want to know what is happening, and the rumor mill seems to churn constantly wherever people gather. When used as a substitute for direct problem solving and honest communication, it obviously can become destructive. When participating in talking about someone else, the essential questions revolve around confidentiality and kindness. Examine how the person might feel if they were present. How would you feel if the object of this speculative verbal chitchat was you?

I choose my words carefully and with respect.

May 18

terroni (tayr-ROH-nee)   Italian
People of the earth.

Rooted in the earth and nurtured by its resources, our existence is fragile indeed. Easy to forget as we stroll down a supermarket lane, that everything the billions of us consume each day depends on agricultural labor and the sustainability of our planet. As weekend gardener we can be reminded of and appreciate the forces that must be contended with to obtain the basics of a late summer harvest. Yet so often those who work the land are stereotyped as uneducated, uncouth, unrefined, vulgar or rough. To be married to the farm is equated with a lack of appreciation for the "finer things" of civilization. Such is the meaning of *terroni*, a somewhat derogatory expression used by industrial-based citizens of northern Italy to describe agriculturally centered people of the south. Rather than honoring the importance of intimately knowing and connecting with the earth, many people express disdain. Perhaps it is a fear of dependency and the entrenched view of peasant's work as less important. City dwellers know that their food is grown by someone, yet prefer not to think about it. Pausing before a meal to express thanks for the effort involved in producing the food enriches one's own bonding to the earth.

I respect the contributions of those who toil to create the food I consume.

talelo (tah-leh-lo)   Tamil
The refrain in a lullaby that put the Hindu god Krishna to sleep as a baby.

Krishna's purpose in life was to dispel evil and show mankind how to live in peace and joy. Many tales are told of his time as a young infant and boy living in the forest with the simple cowherders. He performed many miracles as a child and often spoke of the wonder of nature. He would ask his friends to look at the nobility of trees, which protects those who shelter under them, bearing the brunt of storms, rain, snow and fierce winds. They are gracious as they offer their gifts of shade, fruits, leaves and fragrance. Never do they refuse anyone. This is how all should live: serving others with compassion. The *talelo* reminds us of the comfort we all seek. Imagine what sounds and music might put a baby god into a relaxed tranquil sleep! As we curl into a fetal position, sit before a warm fire or sway gently to the rhythm of a heartbeat, we tap into primal memories of reassurance and safety. Many of us still cook comfort foods when we are sick, or take a healthy dose of that special family remedy. Showing compassion toward ourselves makes it more possible to extend it to others. It is good to remember what soothes you, and to give yourself the gift of solace regularly.

Every day is an occasion to console my mind body and spirit.

May 20

ai (eye)   Chinese
The slow unfolding of a heart relationship.

If at times you find yourself trapped in a secret jungle of expectations, restrictions and misconceptions, searching for the new position, plaything, practice, or partner that will penetrate into the cosmic chamber of a fulfilling love relationship, then pay attention to the essence of the term *ai*. Intimacy is the desire to know another's inner life and the ability to share your own. It is a bridge built between two people who are open, trusting and vulnerable. The love for your intimate gives you new spaces within yourself to explore by allowing you to be who you are. Each partner is a whole person seeking a relationship that adds new dimensions to their life, broadening and enriching it. Like happiness, this occurs when conditions are right, but it cannot be forced or sought directly. It is an attitude, a way of being and relating to another with special closeness and connectedness, that still recognizes the importance of autonomy. Both people choose to be totally close, giving each other total permission to become fully independent. The focus is on sharing your desires rather than filling all your needs.

I am still capable of learning about true love.

skansen (SKAHN-sayn)   Swedish
Open air museum.

History comes alive when we experience the fabric of daily life patterns of long ago. Holding the tools, walking through historic structures, and sampling heirloom foods transport us in ways no video or book can. Such excursions place our own difficulties in a different context and can expand our appreciation for the comforts we take for granted. A visit to a *skansen* can also trigger feelings of loss, as we reflect on our current weakening bonds of community or the disappearance of basic survival skills that were formerly commonplace. It can touch our core deeply to know that we lack the abilities to shod a horse, churn butter, make soap, tan hides or weave a strong basket out of local materials. You may also perceive an unspoken sadness at being so separated from the earth in a world full of office buildings, computers and fast food. There is a hunger for what we may perceive as simpler less hurried times even with the awareness of the challenges our ancestors faced. We can reflect on these things and be thankful that such heritage is preserved in a form wherein we can access both the lessons and the wisdom our cultural history still has to teach us.

There is much to explore in my cultural past.

May 22

hozhooji nitsihakees (HO-zho-QJEE neets-aj-HA-kay-ees)
Navajo
To think about and honor our differences in good ways.

Judging someone without knowing them is a sure sign of an unde-
veloped mind and a wounded spirit. Bigotry and prejudice are
transmitted so easily through families because of lack of contact
with different peoples. We constantly get misleading information
about each other. Every encounter is really a cross cultural meeting, for no two people have similar histories and perceptions.
There is much wisdom in the concept of *hozhooji nisihakees*,
which speaks to both attitudes and actions that foster a celebration
of diversity. While growing up we all wanted to fit in, to not be
excluded from the group, and the notion of difference as something wonderful seemed absurd. As adults we still struggle with
those ingrained patterns and a basic human xenophobia. When
you expose yourself to the richness of different cultures you
expand your understanding of the human family. Your stereotyped
perceptions of groups are replaced by the unique understanding of
individuals. It is only by moving through our differences and conflicts and dissimilar worldviews that we can truly become allies in
the struggle for social justice and equality.

The pictures on my fridge and the friends I invite to my house reflect my
embrace of diverse peoples.

temenos (TEH-meh-nohs)   Greek
A magical circle in which extraordinary events are free to occur.

 Magic is the lifeblood of the universe, and your inner magician is an agent of awakening. He or she shows you the way to enter sacred space, to climb to the top of the mesa of awe and mystery, to transform, and open yourself to regeneration. Wizardry is simply a heightened state of perceptual awareness. It is remembering that ritual slows you down, removes you from your habitual ways of seeing the world, and reminds you of your possibilities. We can create a *temenos* whenever we need to harness our own power to see things differently. We thus invoke the synchronicity of the universe—those propitious, implausible conjunctions of events that occur more than by chance alone. They often appear with greatest frequency during times of intense growth, and can be cultivated by listening and acting on the guidance that presents itself in the circumstances of each day. Your inner magus sees clearly the meaningful coincidences of outer and inner events that are not cause and effect, but rather the mysterious, unspoken dialogue between the world and the needs of your inner being.

I invoke the magic of altering my ordinary perceptions of reality.

May 24

namaste (naa-MASS-tay)   Hindi
A greeting that honors the part of you that is the same as me.

Each of us has moments when we are all connected and interdependent. We grasp that the misery of all humans is at its core the same, and only fear keeps us separate and isolated. We are all seeking to avoid suffering and find happiness. I can never be fully who I am until you are as well. The tiny separate consciousness we each seem to inhabit is really an integral part of the whole. This awareness is manifest when we utter the greeting *namaste*. It is to say that I honor the place in you where, when you are in that place in you, and I am in that place in me, there is only one of us. To speak this word is to remain hopeful. It is to declare that although as an individual being you may not always be able to act out of that commonality, you do remember that such a connection is always present. The more you allow this insight to penetrate your daily living, the wider the doors of compassion are flung open. Compassion is not pity or sympathy; it is a way of walking through life valuing all of creation. It is the beginning of the circle of kindness and caring that ultimately brings us to inner peace.

I revere the unity of all living beings.

csardas (CHAHRR-dahsh)   Hungarian
A dance with sudden alterations of tempo.

The infinite passion of life bursts forth in music and dancing. To feel the body move through space and dissolve into the rhythms that carry it is to experience an uplifting sensual bliss. Music is a living entity, a vital presence in your body which consistently alters consciousness. Its patterns pervade your senses and you vibrate emotionally in a sea of percussive harmony. The repetition that is at the core of measured accents connects you to the patterns of your internal cadence and those of the planet and the universe. Your heart repeats its beat, you rest and are active, seasons cycle as does your life. Every culture has found its unique expression of these rhythmic phenomena, and *czardas* is particularly energetic. Musicians and dancers engage in ritual dialogue, creating a dense tapestry of sound and motion. Reflective of the movement of our lives, the varying pace is sometimes hard, soft, fast, slow, up, down, focused, scattered, silent. It is the edge, the contact with that other reality, on which you dance. Like our existence itself, the point is not to get somewhere but rather to be somewhere in time dissolved in the joy of this present moment.

When I dance I merge with the rhythms of the cosmos.

May 26

Alpaufzug (AAHLP-owf-tsook)   Swiss German
Ascent to the mountains festival.

The urge to flee can become unbearable. To be out under the vast blueness as all of life springs forth in abundance and celebration is all that matters. The call to be outdoors is too compelling and it is impossible to rest until it is answered. Such is the delightful energy of *Alpaufzug*. It is a time when herders drive goats and cows to higher alpine pasture, with traditional costumes and festivals to honor the desire present in each of us to climb still higher and experience more of the glorious gifts of nature. Those who spend much time in direct contact with the planet have a certain clarity, an enduring discernment of natural truths as a result of years of sharpened senses and paying attention to whatever is unfolding. When you feel those urges for contact with the woods or the beach or plains or flowing water it is imperative to just go. Something vital is summoning, and the rewards are immeasurable. You can trust that your body will lead you where you spirit most needs to be. The sanctuary of the landscape is always open and receptive.

When nature calls, I listen.

ichimyaku tsujiru (eeche-me-YAH-koo tsugee-roo)   Japanese
To have something in common.

Attraction to another person is often a mysterious process. At times the sexual pull is obvious. At others we feel an overwhelming sensation of recognition, of two old souls reuniting. We seem to have had a relationship before. So many things seem to fit easily: our rhythms, desires and visions. The match in sharing what we love is effortless and leads to a sense of immediate intimacy. To encounter this dynamic of bonding and attraction is *ichimyaku tsujiru*, literally to understand someone's heartbeat. Because many of us have been wounded by following initial impulses in relationships we tend to not trust these feelings. Yet they compel us to explore, to open ourselves despite the danger and vulnerability. It is rare for two people to experience compatibility in every aspect of their beings. But when the physical, mental, emotional and spiritual ways of their journey are similar, harmony is the dominant chord. Over time we may take note of the areas of struggle rather than the blessings of what is shared. It is in both the foundation of commonality and the arenas of conflict that we discover the potential for continued growth and healing.

I can focus on the wonderful aspects of my close relationships.

May 28

hii' (he-ee') Malaysian Semai
The band; all of us here together.

Our individual problems are linked to the difficulties of our larger social institutions. The commonality of the pain and confusion we all carry is obvious. Yet our current society destroys community faster than it can be built up, and most people have grown accustomed to isolation and loneliness. Do you still believe that the only really safe space is to be locked up within yourself? You are as sick as you are secret, and the more secrets you still keep the more your emotional health suffers. When you find your *hii'*, you begin to see that it is possible to be vulnerable and safe at the same time, to depend on others without losing your independence. In tribal societies throughout the world, one's place within the larger unit is clear. A powerful resiliency comes in knowing one's position in a supportive alliance. Although it can be challenging and even scary, trust is built upon such connections and interdependency. At every stage of life, intimacy is deepened by letting yourself be known.

I choose to spend time with a group of people I trust.

pagodes (pah-GO-djessh)   **Portuguese**
A samba center where musicians gather to jam.

Idiophones such as drums, two sticks or bones clapped together, a string of shells tinkling around the ankles, a dried gourd with seeds rattling in your hand, were some of the world's first musical instruments. Even the sounds of the names of different kinds of drums invoke the excitement they hold. Ngoma, dauli, tupan, murumba, kalungu, babba ganga, atumpan, duono, embutu, tumyr, isigubu, mujaguzo, dumbek, naqara, tar, darabukke, damaru, tabla, mridanga, hoop, bass, snare, tom tom, conga, timbales, bongos, bata, pandeiro, atabaque, okedo, daibyoshi, tsuri daiko, tsuzumi, ntenga, koboro. Enter into the dynamism of a *pagodes*, a place of raw energy in motion, spontaneity, risk, unfettered gusto, and the source of passionate desires. Here there is the awe and mystery of the untamed parts of who you are. The centering power of the drumbeat becomes the voice of the universe. From beginner to master, all walk the path of exploring the sweet bliss of blending hearts and hands together. You must allow some creative expression for the wildness within. The impulse to drum is an invitation to partake of a primal banquet of the soul.

I accept the innate desire of my hands to make music.

May 30

nisse (NEES-say)   Norway
Good luck trolls.

The notion of beneficent beings intervening on the part of humans is an ancient and widespread belief. Over time this help may have come to us in the form of spiritual guidance, enhancement of material status, or protection from harm. Such assistance is often unbidden, a result of need or difficulty. The beauty of the beings' involvement is that it is spontaneous. They show up when we most need them. Many children report the presence of a light or a palpable presence when they are seriously ill. One can easily imagine these magical beings scrambling about the planet on their missions of joyous compassion. Whether we choose to call them *nisse*, angels, light beings, or fairies, their existence is an important aspect of our creative imagination. How would you greet one if it briefly revealed its physical form? Perhaps we have already made such an acquaintance in a special partner, who stands by us quietly and invisibly throughout our life passage. As silent and powerful guides, only their gifts are obvious. It is possible that the more we open to their presence, the greater the opportunities for interaction and connection.

I can invoke a powerful spirit ally.

natchnienie (nat-HEN-nie)   Polish
A moment of soulful inspiration.

It is an unspoken law of the universe that unexpressed creative energy will engender destructive behaviors. We often see evidence of this in the lives of troubled young people. With few opportunities to express their originality positively, the tension release is often destructive and impulsive. Yet when given a chance these young ones produce gorgeous and profound art, music, drama or uplifting community projects. When we make space for imaginative artistic expression in our own personal evolution, we enlarge our perspectives of what life is all about. This generative capacity in each of us is embodied in the notion of *natchnienie*. Opening to the source, we achieve that exquisite twinkling of an eye, time is suspended, and what flows forth from our paintbrush, pen, hands, voice or instruments is pure and inspiring. The internal critic has drifted off to sleep, the muse is out to play, and it feels wonderful. For these moments the struggle to release the inner artistic vision is diminished. We experience healing too, as the incubation of life's experiences now bursts forth in the splendor of creative expression. You simply surrender to its stream and marvel at its gifts.

I can harness joy through the medium of my own artistry.

JUNE

Raven on the wing
Surrendering to the flow
Embracing it all.

wakanta logony (wah-KAHN-tah lo-GON-ee)   Osage
The great mystery is good.

One would think that since we spend so much time in the realm of "I don't know" we would learn to embrace and welcome this reality. So often we feel confused and uncertain of decisions that demand attention. Despite our best efforts to understand the nuances in a current dilemma, no clarity arises. Time to surrender and utter *wakanta logony*. Everything that surrounds us is alive and changing and moving. If we could penetrate these secrets we might obtain more insight into our human quandaries. To acknowledge the fantastic adventure and enigma of our existence is to truly feel at peace. Gazing at an endless array of night stars, or discovering the small miracle of budding fruit trees that survive a late frost because they are enclosed in snow remind you that your life is not a puzzle to be solved but rather a journey to be lived. You can rise above your mundane concerns and greet the profound with awe and admiration. You can rest in the comfort of the benevolence of the great unknown. There are no mistakes, only lessons; whatever road you choose will eventually lead you home.

I can relax and value the goodness of all I don't understand.

June 2

machetunim (MAJ-uh-toon-im)   Yiddish
The mother and father of your child's spouse.

What begins as a joyful union between two families often slowly becomes a war zone of major and minor skirmishes. Impassioned speeches and tearful wedding toasts may give way to squabbling and bickering for the time and attention of the young couple. Trying to please both sets of parents results in simmering conflicts which become more volatile as grandchildren enter the mix. Birthday parties, vacations, holidays and spiritual celebrations become even more critical events. In a society where the rules are no longer clearly prescribed about where the new couple is expected to reside and to spend more time, we really need the concept of extended family that lies behind *machetunim*. Just the fact that the English language lacks this notion indicates how little importance we directly place on this relationship. Designated as official members of the clan, these family members are automatically imbued with recognition and respect. Recognizing that there are both responsibilities and joys inherent in such a designation can reduce awkwardness and competition. Honoring the expanding family allow us to expand the circle of love and connectedness.

I can view the parents of my child's spouse as relatives rather than rivals.

honami (ho-NAH-me)   Japanese
Study of the way in which different plants wave in the wind.

Its leaves flutter silently in the warm breeze, like prayer flags paying homage to the sacred sun. Buddha chose a bamboo grove after enlightenment as one of his homes. For centuries the bamboo has been associated with the growth and development of inner life, and many cultures revere certain trees as guardians of wisdom. What is neglected in the garden of your life, and are you conscious of the optimal conditions for your own personal evolution? How you are coping with the winds of change might be enhanced by applying the discipline of *honami* to your inner life. To invite such an aesthetic into awareness inspires resilient approaches to hardships. Yield but do not give up. Hang around people who affirm you. Stretch upward. Create new experiences for yourself. Send down more roots, and recommit to doing what you know is good for you. Weed out old ways of dealing with a situation. Appreciate each step of your growth, and strive to accept the flow of events. Wait, and let the summer thunderstorms share their secrets. Flow with every fiber of your being, relaxed yet centered.

To yield gracefully with difficult situations enhances my strength.

June 4

paho (PAH-ho)   Hopi
Prayer stick.

Like sand in an hourglass, we want to stop an addictive pattern yet we can't help being carried along. The mood altering experience or substance imprisons us, even as we watch the life damaging consequences emerge. The turning point often comes when we embrace the wisdom that we are not in control. We must turn the situation over to a higher power. Prayer again becomes meaningful as a vehicle for transformation. Beyond the rote repetition of early childhood supplications we discover the power of humbly asking for assistance. Beads, bells, incense, an altar, or a *paho* may be employed as points of focus for a conversation of the soul. These material aids help us see that Creator sees the goodness of our struggles, the light and dark within us. Such a special object achieves significance because it becomes rooted in endurance, dealing with difficult issues, and the certainty that by staying with the process some guidance will manifest. In the search for self we recognize that faith is about daily practice.

The way is revealed one day at a time.

wiitokuchumpunkuruganiyugwivantumu (Uto-Aztecan)
They who are going to sit and cut up with a knife a black female buffalo.

The hunter stalks his prey, calling to its spirit. Because he is always respectful and sincere, a bond is formed which draws that which he seeks inevitably toward him. Patience, skill, cooperation and cunning guide him. Success is his and there will be a feast; the entire community will share in the work of preparation and the joy of celebration. Tools are gathered and songs are sung as *wiitokuchumpunkuruganiyugwivantumu* prepare for their task. Nothing is wasted, and the sacredness of the encounter with a being that has surrendered its life so others might survive is maintained. What aspects of your life have such a sense of ritual and completion within the embrace of community? Whenever the beginning of our quest is imbued with the sacred, we honor the source of all that sustains us. When we take the time to share the abundance of our labors in a way that supports those we care about, we bring reverence to our work. As we balance individual creative expression with a sense of service to others, we step into our power to do good in the world.

I will bring reverence to my work, no matter what it is.

June 6

kesho (KEH-sho)   Kiswahili
Relaxed pace of life.

Before enlightenment, fax, use the cell phone, and check your E mail. After enlightenment, fax, use the cell phone, and check your E mail. We are all conditioned to skim the surface of experience and then dash on to something new. In the midst of a busy everydayathon, it is vital to timeshift, to compress and transform certain moments into the realm of deep significance. To saunter instead of speed through the landscape. Or to consciously embrace a fast pace because that is what a situation demands. Our whole way of being can evolve into *kesho*, as if we were gathering a string of pearls slowly over time. This tempo lies in the middle way between fast and inert, the two walls we often bounce off of in our ongoing duel with the big watch. Finding your natural rhythm in a hurry-addicted world frees you to seek serenity rather than sensation, peace instead of productivity. Future-tripping dissolves as the cadence of now now now becomes the pendulum beat that captures us. We embody a pulse that resonates with the spontaneous. We stop waiting patiently (or otherwise!) and begin encountering.

Speed helps me forget; slowness invites remembering.

tki'o tjuiks (tkee'o tyoo-eeks)   Tohono O'odham
It looks like it may be going to rain on us.

Rain in desert environments strikes outsiders as something lacking, an element missing in the terrain. Those who live in such places are intrigued by the unpredictability rather than the paucity of falling moisture. A months long dry spell can shift with a prolonged torrential cloudburst. Unseasonal storms, and droughts during customary rainy seasons throw patterns into turmoil. The common statement *tki'o tjuiks* reflects such unforeseeability. Events are viewed in this phrase from the lens of the probable without any firm assumption that something will happen for sure. Few are willing to confirm that something will happen until it does. This notion of not anticipating is so ingrained in the structure of Tohono language and reflects the element of surprise in all life. It is such an intriguing notion to view uncertainty as a great gift, a blessing, and to see the folly of viewing one's life as predictable. Entering into a mindset that abhors assumptions and embraces uncertainty is refreshing to the spirit.

I welcome the astonishment in daily occurrences.

June 8

Danonal (dahn-o-nal)   Korean
Cold water shampoo day.

We are drawn to flowing water like moths to the light. We gain a sense of peace and calm in our bodies when we sit quietly by a stream or waterfall. The sounds and smells form an intricate bouquet of delight that speaks of simpler times and quiet contemplation. A celebration that reflects this communion is *Danonal*. In a ritualized effort to avoid heat related illness during the coming year, people gather for the day near a body of cold water, where they bathe and wash their hair, picnic, and compose poems. Later, customary offerings are also made at family shrines, as ancestors are honored and thanked. The date of the festival, which usually falls in late spring, is determined by a lunar calendar, and it is a wonderful opportunity to revel in natural settings. While we are often ready to use anything as an excuse for a party, the idea of dedicating a day to both fun and introspection seems confusing. Bathing is sanctified in many cultures as an expression of cleansing mind, body, and spirit. Such ardent sensuality makes visible the longing to release tension and anxiety. It is an act of self love and enduring joy.

Washing in a source of naturally flowing cold water invigorates all aspects of my being.

asbestos gelos (ahs-BEHS-tohs GEH-lohs)   Greek
Unquenchable, inextinguishable laughter.

Human laughter has been called internal jogging. It shakes us up and turns tension inside out. Lost in the sweet abandon of a spontaneous giggle, we become childlike again. At its very highest intensity, laughter is composed of twelve separate and distinct gestures, including throwing back the head, opening the mouth wide and pulling back the corners of the mouth. Most often there is an accompanying hooting or barking sound which so distinguishes each individual style. The term *asbestos gelos* causes much reflection upon the nature of human endeavors from a god's perspective. Our pitiful human condition inspires both tears and raucous laughter. The joke is truly on us whenever we take things too seriously. The basis of a visual or verbal joke is that something strange or shocking occurs, but since it is not to be taken seriously the slightly frightening sensation gives way to relief. Laughter is uplifting because it sometimes represents an expression of danger encountered but escaped. We also surrender to laughter out of pure delight, in appreciation, or when confronted with the absurd. It is our ticket from endless tears to unmitigated joy, a round trip we will make over and over again.

I can be jubilant and full of laughter for no reason at all.

June 10

a piacere (ah pee-ah-chay-ray)   Italian
At your pleasure; whatever tempo you wish.

The mood of the moment shifts imperceptibly, as the melody moves on to new rhythmic territory. We catch our breath as the symphony of daily preoccupation composes itself into a new beat. We may stray far from the music of our souls, from what we are meant to do on this plane of existence. Although mostly used in a musical context, the signature *a piacere* encourages broader rhythmic interpretation. A life well lived is one in which we cultivate changing tempos by playing and resting and creating a little each day. It is to dance to our own tempo and find open arms waiting to embrace who we are or who we are not. Freedom sings as you dare to be outrageous and sullen, feisty and silent, poetic and unintelligible, exotic and mundane. All the songs playing deep within your eyes seek to manifest whatever dream you hold inside. Once you have heard the inner call there is no retreat, only the constant variations of the song that will bring you home. You need only be yourself, in synch with the beating of your own heart.

I find delight in the many rhythms of my mortality.

la perruque (lah pay-RIEK)   French
What you do for yourself while apparently working for another.

We may do nothing for what seems like forever, or work ourselves into a frenzy to get a project out. Is it the hours or the results that count? Under the cover of working at our jobs, we may engage in some personal activities. A little grocery shopping or a stop at the bank on the way to a meeting, a few family phone calls from the office phone or making a list of errands for later in the day represent common examples. What we do for ourselves while apparently working at what we are paid to do constitutes *la perruque*. It is a small sleight of hand, a secret life of sorts, that demonstrates that the boundaries between public, personal and interior lives are thin. Daydreaming at work is balanced by thinking about the office while on vacation. The real question is who are you fooling? You strive to be a whole integrated being. Remove the mask that hides the luminous gifts you have to contribute in both settings.

Today I can effortlessly balance personal needs with the demands of work.

June 12

kilesa (kee-LEH-suh)   Pali
Torments of mind.

The great war within seems to rage on endlessly without hope of
a cease fire. Sometimes as soon as we emerge from the realm of
dreams and open our eyes we can feel the pressure of the
"shoulds," "have to's" and regrets marching into our heads. The
pain we receive from others pales in comparison to the damage
we do to ourselves with an untamed mind. We may see the suffering of *kilesa* clearly, yet still be unable to free ourselves from
this distress and anguish. The path is to simply let go, to surrender and release the desires and delusions that hold us prisoners
within ourselves. You are a captive, polishing your own prison
bars, waiting for escape when the door is unlocked. Once you
fully acknowledge the pain you create for yourself, it is possible
to cultivate peace and serenity instead of repeating the endless
cycle of unfulfilled expectations and disappointments. When
you spend time in meditation or exercise or celebration, the futility of clinging to anything becomes obvious. Your power grows
in that acceptance, and what you seek the most will be found by
letting go of the struggle to find it.

Moment to moment I can welcome peace instead of affliction.

takuan (tah-kwan)   Chinese
To have seen through life and thus to take things lightly.

The cosmic joke really is on us. One need only look around to see evidence in abundance. Someone works really hard to retire, and then dies within a month of the event; just when a friend finally gives up the idea of a serious relationship, love blossoms unexpectedly; personal debt is overwhelming and a sudden inheritance arrives, changing everything; the promotion comes in, and as a result you lose out on another important opportunity. There is no pattern to the astonishing twists of fate we all encounter along the way. Paradox and surprise rule! To fully perceive this as the nature of reality through the concept of *takuan*, is to enter a profoundly liberating state of mind. We realize the absurdity of thinking that we are in control, and there is a lightness to this web of events beyond our comprehension. You are still asked to continue, to embrace the work of living, yet all of the ups and downs are held in the arms of a comforting presence, a sureness as deep as the center of one's own being. The burden of seriousness is somehow lifted. This is an awareness that comforts, a spiritual dose of nourishing chicken soup, an uplifting breeze of illumination.

I can let go of trying to control my dilemmas.

June 14

tiep (tee-YEP)   **Vietnamese**
To be in touch with oneself.

We do so much to forget ourselves. Lost in the web of our own wanderings we constantly invite something else to enter. Whether it is television or sports, politics or a book, we seek escape more than engagement. To practice *tiep* is to caress the source of wisdom, understanding and compassion within ourselves, within the context of a large community of others who are similarly engaged. It is to be fully aware of what is going on in our bodies, our minds and our feelings. Contact is made with the inner being that is already enlightened and for whom the insight of generosity is tangible and effective. This idea also includes a sense of continuance, the act and art of making something long lasting. The wellspring within us is part of the ongoing existence of the source of true understanding started by evolved beings eons ago. Our careers in peaceful compassion were begun before we were born. Beyond the individual, it reflects the interbeingness and interconnectedness of the community seeking to enlarge and stabilize these qualities. We can rest assured that the flames of wisdom and the flowering of compassion will continue long after we have passed on.

I am part of the many for whom compassion is a way of life.

diyan lang (DE-yahn lahng)   Tagalog
Wandering around; response to Where are you going?

Many cultures have some expression defining the process of just flowing along, drifting on the breeze of adventure with no purpose or destination in mind. They honor and accept the importance of such activity. Meandering is quite easy to do as a stranger in an exotic land, but also possible in one's own home town. Walking around in this manner reflects an openness to perceiving the world differently. Being and allowing rather than doing and making. Where are you headed? *Diyan lang!* It is an invitation—no, a declaration—that you are off to ride on the wings of the now, to listen to the call of immediate desire, to see the world unfolding in all its exquisite magic. How delicious it is to both wander and wonder around, like a toddler at the beach, full of sensual pleasure and giggling delight. Such self indulgent time serves a higher design. The connection to all of life is deepened, mystery is reawakened, and the sense of satisfaction with the basic gifts of life is affirmed.

I give myself the gift of roaming about with no destination.

June 16

simpatico (seem-PAH-tee-coh)   Spanish
Instinctively attuned to the moods and wishes of another.

Whenever we meet another, we try to establish points of connection. We search for something familiar that can reassure us that this stranger is trustworthy and somehow not really that different from us. Long before discussions of politics, religion, or the stories of one's past, we tune into non verbal expressions and manners, and a basic sense of how the other is in the world. It is one of the reasons that cross cultural communication can be so difficult, and require so much time, as potential layers of misunderstanding gradually get clarified. Along our journey we meet people with whom we feel an immediate ease, a mutual worldview, a sense of always having known this person. Sometimes this develops over time, often it blooms quickly, a result of a shared history of oppression, difficulty, challenge, or multiple common interests. Like two notes in harmony, there is an undeniable resonance that fills every interaction. *Simpatico* implies an understanding beyond words, a connection deeper than lifetimes, a joy in finding a lost brother or sister who really understands where you are coming from.

I am grateful for the deep connections I have with some people.

ma (mah)   Japanese
Empty space, the huge meaning carried by small silences.

Sometimes we use talk as a crutch to move through fear and discomfort. At difficult times when we are "at a loss for words," we still struggle to jump on the lifeboat of verbal expression, clutching at some phrase or expression that might guide us through. We talk to ourselves all day long, reassuring our egos that all our little plans and desires will get fulfilled, or battering ourselves for our less than perfect actions in the world. When we embrace the essence of *ma*, we validate empty space and free time as having value. We also create a significant new communication tool. The impact of the moment of silence before we praise our child's report card, answer yes to a lover, or reject an offer is immense. When we pause before going on with a tale, to let the meaning sink slowly into the souls of our listeners, or share a quiet moment with a grieving friend when nothing needs to be said, we deepen our practice of silent voicing. The rich nuances of such expression hint at a universe where one can learn to see and feel space, to dance in the interval of emptiness and discover significance.

I can consciously bring forth the space of silence into my interactions.

June 18

senge (sehn-guh)   Sango
Naked, nothing; A response to How are you?

One out of five people on this planet goes hungry everyday. A similar multitude do not have access to clean water, nor adequate fuel for cooking or keeping warm. What keeps one alive in the face of such difficulty is often a sense of humor about life's condition. Thus in parts of the Central African Republic the response to an inquiry about one's well being, is simply *senge*. I have nothing, I am nothing; there is zero happening. Yet it goes deeper to a more expansive truth. I also stand before you naked with nothing to hide, nothing to covet. I am simply who I am. Compassion for the suffering of others can help us examine our own sense of deprivation. If less is really more, than what have you actually gained by immersing yourself in the material world? Are all the pressures and deadlines and living by the clock worth the payoff? Have you exchanged an abundance of material goods for the deeper loss of spiritual meaning ?

Those who have little often have much to teach me.

aloha 'aina (ah-LO-hah ah'-ee-nah)   Hawaiian
Love of the land, one of the three essential principles of the Hawaiian culture.

When was the last time you directly expressed your affection for the land that nourishes and sustains us all? What did you do? Perhaps it was a simple thanks as you ate something from the garden, or were swept away by the majesty of old neighborhood trees. Or maybe you engaged in a more direct action by planting a tree or working to preserve a piece of land. *Aloha 'aina* is such a vital thread in the tapestry of daily Hawaiian life that one is struck by how palpable this respect is when visiting these wonderful islands. Offerings, feasts, flower leis all speak the language of gratefulness. To see the earth more as part of sustaining one's heritage, rather than as a commodity to be bought and sold is to invigorate and sanctify a unique bond. It is in our nature to become attached to special places. Perhaps it is a stretch of beach, a favorite forest grove, a rock outcropping on the plains, or just a city park or neighbor's garden that calls to us. When we suffuse it with affection, and care for it, we learn something about this ancient Hawaiian connection. Like a babe evolving inside a womb, we actively create relationship with the land, and grow together in harmony and beauty.

I can find new ways to expand my relationship with the land.

June 20

biga peula (BEE-kuh POOL-uh)   **New Guinea Kiriwina**
Hard words; potentially disruptive true statements.

The truth will set you free. Honesty is the best policy. The truth never hurts unless it ought to. Such platitudes are not strong enough to outweigh our collective desire to avoid conflict, shame, or embarrassment by leaving unspoken that which might cause harm. We all know that you can get in serious trouble for saying out loud what everyone knows to be true, whether within a social, family or work related context. Yet we also appreciate the benefits of someone revealing our unpleasant blindspots. What may be hard for us to hear ultimately serves. To utter a *biga peula* is to invite disruption of normal social amenities. Doing so often shifts things enough to create a significant breakthrough, but not without the risk of fracturing relationships. Timing and awareness become important allies. Hurtful words, even though true, spoken in anger or as punishment for perceived wrongs, only increase our collective suffering. To use this concept skillfully is to uncover secrets that must be revealed for healing to occur. The motivation must be clear, the intention sincere, and the outcome beneficial.

I use the truth as a revitalizing balm rather than as a weapon.

kismet (KISS-met)   **Arabic**
Fate or destiny.

Our desires create the energy of life. We throw our intention forward into the future and the force of our will carries us toward it, like a ship moving steadily to a lighthouse, a plant reaching for the sun, a migratory bird seeking familiar nesting grounds. In the process we discover more of who we really are. Yet this movement does not occur in isolation. Every society accedes to the unseen forces that shape an individual's sojourn. To align oneself with *kismet* is to multiply the bounty available. We can rebel as much as we want, waving free will banners in the air, rejecting or ignoring the assistance that comes our way, or wailing against the unfairness of it all. In the end it is clear there has always been a certain direction to your life, an inexorable flow that guided, cajoled, and when necessary forced us to enter where we feared to tread. To accept this reality is to welcome and resign yourself to the bends in the river, both the difficult passages and the gifts of smoother going. There can be no momentum to your growth without surrendering to the invisible power of what is meant to be. Destiny entices you forward while dancing in your rearview mirror.

How exciting to see what surprises fate is yet to reveal!

June 22

banjar (BAHN-jahr)   **Indonesian**
Cooperative groups of neighbors bound to assist each other.

Given the increased mobility of our society, for many of us, a sense of community arises not so much from neighborhood, but rather from the loose assemblage of friends and acquaintances. Even if scattered across the country, these relationships seem more solid than the shifting dynamics of who happens to live across the street. It is hard for us to imagine the stability and sense of defined place inherent in the concept of a *banjar*. Its roots lie in the daily pressures of village life, where survival means having neighbors you can count upon. That such intricate responsibilities are openly declared and discussed is testimony to the cooperative nature of such cultures. For us, lending a hand occasionally or helping create a block party or crime watch is easy. The challenge is to incorporate into our daily awareness the importance of supportive interaction with those around us. In the giving there is always receiving.

I will open myself to those who live around me.

yawari (yah-WAH-ree)   Xingu
Ritual insults that follow certain rules and are spoken in the presence of bystanders.

Growing up the flurry of insults one had to defend against seemed endless. Someone was always making fun of our appearance or behaviors or of those of our family. Even if untrue, we often got hooked by the exchange. The oft repeated notion that "sticks and stones can break my bones but words can never hurt me" is rapidly discarded in the heat of the encounter. As we have moved from fists to guns, the potential lethality of "dissing" or insulting someone has increased considerably among our youth. A look perceived as disrespectful can bring a bullet to your head. Enter *yawar*i as an alternative. Though not exactly a form of dispute resolution or conflict mediation, it can be a method of de-escalation nonetheless! With such a practice we can teach young ones the ability to keep one's center when facing insults and let the remarks bounce off harmlessly. Like the Starship Enterprise when encountering a potentially hostile presence, one might train in the art of "shields up and open a channel." We can teach them to stay focused and listen, yet not to engage in increased hostility. It is possible to add to the choices of fight or flight the valuable notion of flow.

I can instruct young ones to deal with insults in a violence free way.

June 24

ravda (RAHV-dah)   Romany
Strength that comes from being emotional.

"Why don't grownups cry more?" queries a five year old. The young ones know how to bring pain up to the surface fast, while adults tend to forget or repress the essential purification available by just letting it all go. One feels and has more *ravda* if you cry and sob and scream, and get everyone on the phone or over for tea, and yell and hash it all out. Perseverance and tenacity are fed by this wellspring of shared emotional release. People can go through the worst things and crack before your eyes and still keep going because they sob when people are hurt or killed. The shell of protection in one who admits no pain or fear will ultimately break apart in destructive ways. Better to give yourself permission to allow the torrent of tormented sensations to find its way out. With open hearts to listen, tender faces to encourage and loving arms to cradle you, there is no better path to a deeper more sustaining fortitude. By letting go you are better able to hold on and continue.

I find solace and strength in expressing my deepest feelings.

takwatsi (tahk-WAH-tsee)   Huichol
A basket used to hold shamanic power objects.

It is a tradition as ancient as it is potent. People have always imbued natural objects with special powers. Rocks, crystals, feathers, shells, various animal parts or crafted objects became repositories of sacred energy used in seasonal ceremonies, healing practices, and as a significant form of protection against unseen forces. Reflecting traditions carefully preserved through generations, the sacred objects of the people were shielded and carried in a *takwatsi* in a way that honored their powers, and so that their intense properties would not be dispersed or used improperly. The concept of such a container can enrich our present day lives. When you create a spirit bag of your own, you embark on a journey of personal healing and helpful objects will be drawn to it. Some may be significant because of family history or stories associated with their discovery; others will simply feel like they belong. Each expands in its own way your link with the sacred. When you learn to use them as a source of renewal, you declare your willingness to stand in relation with transcendent practices still accessible by anyone.

I invite symbolic objects into the abode I have created for them.

June 26

qaqayuq (qah-qah-yuuq)   Inuktitut
One who likes being the center of attention and shows off.

"Mommy, daddy, look at me! See what I can do!" As children we instinctively seek to fill a well of self assurance we will drink from the rest of our lives. From the earliest age, we crave the attention and praise of those closest to us. With their caring presence, these loved ones reflect to us what the big scary world is really like, and in that light or its absence we slowly form an image of our self. For a short time, we are indeed the center of the universe, effortlessly drawing what we need toward us and demanding that those in near proximity pay attention. Especially in Western culture, we continue to want to be regarded for our uniqueness, our individual expression, the inimitable expansiveness of boundless ego. Possessions, style of dress, school and work accomplishments continue to feed the insatiable desire to be noticed. In cultures that place high value on cooperation and group process, such attributes are often viewed as childlike. If someone is said to be *qaqayuq*, they are laughed at and thought to be silly. While their antics may be entertaining, such extroversion is seen as a quality far less important than the ability to get along and contribute to the collective efforts that insure survival. We can strive to continually let go of ego and laugh at our own tendencies toward self importance.

I can notice when I especially want to be noticed, and laugh.

gule gule (gu-leh gule)   Turkish
Go smiling; form of Goodbye.

We seldom reflect on the possibility that when we bid farewell to someone, it might be the last time we ever see them. Yet with every person close to us, that experience will occur if they pass on before us. It is very interesting to contemplate how different cultures proclaim the essential commonplace ritual of departure. There are many variations of blessings, and the "until we meet again" sort of withdrawing salutes. *Gule gule* is quite remarkable for its profound simplicity. We wish for those who are departing what we most desire for ourselves. "Hold happiness in your heart. May you have much to delight in!" An element of conflict resolution is also manifest. "If differences are present let us set them aside. Never should we leave each other in anger or with bitterness in our hearts." And finally, there is no better way to hold in one's memory the last image of a dear friend, than of them smiling as they exit.

This week the language of my goodbyes is laughter!

June 28

dak (dahk)   Urdu
A stopping point or resthouse for long distance travelers.

Every step is a passage to eternity. Along our journey fatigue may cloak us like a heavy garment. Body mind and spirit crave the ancestral fire, the nurturing warmth of a meal and a bed. Time to give thanks for the *dak* just over the next pass. In Pakistan and India, lands where pilgrimage is common, and many villages still flourish in isolation, such places of respite offer unpretentious necessities. No hotel amenities here, just the basics of nourishment and a bed, which are embraced with an appreciation only the hardship of rugged travel can engender. We realize how little we really need to survive and experience the freedom of fitting all our essentials in one uncomplicated bundle. When you seek such islands of serenity in a frenzied "more is better" world, you welcome extraordinary spaciousness into your life. The doors of perception are thrown wide open, and the journey is a good one. Lessons appear in vivid, more comprehensible forms.

Whenever I can, I enjoy the clarity that comes with living simply.

fado (FAH-doo)   Portuguese
A haunting blues style music rooted in African slave songs.

The wail of ancestors tumbles through the subtle harmonics. A deep longing is evoked, the promise of a freedom not yet fully tasted. *Fado* brings tears to its listeners and tears at their hearts. It is musically demanding for performers and emotionally draining for the audience. Both are transported to an era of slavery and oppression and survival. The tones invite us to participate in a passage of healing remembrance, to reflect, and to never forget. Through the music we become the slave owner destroying families; we become the slave child who is loved despite the misery; we feel both the unexpected gestures of kindness and the flailing crack of the whip. The melodies implore us to find new ways to relieve the suffering of those who are still marginalized in our society. There is no demand for a deepening of guilt and shame, but rather an invitation for an expansion of compassionate action.

I am an instrument of hope in reducing prejudice and discrimination.

June 30

hadai (bih-DA-ee)   Navajo
The special relationship between a boy and his maternal uncle.

The teachings of gentleness and strength, caring and support are strong and deep. Slowly the boy embodies the rhythms of manhood. He learns from an older male presence how mind body and spirit work together in the masculine realm, through the consistent bounty of time and energy. Like no other guidance he will receive in his life, this exemplary kinship resonates with the beauty of a gift passed on through centuries of tradition. The term *hadai* implies not just the existence of a blood relationship, but a circle of expectations and responsibilities. How much we might learn from such a bonding in an era when many young people seem lost and adrift. In adolescence a young man often rebels and withdraws into isolation and separation, especially from his parents. At this critical time other significant men in his life may still be able to reach him. But only if a bridge of love and trust has already been forged and stabilized. Whenever we are creating such a linkage, we honor the truth that every young boy needs both the masculine and feminine to be complete.

I can be a positive male force for a young man, or find someone who can.

JULY

Each being must catch
The secret wave of their heart
And ride into life.

funktionslust (foonk-tseeh-OHNS-loost)   German
The pleasure of doing, of producing an effect.

Children create a new universe everyday. By manipulating whatever and whomever is in their immediate environment, they produce an impact and foster change. As children, each of us learned
to stimulate our own growth by the cyclical process of formulat-
ing a new situation, responding to it, and then pushing the edge
of our skills toward mastery. And we did it all while playing and
having fun! The joy of *funktionslust* seems hardwired into our
intelligence. There can be no mistaking that relaxed stance of the
body, the clarity of purpose and intent, and the evident delight
that permeates an individual fully engaged in what they are
doing. One of the first questions we ask a new acquaintance is
some variation of "What do you love to do?" Baking, gardening,
building, sports, and other forms of creative involvement feed a
hunger for expressing ourselves in the world. The inherent enjoyment is magnified when we invite its presence into even the sim-
plest of daily activities.

*I can find happiness in brushing my teeth, putting on my clothes and
other simple tasks.*

July 2

hoo ha (hoo ha)   Yiddish
Expression of surprise, astonishment and admiration.

We experience times in life when our whole being responds positively to something. There is no time for editing the reaction—our breath is taken away. Maybe we are excited by an astounding come-from-behind finish to a race, or the dramatic unveiling of a gorgeous work of art. Perhaps we stand stunned by the finale of a piece of music performed by a virtuoso soloist, or the absolute beauty of our daughter walking down the stairs on prom night. A common theme from all of these examples is that, for a brief instant, humankind really has achieved perfection. *Hoo ha!* The expression rolls out of your mouth in an exaggerated fashion, relishing every second of the experience. You surrender to the magic of the moment, realizing its transitory nature and yet clinging to the sense that time has been suspended. Previous limits have been shattered, any expectations surpassed. It is a blessing that your senses have been overwhelmed, and this expression enlivens even the more ordinary moments to follow. You feel fully alive, satisfied and complete.

I cherish times of amazement.

wa (wah)   Japanese
Sense of harmony and well-being.

Life's turbulent waters always seem to be stirring something up: concerns about material goods, a variety of physical and emotional aches and pains, and the anxiety of our crazy minds worrying about it all. Even if we are feeling pretty good, someone we know may be suffering and that increases our own distress. It seems that the norm is to live with the mindset that things are never quite right. To choose instead a worldview that *wa* is always accessible requires changing some fundamental habits. As we focus on discovering peace, the old patterns will wither of their own accord. Drink serenity in like water from an oasis or nectar from a flower. Breathe tranquillity into every fiber of your being. First you must believe that you deserve to nurture yourself in this way. Then it is possible to allow this sense to permeate your being. The floodgates will open, and a river will flow within you from a calm center, available when needed for yourself or others.

I carry with me always the capacity for inner peace.

July 4

intelleto (in-teh-LEH-toh)   **Latin**
Visionary intelligence.

We are each an unsculpted block of time, a roughly hewn work in progress. Like Michelangelo in his studio, we slowly remove the apparent surface of our lives to reveal the sculpture hidden underneath all along. Like an archeologist on a field exploration, we bravely uncover layers of conditioning in order to see our original nature. We seek not something that is learned or crafted but what has always been there, the wellspring of our humanity. We are guided there by the faculty of *intelleto*. This quality of perception is not merely rational intelligence, but a more expansive capability of seeing through appearances to that which is as yet unborn, unseen, unformed. This inner eye applies not only to self examination, but plays a role in most creative endeavors. Possessed by every one of us, the quality of intelleto is the language of inspiration. Whenever out-of-box thinking is invoked, you open a channel to your own consciousness, and beyond to the source. When you utilize this attribute to reduce suffering, whether by drafting a meaningful document, inventing a useful item, or creating a healing work of art or music, then you truly discover the power of this gift.

I welcome the property of seeing deeply into my life.

petana (peh-TAH-nah)   Keres
Cornmeal, which is considered sacred and often used as an offering.

In some Native North American cultures, the growth of an individual is perceived as analogous to that of a stalk of corn. From the sowing of the seed, to the development of strong roots, to the aged withering of the plant, each stage has its parallel significance in human life. Corn needs good soil, water and light, and the company of its brothers and sisters in the field. So, too, babies need a physically healthy start, love, kindness and a supportive community. The word *petana* evokes spiritual power. It reminds us that we are sustained by the goodness of this earth and by Creator, as well as our own efforts. The Corn mother of ancient myths of Southwestern tribes of the United States planted bits of her heart to yield the first grain. Cornmeal is therefore considered sacred, and is often sprinkled on the ground as an offering expressing gratitude before taking something from nature. To give thanks can become a way of life for us. We are grateful for the rain, when it comes, for without it there can be no harvest. We are also appreciative of our suffering and hardship, for without them our spirits could not grow strong and complete their journey.

Remembering to give thanks connects me to the beauty of creation.

July 6

pasalubong (PAH-sah-loo-bong)   **Tagalog**
Gift of food one brings back after travelling.

Music, babies and food are the vernacular of life. Understood and appreciated across cultures, they transcend the inherent limits of language. Universally accepted as an expression of good intent, they smooth the way for a variety of social encounters. From the earliest ancestors who thought of bringing some wild berries back to the cave, sharing food has been an essential aspect of human interaction. Partaking in a meal together is a standard form of bonding and communicating. Like Marco Polo returning from a quest, bringing home both stories and food to eat while telling them seems a winning combination. The more exotic the *pasalubong* the better. From spices to coffee to sweets or snacks, the present is a token reminder that the family was carried along in our minds and hearts on the travels. Loved ones were missed and thought of while the voyager was away. Now one is home and all are together again. It is a time to celebrate and to show appreciation for a safe return.

There is much to share when returning from a trip.

Kukulkan (koo-kool-KAHN)   Mayan
The god of wind, symbolizing light, water and motion.

In our daily lives we can touch the ancient ways of finding godlike qualities in every aspect of nature. Swept away in the dynamic beauty of our changing sea and landscape, we can pause and marvel at both the sustaining power and seeming indifference of nature to human affairs. The sun rises, the wind blows, and rain falls, supporting our lives and yet occurring without regard for our individual wants or needs. How insightful to honor a deity such as *Kukulkan*, and thus recognize our planet as a living entity. With each rising and falling of your own chest, you resonate with the larger respiratory winds of the world. With every shift of inner light and shadow, you shine with the brilliance of a species struggling to find a sustainable connection with its home. Your bloodstream pulses with the memory of its ocean origins. Your steps upon the earth are a spiritual path, your voice on the wind a supplication for the peace and harmony we all seek.

Feeling the movement of wind and rain and sunshine is a form a prayer.

July 8

bodhisattva (bo-dhee-SAHTT-vuh)   Pali
One who has attained enlightenment but remains to help others attain salvation.

Compassion is a power that is asleep within each of us, a trembling of the heart that simply asks "How can I help?". To aspire to become a *bodhisattva* is to develop a courageous altruistic attitude and to take responsibility and work for the happiness and well-being of all sentient beings. It is to cultivate a gentle generosity that doesn't depend on conditions, and is all inclusive. Through compassion, you keep expanding the edges of who you are able to love and accept just as they are. In this simple yearning for individuals to be joyous there is no holding back of affection because they don't act as we want them to. The domain of compassion is all encompassing, and at the very least finds expression in not wanting to harm others. Through practice, your capacity for loving extends gradually beyond friends to your worst enemies. Like a large tree, your shade is offered to everyone. Like the sun, your light shines upon all beings.

I vow to practice compassion in my daily life.

koinonia (koy-NOH-nee-ah)   Greek
A community discovered through a shared story or other commonality.

There are those who believe that community is found rather than made. It is discovered when we meet others who are on the same voyage, people with whom we are linked through circumstances. In telling our history to someone, we enter into a bond of trust and begin to reveal that which is normally hidden. The relating and hearing of an experience draws on the strength and hope of others who know that same truth because they have been there in their own lives. This is the essence of *koinonia*. Like former strangers at a twelve step or other support group meeting, there is an intimacy that is possible simply through the sharing of similar tales. In the process of emptying ourselves to others we create a fullness and richness for all who are present. You are never truly without company. There are others who lost their mother when they were young, or struggled with substance abuse, or got up in the middle of the night to watch a comet, or have a yarn about falling off a horse. It is comforting to appreciate that many people have had similar episodes in this great shared adventure of life.

Shared anecdotes are the lifeblood of human connections.

July 10

kaas (kahs)   Yiddish
Anger, wrath and sorrow.

In Western culture, men are encouraged to express their anger.
Might makes right, we are told, and righteous anger is so sweet.
Men are not encouraged to admit to fear or pain. Big boys don't
cry; they are like tough, sturdy oaks that feel no pain and fear no
one. If you have grown up male, these messages live in your
body. They were passed on to you by your father and other men,
more by temperament than by teaching. The ripples of such poor
training continue to adversely affect the lives of many. How
refreshing to be exposed to the sense of *kaas*. Inherent in this
term is the understanding that beneath most vented anger lies a
layer of fear or grief. It is a mixture of emotions that temporarily
color our reality. This term implicitly transcends the notion that
men should funnel all their sadness and apprehension into a
blind storm of rage. Better to acknowledge and taste the sorrow
and grieve appropriately for when you cannot cry, your ire will
only bring tears to another. You cannot fight your anger or control it. But you can with time and patience, accept it, treat it with
tenderness and heal the pain and fears that give it life.

I can be free of anger only when I embrace my grief.

nimewisha kabisa (nih-meh-WIH-shah kah-BIH-sah)   Kiswahili °
I'm beat, done for, exhausted.

Your body is your teacher. Through it you learn what is necessary
for survival and for growth. You have been with this teacher since
birth, but how observant a student have you been? Do you regularly pay attention to the messages it is offering? We can get so
wound up in stress and tension that we begin to think it is normal,
ignoring the muscle tightness, anxiety, sleeping and eating difficulties. When we experience such reactions chronically, our resistance breaks down, and we become physically or emotionally ill.
We start blaming others for our feelings of increased frustration
and failure. Entering a declining spiral of emotional volatility, we
become more irritable, isolated, argumentative, noncommunica-
tive, and hostile. You want to shout *"nimewisha kabisa"*! The
well is dry, there is nothing left to give, you are emotionally and
physically spent. How much more sane it is to notice our stress
before things get to this point, and to ask for help, or use other
coping strategies. Through meditation, or exercising regularly,
we can effectively defuse stress before it overwhelms. Saying no
to others is often a stress reducing way of saying yes to yourself.

*I am more aware of early signs of stress as feedback to do things differ-
ently.*

mithuna (MITH-oo-nah)   Hindi
Statues of amorous couples.

Temples throughout the world honor a diverse pantheon of powerful beings. While all cultures engage in sexual fantasies, most do not spend years carving them out in exquisite detail as have Indian sculptors. The parade of erotic poses is endless, with gods, goddesses, nymphs, handmaidens, and voluptuous humans all engaged in a frenzy of love and lust. This land of *mithuna* speaks not only of carnal passions, but also the tenderness and peacefulness of sharing the bounty of human sexuality. To bring just a taste of Tantric notions into one's life can be revolutionary. Imagine that woman is seen as the dominant force of creation, and that indulgence in the senses is a path to god. Whatever one's religious background, the beauty of your sexuality is clearly a gift from on high, a portal we experience that can transport you to timeless realms where the pulse of the universe is palpable. To see sexual energy as an exchange of loving vitality that worships all creation is clearly an appealing philosophy. When you consciously use sensual touch for pleasure and celebration, you invite the divine into your union.

I can deepen my connection to another by seeing our shared sexuality as sacred.

kasa (kah-sah)   Korean
Lyrical form of poetry expressing attachment to the beauty of nature.

Nature calls to each of us with a unique voice. Whenever we answer we are taken on a special journey to the center of ourselves. Natural beauty is like a healing salve, drawing out of our bodies and spirits fatigue, depression and loneliness. A riotously colorful field of wildflowers, the soothing sound of the surf, the immensity of a forest at dusk compel us to surrender to forces that embrace us in wonder. The artistry of *kasa* reminds us of the depth of our connection to our wilderness environs. It provides an opportunity to be doubly moved. It can trigger memories of past meaningful outdoor encounters, and remind us of that universal place within that is always aware of our intimate relationship with natural phenomenon. The existence of such a specialized form of verse bespeaks a culture deeply rooted in appreciation of its wild countryside. To lyrically express the bond that exists between people and mountains, trees, rivers and the sea is to enlarge our capacity for reverence. It is to acknowledge that our interactions with the wilderness are symbiotic, not only at the physical level but on the spiritual plane as well. Those times when I am especially drawn to make contact hold the promise of messages that cannot be ignored.

I pay homage to the summons of the natural world.

la couler douce (say-lah COOL-dooss)   French
To flow sweetly through life.

None of our suffering goes to waste. It polishes the edges of our perception. Like the forces of wind and water upon rock, the face of our compassion is slowly altered by tribulation and misery. For some people life seems to always be easier. Beyond believing in their good luck, we suspect they have been lifted above the morass of common hardships. Somehow they seem to possess the capacity for *la couler douce*. Apparently endowed with natural talent, and blessed with the right opportunities, they easily provoke the envy of others. Instead of feeling jealous, we can learn from what they seem to be doing right. Such a lightness of being in the world is mostly a function of attitude. We can realize again that everyone experiences pain, though it may be well disguised in some. A useful meditation when you encounter such beings is that of sympathetic joy. To visualize them and say "May your success and joy increase and multiply." This practice is very liberating and increases your own happiness. It enlarges your own appreciation of the ever changing ebb and flow of goodness.

In wishing others well I enhance my own progress.

chwarae teg (HWAH-ree TEHG)   Welsh
Fair play; what is right and just.

The rules of the game are not always lucid. Someone is usually bending them in unexpected directions. Where do solutions lie to our pressing dilemmas? Is it wrong to produce landmines that continue to cripple children long after a regional conflict is over, or to export drugs and pesticides we do not deem safe for use in our own country? Is it right for fathers to support their children financially and emotionally, and for society to make amends for past abuses to people of color? To see through such questions to a more palpable truth is the quality of *chwarae teg*. How well we treat our most vulnerable planetary citizens reflects most clearly our moral development. You can start with creating a personal circle of justice that is well defined and irrefutable. Through self reflection and dialogue with others, social change does occur. It is in the leap from personal clarity to public policy where conflict arises. Your commitment to engage the vast spectrum of difficult questions, without harsh judgment of others, can be a guiding light for others.

I am willing to live a principled life.

July 16

hanbleceyapi (hahn-blay-chay-YAH-pee)   Sioux
Vision quest.

Among Native peoples the deep commitment to spirituality is present in every aspect of relationship to the natural world. Such faith is a unifying force among Native peoples. By undertaking *hanbleceyapi* a specific plea is made to Creator for guidance, a request for an infusion of supernatural insight. First one's body and mind have to be purified, through the smoke of sacred herbs. Then one goes to an isolated forest or hilltop and fasts for days, praying that a deeper understanding might emerge. A waking vision, often in the form of a human or animal power, is finally manifested, often requiring further interpretation by an elder. A medicine bundle or shield is often created afterward, based on contents of the vision, to serve as further counsel and protection. Perhaps it is time for you to devote some ritual time to soul searching. At the turning points of life—reaching a certain age, marriage, the death of a parent, divorce—the call to a deeper questioning can often be felt.

To ask for deeper spiritual acumen is itself a healing act.

hytter (HEET-tayr)   Norwegian
Cottage that is close to nature.

For many indigenous peoples, the notion that one would own the earth is absurd. The land is bountiful and for the use of all, belonging to none. It nurtures the body and spirit of humankind without exception. We have evolved in close relationship to the wildness of our planet. No wonder there is such a primitive urge to "get out" into it. For most of us, if we have been absent too long, there is a palpable sense of the need to return home, if only for a day hike, to the vastness of natural creation. The *hytter* makes the journey a bit easier. To escape to a rustic structure deep within the embrace of nature is to find a solace not otherwise available. When you create such a retreat, and share it with friends and family, you acknowledge the importance of an ancient connection. In effect, you declare that the time, energy and attention spent in this way is a valuable way to invite the gifts of peace and quiet and community into your busyness. You breathe in the joy of simple inspiring beauty.

Finding a space away from it all renews and uplifts me.

July 18

hoomaikai (ho-o-MY-ky)   Hawaiian
Grateful.

We have much to celebrate. Our being alive, awake and aware, and able to survive are great blessings. Most of us can feel the wind on our face, listen to early morning birds, sample the fragrance of fresh cut blooms, treasure the visual magnificence of a moonset. When we gather in community to share our gratitude for all of life's gifts, we create an opportunity for social bonds to be strengthened and past transgressions forgiven. The idea of being *hoomaikai* is woven deeply into the fabric of Native Hawaiian island culture. Music, dance, the exquisite variety of fine artworks, and personal adornments all function as expressions of thanksgiving. When you focus more on what you have, than on what you want, a space of abundance is created. Happiness is indeed wanting exactly what you already have. When we take time to recognize and actively give thanks for all the goodness that is, we complete the circle that began with the asking and receiving.

Appreciation is a pathway to contentment.

rebbilib (rrehb-bee-leeb)   Marshallese
Navigational aids based on the feel of the waves and swell patterns.

Imagine the earliest sea travellers, setting out across vast stretches of ocean to discover or visit distant new lands. Guided by stars, the patterns of clouds and migrations of birds, these early navigators also learned to intimately read the seascape, and to record their observations for others. Plotted over the course of generations, and recorded in "charts" of palm and shells, these *rebbilib* were simple yet elegant reflections of local wind and wave regularities. What might a construction of your own ancestral practices reveal? A family picture album, heirlooms, and bits of stories passed down could contribute to the mapping of the rules and guidance you received in your early years. How relatives coped with life's turbulence, and what new lands of awareness they encountered offer insight into your present day concerns. Perhaps you are repeating rather than learning from past mistakes. An awareness of familial customs and models can steer you to a new and happier reality.

I can sail away on the ocean of my reflections, and find new meaning in old family routines.

July 20

munkumbole (moon-koom-BO-leh)   Arunta
Shamans who specialize in clairvoyance.

Ancient psychic power. The words fill us with anticipation. In historic Aboriginal cultures people wake in the middle of the night with the awareness of distress, and travel hundreds of miles to be at the bedside of a sick loved one. Tales abound of shamans knowing about activities in remote locations, predicting natural disasters, and even knowing in advance the day of a person's death. Through the existence of *munkumbole*, some societies still keep the ancient talents of clairvoyance alive. You probably sometimes intuit who is calling on the phone, get a vague sense that a relative is in distress, or receive counsel about a decision in a dream. Perhaps these phenomena are more widespread than we know, but selective inattention relegates these important experiences to simply being "weird." When messages from dreams or other forms of psychic ability are met with fear and discouragement in a culture, it is not likely that budding practitioners will have the guidance needed to hone their inborn skills. Yet through our intuition is it possible that our collective brains are trying to rekindle the memory of this human gift?

I welcome my ability to perceive through extrasensory channels.

jihad (jee-HAAD)   Arabic
A righteous struggle.

The Koran declares that reforming the earth is the ultimate purpose of human endeavor. Practitioners of Islam are encouraged to do their part by following the five duties of this religion. These include a profession of faith and commitment to monotheism, five daily prayers, regular almsgiving, fasting, and pilgrimage. The term *jihad* speaks to this endeavor to raise humanity above its pettiness and selfishness. Rather than referring to territorial expansion, or forcible conversion of people to Islam, the intent is to use political power to implement revered principles through public institutions. Instead of a separation of secular and religious interests, the emphasis is on merging the two in daily existence. Education, laws and customs support the community commitment to living life based on moral and spiritual behaviors. You can recognize the power of this worldview in your own personal quest. When you build a community that supports your individual journey to wholeness, and encourages healthy practices, your attempts to develop are reinforced.

I work peacefully to infuse spirituality into daily life.

July 22

passeggiata (pah-say-DJIA-tah)   Italian
Community ritual of strolling back and forth down the street.

Just knowing there is a place to gather, where people move slowly on foot, and have the opportunity to look each other in the eyes, is remarkably comforting. We join the celebration, preening, grooming and dressing our best to impress others. There are variations on this theme wherever young people gather. Whether it is cruising in cars, walking the malls, or circulating at a party, being seen is clearly important. The *passeggiata* is a time honored Italian tradition of observing and being noticed. A simple, flirtatious choreography of sensual expression. A gaze, a laugh, a wink, a smile, transmits so much in a fleeting moment of contact. The inviting look of desire becomes a visual poem that articulates the unspeakable. The groups of participants move slowly in a transparent, transcendent dream that is so simple and enriching. We can learn much from such a healthy way to explore attractions, and exchange pleasantries.

I enjoy my own desire to be noticed.

pistarckle (piss-TAR-kl)   English Creole
Confusion; a group gone out of control

Each of us possesses a sense of personal space, an invisible territorial bubble that surrounds our body. If this mobile enclosure is
invaded without our permission, we feel threatened and tense.
Sometimes in a crowd, we suspend the usual boundary and act
out of a herd instinct. Jammed in an elevator, or a packed room,
we cannot avoid body to body contact, but we usually minimize
social interactions. Our faces become less expressive, and we stu-
diously ignore those around us. A crowd that is jostling about,
rather than focused on the common spectacle of a sports or theater event, can be frightening. When a *pistarckle* develops, the
result can be intimidating from within, and somewhat hilarious
when viewed from the outside. Everyone is shouting and gestic-
ulating all at once in a gathering that no longer is following the
rules of social etiquette. Like the frenzied pace of schoolchildren
at recess, the disorder of post performance backstage revelry, or
the antics at a wild party, the boisterous result eliminates normal
social inhibitions. The group frenzy builds upon itself until a
threshold is reached and the crowd begins to calm itself, like a
fire peaking and then smouldering down to embers.

By keeping my own center, I can feel safe within the exuberance of a
group gone wild.

July 24

enlaki (en-LAHK-ee)   Kayapo tribe
"I'm another you";greeting used when another is heard nearby
in the rainforest.

"Remember, we're all in this . . . alone," jokes Lily Tomlin. We constantly seek both social contact and time by ourselves. When these needs are balanced, we feel relaxed and at peace. Otherwise we may vacillate between the extremes of isolation and loneliness, or feeling invaded and exhausted. The reality is that we are always connected, even though physically apart. The use of *"enlaki!"* dramatically illustrates this awareness. The response offered to the unseen greeter is simply "alakim," which translates roughly as "you're another me." There is such inherent respect and caring in this salutation, an acknowledgement of the universal lifeblood we all share. Beyond the practical aspect of not being mistaken for a form of edible game moving through the dense growth, there is the simple joy of recognizing the presence of another human being. To use this expression and its response is to surrender to the mystery of our shared journey in this lifetime. It is an opportunity to expand our compassion and understanding. Yes, just like me, you are seeking to find happiness and avoid suffering. Whenever you feel the pull of judging mind that wants to put down others, you can remember this basic commonality that transcends all differences.

I can be alone and apart while also feeling bonded and connected to others.

pingnguaq (peenj-NJU-ahq) **Inuktitut**
Playful and not taking things seriously.

"enLIGHTEN UP!" reads the bumpersticker on a passing car. Those beings who have managed to become masters of love and compassion radiate a gentle effortless quality of being. It is as if the burdens of everyday concerns have been permanently lifted. You can feel their presence, uncontaminated by future wants or past concerns. When we experience moments of this, we know something about being *pingnguaq*. To cavort with life, and see it all as a game of wonder and delight is a gift we give ourselves. It is a perspective that is always valuable when invoked. Children are often skilled at transforming mundane tasks into opportunities for creative enjoyment. Grocery shopping, preparing a meal or doing garden chores emerge as portals to enchanting adventure. Even negotiating a business deal or preparing a report can be part of the realm of joyous abandon. You really do get more done when you're having fun. It is a matter of letting go of how things are supposed to be, and allowing high spirited behavior to emerge.

Playful ecstasy can lead to delicious release.

July 26

kashim (KAH-shem)   **Kodiac Island Russian dialect**
Ceremonial house.

The spirit world of the indigenous people of Kodiac Island swarmed with supernatural beings that had to be placated with a variety of taboos and amulets. Neither good nor bad, spirits affected people's lives, and individuals try to be in good standing with them through the use of prayers, magical charms and talismans. The *kashim*, like the kiva of the Pueblo people of the southwestern United States, served as a focal point for ceremonial dialogue. Through the ministrations of a shaman, preparations for a hunt or ceremonial gestures of thanks were performed at the kashim. Care was especially taken not to offend the spirits of animals that provided the sustenance of survival. Modern day churches and synagogues serve a similar sacred function. Although these spiritual structures mostly remain empty, their existence is testimony to the human need for a sacred space that is always welcoming and inviting. It is a place of practical worship, where a community can gather to petition and to celebrate.

I embrace all the diverse paths that lead to contact with a higher form of being.

hamam (ha-MAAM)   **Turkish**
Bath.

We can bring mindfulness to every aspect of our daily living, and thus invite a marriage of practical and spiritual activities. The light of awareness can illuminate even the most ordinary activities, filling us with appreciation and happiness. To cleanse the body is such a commonplace occurrence, a habitual action that most often provides a fertile space for wandering thoughts. The stream of a hasty shower water mimics the flow of random ideas. Taking time for a bath slows down the pace a bit, offering a cleansing of both mind and body. Then there is the *hamam*, a class unto itself. This hot and steamy soak in a communal bathhouse is designed to placate both the spirit and its temporary corporal dwelling. Communal yet deeply personal, the hamam experience often includes a scrubbing massage that takes away layers of old skin, and the application of fragrant oils to animate the senses. A vital relaxation begins to emerge as eons of stress dissolve. More than a self indulgent ritual, it awakens the passion of being fully alive.

Washing myself affords new spiritual insights.

July 28

mushairah (moo-SHY-dah)   Urdu
Open air recital of poetry dealing with devotional or erotic love.

The task of consciously loving another is a journey of awakening. In the acceptance and giving demanded by such an undertaking lies the opportunity to discover godlike qualities in both ourself and the other. To remain both individually whole and still join together to form something greater than each is part of this divine mystery. From our earliest personal attempts at poetic expression to culturally popular love songs, we seem driven to somehow relate to others the depths of our feelings. In the Pakistani tradition of *mushairah* people come together from far and wide to enjoy the passion and festivity of poetry. Food, music and dancing fire the revelry, inspiring yet another round of lyrical exploration. This dramatically intense poetry is not meant for silent reading. Designed to roll off the tongue in sensual rhythms, its ardent delivery is as essential as its profuse proclamations of infatuation. Whether invoking subtle invitations to pleasure, images of loyalty, or an endless array of the beloved's finer qualities, the phrases stir places in both men and women that long for release.

Writing and receiving poetry and love letters feeds my passions.

zou ma guan hua (tzo mah gwahn hwah)   **Chinese**
Too much in a hurry; trying to observe flowers while galloping on horseback.

We run so fast because we are afraid of ourselves. The noise of our own thoughts is too immense, and the cosmos too vast to make stillness and silence a desirable experience. Early on we are taught that to keep busy is to be productive and worthwhile. Accustomed to a super physiologic pace, we feel uncomfortable when forced to "waste" time because of weather, a traffic jam, a computer glitch, or a line at the market. If we experience being still in the course of a day, it is often scheduled. Time to meditate for twenty minutes right now! The expression *zou ma guan hua* captures the core of the widespread malady of rushing about. We jam our senses with so much stimuli in order to convince ourselves we are truly alive. What we often get is frustration, fatigue and a gnawing sense of desolation. It may feel like someone is always pushing you from behind, until you realize it is just yourself. To achieve balance we can aim to live at a more relaxed pace, to make choices that simplify rather than complicate, to feel open and flexible rather than rigid and closed.

When I slooow down, I increase my ability to enjoy life.

July 30

nanwatai (nahn-WAH-tie)   Pashto
Formal submission of the vanquished to the victor.

History is replete with tales of the ebb and flow of dominance over others. The act of *nanwatai* carries a unique perspective. More than just a formal surrender and acknowledgement of defeat, its intent is to provide a public forum so that the magnanimous benevolence of the winners may be demonstrated. Rather than increasing oppression, it is designed to create a climate of forgiveness for all participants in the conflict, and to affirm that suffering was experienced by both sides. A return to peaceful co-existence and relative normalization of the relationship is seen as beneficial to all. Such an approach has validity in our own lives. When you are willing to let go of a power struggle, to get off the need to be right, you open the door to grace and generosity. To yield is not to give up, but to retain the ability to bounce back from adversity, like a willow in a storm, or a raven on the wind.

True defeat lies in remaining stuck in patterns that are not working.

bilibong (bih-lih-BONG)   Arunta
Waterhole which our spirits emerge from at birth and return to at death.

The path travels outward in an ever widening spiral as your journey to wholeness unfolds. Early footfalls eventually evolve into a pace and stride that feels right. At some barely perceptible moment in time, there is a turning point, when you have wandered far enough from the center of your being. Often it is a dramatic event, a distinct unexpected upheaval; sometimes there is just the knowing that the load is somehow lighter. Your steps are now more focused, with clearer intent. As the voyage winds inward, there is an increasing sense of peace and satisfaction. The *bilibong* in the Australian outback patiently awaits your reunion. There is always the memory of that source, faint and distant perhaps, but palpable in the hidden recesses of one's own heartbeat. The process of awakening is the thread that reels you out and pulls you in. Home has been the destination all along, and it shimmers brightly, though it may be years away. You begin to see the light that is your breath, to finally allow expression of the more eternal levels of the self.

Knowing that I will return from whence I came is comforting.

AUGUST

Sensuality
Twilight and blooming jasmine
Let your spirit sing

ibota (ee-BO-tah)   Nigerian Bini
A family gathering time for stories.

Half of the world lives in 2 million villages, and most feature a public shared space, where great tales were developed and passed down through constant retelling. The Bini in Nigeria look forward to the *ibota*, a family gathering in the early evening, in which songs and stories are mingled together, offering advice on how to live. Held in someone's lap the young ones feel the teachings of the narrative enter directly into their bodies, the motions of the characters experienced with their own limbs. There is a comfort in hearing stories over and over until they gradually become a living tradition that nurtures your spirit. The opportunity to see the smiling faces of neighbors and extended family, both young and old gathered together, is rare in our modern world. It is possible for us to recreate the magic of storytelling within our own circle of relatives and friends. We might rediscover some sense of wonder and adventure that we thought was lost forever.

I can carry with me always some favorite recountings, and learn to share them.

August 2

aura (OW-rah)   Greek
First breath of air at dawn.

Reluctantly we leave off dreaming and enter into full awareness as the earth bestirs itself. Birds often begin the stirring, just before a yawning glimmer of light appears at the eastern horizon's edge. The clear air resonates with a crisp vitality, a gentle breeze tossing off the covers of the night. To rise with the sun, and enter the activities of the day gently is a quotidian slow dance of infatuation with the glory of being alive. The *aura* of the day is exquisite. Drink in the auspicious caress of a waking world. Allow the sighs of the morning sky to whisper their secrets. Do you start your day the way you would like? Creating a morning ritual summons the unfathomable to reveal itself. This is not just something else to add to the list of "have to do's." It is an invocation of petition and thanksgiving. You tune the strings of your being to the voice of the cosmos, and enter into dialogue with the rhythms of your immediate world. Doesn't such a beginning sound better than a jarring alarm clock, a rush to dress, and two cups of coffee so that you can function?

Early morning beginnings set the tone for my day.

mide (MEE-dah)   Algonquin
Mystically powerful.

In the laboratory of our lives, we seldom invite mystical meta-
physical manifestations in for a visit. If they get in the theater at
all, they are relegated to a backseat view. Logic, reason and pre-
dictability hold the upper hand, with scientific explanation the
paramount worldview. Tempted at times to reject these teachings,
and embrace a path of the heart, we are pulled back to reality by
the demands of our complex mechanistic world. To see a vision
in the clouds, hear a message in the flapping of raven's wings, or
receive a gift from an ancestor in a dream would be silly, daft,
preposterous. How restrictive is our existence when we deny the
presence of *mide* events and people in our lives. All the forces of
serendipity and synchronicity hovering in front of your face will
not remove the blinders until you are willing to develop a more
inclusive perspective. Your lessons are those moments when all
you know is that you have been touched by a miraculous presence beyond your ability to grasp intellectually. Your task is to
suspend disbelief and humbly accept the blessing.

I welcome the potency of unexpected miracles, large and small.

August 4

gatha (GAH-tuh)　　　Sanskrit
A phrase to bring one's awareness to the present.

We are all time travelers, dancing between the past and the future, settling only sometimes, like a butterfly, to rest on the blossom of the present moment. Thoughts carry us away, constantly, to distant shores. We enter the landscape of daydreams, playing out future scenarios, recalling past encounters. We can use a *gatha* as a link to the present. As we focus on it, and it fills our mind, we become it, fully and completely for a short space of time. Calming, smiling, present moment, wondrous moment. We take refuge in this island of self, a realm of our consciousness which is always connected to what is happening. We walk the path of relaxed alert presence, and are able to briefly, yet deeply, rest in the arms of the moment. These short verses connect to each other throughout the day, and create for us a well of awareness and vitality that positively affects all those other times when we are lost on the river of thoughts.

To utter spontaneously throughout the day "To be alive, delicious joy, uplifting moment" can be renewing.

nngoma (n-NGO-mah)   **Kiswahili**
Both drum and dance.

Among the Akan of Ghana, drums are placed on the backs of carved animals, most commonly the lion or elephant, which enhance their power through contact with animal spirits. Drums often represent ancestors and may exist in male-female pairs or even families. It is said that on certain occasions the spirit is especially strong and the drum plays itself. The repetition that is at the core of rhythm connects you to the patterns of your internal tempo and the larger ones of the planet and the universe. Your heart repeats its beat, you rest and are active, seasons cycle as does your life. The term *nngoma* reflects this connection. African drumming is highly polyrhythmic, and dancers hear each tempo distinctly, following one with their feet, another with their shoulders, a third with their heads. Drummers and dancers engage in ritual dialogue, creating a dense tapestry of sound and movement. Like an old friend, the cadence of drumming can gently lead you into an open receptive trance in which the present moment dissolves. Drums are the threshold of another reality, which if you enter, you can no longer drum. It is the edge, the contact with that other reality, on which you dance.

My hands can drum and my feet can dance.

August 6

nyaweh gowah (NYAH-weh GO-wah)   **Iroquoian**
Great thanks.

As woodland farmers, tribal groups in the eastern part of America had many agricultural rites. The maturing of corn, ripening of wild strawberries, or even an increase in abundance of game animals prompted a religious show of appreciation. Part of daily life as well was a morning prayer to the spirits that lived in everything, creating a fabric of respect and gratefulness that was woven deeply into one's consciousness. Before taking a journey, using a plant, or eating a fish or animal some form of thanks was given. To express *nyaweh gowah* was to strike the chord of gratitude that lived in each members heart. Besides the honoring of Creator's provision of physical needs, there were the many gifts of community, ancestors and loved ones. You can be especially grateful for all those who have supported you in your life. Parents, relatives and other significant adults nurtured you and from their hardship prepared an easier way. When you allow yourself to spend more time in a state of appreciation than in one of dissatisfaction, you radically begin to alter your inner state of peace and tranquility. You walk more gently in the center of your life.

Each breath I take can be a prayer of thanks.

gamzu l'tova (gahm-zoo lto-vah)   Hebrew
Even though this is unpleasant, it is for the best.

The I Ching, an ancient divination practice, says pain is breaking the shell of understanding. The more we go into our grief, the more spontaneity and aliveness we will also feel. The more we explore our wounds, the less likely we are to inflict them on others. Assigning blame for our hurt, or judging it good or bad, prevent you from feeling it, rather than help you deal with it. When someone utters *gamzu l'tova*, they speak with the wisdom of the larger view. If dealt with skillfully, the affliction of the present moment creates the path to greater freedom. When you grieve, you consciously experience the woe of the soul, and accept the weight of sadness. You have to carry your own pain. Welcome it from the depths. Wallow around in it. Accept and be patient with it. Dance it and be grateful for the growth it brings. Feel the wounds fully, the beauty of the hurt. If you don't, you spend lots of energy building walls to protect yourself. Let those barriers of strength and holding tight dissolve in a cascade of tears.

With tribulation comes release and growth.

August 8

a solare (ah soh-LAH-ray)   Italian
To sit in the sun doing nothing.

Have you ever tried to figure out why you bustle around so much, but found you didn't have the time to answer such questions? The act of deepening the inquiry into why we end up rushing, begins to alter our reality. Why do you speed through life? The usual responses begin with "not enough. . . ." We don't have enough time to get through the endless lists in a relaxed manner. We don't have enough energy to get it all done, so we just move through it as quickly as possible. We don't have enough money. More money, we speculate, would magically translate into less demands in general. Besides the adverse physiological and personal emotional consequences, scurrying as a predominant pace wrecks havoc with relationships, and encourages dangerous practices. The aphorism "haste makes waste", still rings true. Try to come back to breath, and spend more time *a solare*. Daydream, gaze at the clouds, sip a cold drink. Appreciate that you have caught your-self dashing about, and begun to practice the art of slow-mo. Taking time to do nothing allows you to take the pause that refreshes, and begin anew to take it easy.

Instead of careening through life, I can saunter a bit more.

ranz des vaches (rahnz day VAHSH)   Swiss French
Yodels and other tunes sung as cattle calls.

Reflect for a moment on animals in your life. Beyond their role in nourishing our bodies, they have always held a place in our hearts. We love their beauty, their wild spirit, their instincts, and their capacity to interact with our own desires. Children's books abound with anthropomorphized entities whose adventures reflect our own. Their physical presence in our homes provides a comfort qualitatively different than any other. Like the Swiss *ranz des vaches*, peoples throughout the world converse with animals through song. Listen to a youngster interact with a new kitten or puppy, and note that they automatically use a higher pitched sing-song voice. The fact that we continually seek and are able to communicate with our non-human kin is testimony to the sustainable connection that nurtures us both.

All animals deserve my respect and caring.

August 10

ahimsa (aah-HIM-saa)   Sanskrit
The purifying inward force of non violence.

Right now, this moment, the majority of humans are not engaged in killing or unkind acts. Where such deeds are occurring, both the victims and the people who create suffering are worthy of compassion. When we allow this natural tendency of caring to arise, we do away with many negative thoughts, which leads to an openness that fosters communication and trust. The practice of *ahimsa* is an active courage fed by one's own spiritual discipline and evolution. It seeks to find a way in any situation to resist and dismiss malice, anger and fear of one's own death or physical hurt. It is to drop any thought of retaliation for the suffering you endure. One is never passively non violent. Your heart is expanded outward with respect and caring. You blunt the sword of the aggressor through a resistance of the soul. The ultimate bowing down of those who are belligerent is not a humiliation, but rather an elevation above their weakness and confusion. As more individuals learn to increase their inner strength in this manner, then social justice will continue to emerge. The collective effort of the people will show us all the way to the enduring freedom of peace.

On the battlefield of the heart, my weapons are understanding and compassion.

hwan gap (hwahn gabp)   Korean
The celebration of one's sixtieth birthday.

The beginning of wisdom is a firm grasp of the obvious, a knowledge tempered by experience and guided by values. The heart of this virtue is recognizing vulnerability in oneself. In order to truly understand the suffering of others, elders must have become aware of their own destructiveness, lived through their own weakness, and explored their own shadows. The celebration of *hwan gap* recognizes that this special quality of sagacity has truly begun to emerge, and needs to be honored appropriately. One has survived, and moved through five cycles of the entire animal zodiac. Each year focuses on one of twelve different animals and the qualities it represents. At the age of sixty, many people are in touch with their own energies, and know how to focus on what is really important for them—family, giving back to their community, or enjoying activites they had little time for when younger. One often comes closer to balancing the energies of thinking and feeling, being active and passive, independent and dependent, relaxed and serious. It is a time of ongoing appreciation for the unfolding mystery of our existence.

I learn to adapt to the gifts of old age by dancing with my shifting energies.

August 12

lammas (LAHM-mahs)   Old English
The time in-between summer solstice and fall equinox.

Patiently waiting, the time of in-between relishes its moment in the sun. Suspended in its own magic, like a trapeze artist between rings, this period is important because it is testimony to the enormous changes that are evolving. It celebrates the pauses between the notes, the shifting of a season, the fork in the road, the fleeting time when what was, has not yet danced into what will be. A moment to simply notice where we have been, and where the road leads on ahead of us. *Lammas* is an ancient pagan festival of the first harvest, a midsummer marking point between the more celebrated solstice and equinox. No matter whether we are betwixt and between relationships, jobs, houses, or transforming flashes of insight, one can relish the splendor of the situation. This is not the stuff of restless wanderings. It is a resting point of recognition before moving forward on one's unfolding journey of dreams.

From dwelling in the in-between times, I know when it is time to move forward.

hiya (HEE-yah)   Tagalog
Trying to avoid shame or loss of face.

Embarrassment is rooted in the fear of being rejected. Negative attention is cast our way, accompanied by a dose of ridicule, or we are caught off guard by the mention of a sensitive subject. Shame is the experience of also feeling basically unworthy, which deepens the apprehension. Not only is what I have done awful, but the belief grows that one is bad in their innermost core. To reflect on past actions and learn from mistakes is helpful; to wallow in putting yourself down is not. The range of secrets you hold close determines the extent of the repository of shame that still imprisons you. Many societies highly value cooperative relationships, where the will of the group mind, as opposed to individual desires, is the dominant social value. In such cultures, it is critical to engage in *hiya*, to be scanning for the slightest evidence of creating group disharmony. In any situation the automatic response is to placate, to shun both the possibilities of giving or receiving an insult. By consciously avoiding both shaming and being shamed, the hope is that group relations will flow smoothly, generating a healthier interaction for all involved.

I can release the feelings of unworthiness that constrict me.

August 14

sangha (SANG-gha)   Sanskrit
A supportive community for spiritual growth.

Many of us have grown accustomed to isolation and loneliness. Do you still believe that the only really safe space is to be locked up within yourself? When you allow someone to help you, you are helping you. Support is accepting the assistance you need in order to move forward in your spiritual development. The existence of a *sangha* is one of the three gifts of Buddhism. The Buddha himself and the dharma or teachings comprise the other two. Like three legs on a stool, each plays its role in supporting us on our journey towards enlightenment. Just knowing that others are also struggling on the path and are ready to offer assistance by example or deeds is uplifting. It is possible to be vulnerable and safe at the same time, to practice the wheel of both giving and receiving. Finding such balance takes you through new territory, enriching your capacity to be generative, and is at times scary, exhilarating, joyous, and painful. Heartspace is that part of you where you are most vulnerable and open to the world, where others can enter and touch you deeply, and from which you reach out to contact them more fully. The world needs you to be yourself, and to join your heart with others to create a more harmonious, empowered community.

I feel the welcoming arms of others sharing my inner journey.

zayats (zah-jahts)   **Burmese**
Rest places around a pagoda.

A stupa was originally a mound for relics, especially those of Buddha or other Buddhist masters, lamas. Known in various Buddhist cultures as chortens, dagobas, and pagodas, the shrine's basic shape is meant to suggest a human figure hidden in the structure in the posture of meditation. The crossed legs lie in the base, and the body up to the shoulders is represented in the hemisphere. The head rests in the kiosk, whose tiered form suggests ascending states of consciousness, the ascent of the human spirit achieving wisdom by dispelling our habitual delusions and impediments. The whole structure represents a cosmic diagram around which pilgrims walk, praying for the liberation of all beings. *Zayats* cater to the physical needs of pilgrims, providing shade and basic sustenance within sight of the holy place. The existence of such comfort areas bespeaks the practical element that is always present in the Buddhist religion, and the reality that such shrines are visited constantly. To sit and unwind in the vicinity of a sacred site is wondrous.

I am grateful for a special place to rest and reflect.

August 16

hanare (HAH-nah-ray)   Japanese
The moment when an arrow is released of its own accord.

Zen archery involves creating a timeless interval in which the arrow and its target have already become one before actual contact is made. There is a flash of spontaneous release when the bow appears to have absorbed all of the archer's strength and energy. As quickly as an outbreath, *hanare*, the leavetaking, occurs. This motion is simply the natural completion and outcome of all previous movements, as well as the concentration of physical and spiritual dynamism on the part of the practitioner. The holder of the bow and the arrow is simply a conduit for the universal force that flows without restriction and that compels the arrow to fly forward. In such a practice one is liberated from the small self, and opened into the all embracing oneness. How wondrous it is when our intention and our actions are clearly joined. When we can distance ourselves from our clinging to a specific outcome, and just relax into the process of summoning our best efforts. Through diligent exploration and repetition of any form, the everpresent power of all creation can be effortlessly touched, the dissolution of the ego accomplished, if only for a moment.

I welcome increasing synchrony of mind body and spirit.

Kinaalda (keen-nahl-DAH)   Navajo
Puberty rite of passage for young women.

Women have been oppressed in different ways than men. They have been taught in the past to hide their abilities. As mothers, wives, daughters and sisters, many women have been hurt by men, especially by the absent or abusive father or mate. Men especially must understand the depths of this pain, and work to prevent such suffering in future generations. *Kinaalda* is a traditional Navajo ceremonial initiation into womanhood designed to offer girls guidance for leading a healthy and harmonious life. It is a formal communal preparation for her meaningful role in a matrilineal society and the attendant responsibilities and expectations. The songs that are sung activate goodness and beauty in a young woman's mind, reminding her of the respect and caring to which she is entitled. The effort required for her as a woman to accomplish living in a beautiful peaceful way is also affirmed. Blessings are invoked for the future children who will be born into the family clan and welcomed by the community and tribe as a whole. This empowering ritual can serve as a model of adolescent initiation for the people of the white, brown, black and yellow hoops as well.

I honor the young women in my life and affirm their beauty.

August 18

kamayan (KAH-mah-yan)   **Tagalog**
Eating with the hands.

Bringing the hand to the mouth is a universal gesture that communicates that one is hungry and would like to eat. The action of *kamayan* is restricted in some societies by modern propriety. Acceptable with snack foods or appetizers, eating without utensils is rarely utilized for the main courses. Imagine that this veneer of Western civilization is temporarily stripped away. Huge platters of food are placed before you on a banquet table. Like the total immersion of a toddler relishing every morsel on their fingers, you experience joyous sensual pleasure inherent in feeling the texture of the foods and licking your fingers. Many cultures around the world still regularly eat this way, enjoying the unaffected directness of the action. Like sitting and staring at a fire, there is a primal body memory that is activated, which transports you to a time of uncomplicated natural awareness and actions.

It is good to remember my beautiful elemental nature.

buba (boo-bah)   **Sango**
Messed up; refers to anything not working right, including people.

Do we really invite problems into our lives because we need their gifts? There are those days when you just want to shout from the highest peak "No more lessons!" We have so many expectations in the course of our daily activities. We take for granted that the alarm will sound, the stove and fridge will still be working, as will the lights in the house. The car will start, and obtaining needed things at the market will be possible. But there are days when the car breaks down, the line at the bank winds out the door, and miscommunication seems to rule. Everything and everyone seem to be *buba*! This is when the depths of your patience are tested. It is one thing to talk about "going with the flow" when everything operates well; another matter entirely when breakdowns occur faster than they can be fixed. Multiple excellent opportunities arise to strengthen that calm inner center of patience and under-standing. You can fill that well when faced with small challenges and drink from it in times of larger difficulties.

When outer world situations are out of balance, my inner stability sees me through.

August 20

summum bonum (SOO-moom BO-noom)   **Latin**
The greatest good.

Imagine your gravestone reading: here lies a person who did nothing in between the great deeds they dreamed of undertaking, and the small tasks they hated to perform. You can be heroic in the ordinary situations of your daily life. When we hear the term *summum bonum*, our first thoughts might be drawn to the media image of someone who, despite incredible personal hardships, manages to save humanity from some catastrophe. Yet the essence of this concept lies in the quality of making choices through a lens of concern for others. It is to practice a voluntary form of restraint for the good of society and all its members, to root out prejudice, ignorance and greed. It is concurrently a long journey to the shores of your deepest self, and the way is formed by your actions. As the hero of your own personal myth, you give context and meaning to existence through your thoughts, words and deeds. Ultimately the thought and the act are inseparable. Charity given with a poor motive is ultimately destructive; murder which never leaves the heart or mind still strays from right action.

I cultivate the predisposition to transcend myself, and work for the benefit of others.

istiqara (is-tick-ARE-uh)   Arabic
A request for spiritual or practical assistance in the form of a dream.

In the alternate reality of the dreamscape emotions are intensely focused, with a single dominant chord of fear, joy or anger rather than the symphony of feelings occurring in the waking state. Interrupted stories with constantly shifting scenes fill a quarter of a night's sleep, expressing important wishes and concerns of the dreamer. Newborns spend half the night in this state, a form of consciousness we share with all mammals. The Greeks had a temple designed especially as a place where one might encounter healing dreams. Indigenous peoples have their shamans who often have the teachable ability to see dream content clearly. The Muslims have the art of *istiqara*, in which a person seeks answers to a spiritual dilemma through special prayers recited before sleep, in a sacred space of supplication, with the confident expectation that a dream will be the vehicle of transmission for a response. Since many scientists, artists and great thinkers over the years have attributed their inspirations to night journeys, perhaps this faculty needs only a sincere invitation in order to appear.

My ability to extract meaningful messages from my dreams is increasing.

August 22

ziku (zee-koo)   Choiseulese
Peacemaking procedures of exchanging valuables to settle a conflict.

The pattern of vengeance often demands more than an eye for an eye, inflicting greater damage than that received and leading to continuing conflict. Such destructive impulses are a considerable drain upon any group's resources. Even where there is an ethic of peaceableness, or at least a common sentiment that other forms of resolving differences are preferable than outright violence, escaping from the cycle of revenge is difficult. We see ongoing evidence of this pattern of retaliation in individuals, families, gangs, communities and even entire nations. Among the Choiseulese in Melanesia, one coping strategy is to settle things peacefully through *ziku*. A friend who has marriage ties and whose village is at peace with both combatants may be sent to intervene. A preliminary payment for damages on each side may be made by both parties, and a day and place are set for the two parties to meet. On the appointed day the whole army comes to make peace, while at the same time to demonstrate that the warriors are not afraid to fight. After a great deal of oratory and reciprocal transfer of goods, a feast takes place, restoring balance in the relationship, and helping to avert future conflict.

In resolving conflict I can appreciate and honor my opponent's values.

halus (HAH-loos)   **Bahasa Indonesia**
Describing the highest standards of behavior, performance and art.

In reaching upward toward our goals, we purify our character, and expand our capacity for expression in the world. Reaching for what seems barely possible, we often exceed our own initial expectations. Those rarefied times when the exceptional manifests, in ourselves or in others, imbue us with the desire to consistently move beyond previous limitations. We live the ideal for a moment, and that is enough reinforcement to keep going, to continue our efforts. When something is *halus*, the art of excellence reveals itself. This realm arises from traveling the path of disciplined practice. It is not a "have to" or "should" imposed from without. By consistently doing what we know to be true and good for us, we embrace the practice of our art, or of life itself, as we would a lifetime lover. We discover the paradise of the highest and best of which we are capable.

I acknowledge excellence whenever it occurs, in myself or others.

August 24

tocayo (toh-CAH-yoh)   Spanish
One who shares the same name.

When a person is given a name, their spirit is expected to accept it. Wrapped in the meaning and sound of the name itself lie bits of one's destiny, a cradle of family expectations and hopes. We slowly grow into our given name, learn to dance with its deeper implications that are revealed piecemeal along the way. In a variety of traditions, an individual takes a second name as they enter puberty, often reflecting their unique character and interests. Many in our diverse world straddle two cultures with names that operate in each: one for outsiders, one for close relations. Calling someone our *tocayo* is an endearing term in and of itself. There is an unspoken brother- sisterhood present when contemporaries carry the same appellation. A sense of shared fate and fortune is present, especially when the name is less common. When we are named for someone, we somehow embody some of their strengths, and become a distant blossoming of their dreams through the generations.

However far the stream of my life flows, my name helps me to remember its source.

waka (WAH-kah)   Xingu
Ceremonial messengers.

Such brave souls, these beings chosen to walk into an enemy camp armed only with potent aspirations, or asked to deliver news likely to instill anger in the listener. The functions of the *waka* are part of a political and kinship organization among the Xingu tribal society of Brazil specifically designed to promote peace. Ambassadors of intertribal relations, they invite other tribes to ceremonies inaugurating new chiefs, or mourning rituals for those recently deceased. They formally lead guests into the community, guide them through the various aspects of the observance, present them with food and gifts, and facilitate an honorable departure. They are symbols of the friendly intent of the host tribe. When tensions are high, they may not be treated so well by their neighbors, but their larger purpose sustains these truce carriers. At the office, within our extended families, and in our communities our peaceful intentions and actions can be bearers of the message that nonviolence works.

In any situation, I can strive to be an emissary of peace.

August 26

**wewepahtli iktzeilwitl (way-way-PAH-tlee ikt-tseil-WI-ti)
Nahuatl**
Greatest medicine; natural healing powers.

Healing is an active process, requiring our intelligent participation in directing our energies with the awareness that changes in one aspect of our being affect all the others. For example, taking better care of your physical self alters emotional moods. Finding a spiritual path transforms the mindset brought to each day. For most tribal societies in the world, healer and priest are one, in recognition of the fact that the state of the body is connected to the condition of the spirit. As a result of this perspective, complex systems of revitalization were developed, such as *wewepahtli iktzeilwitl*, with a holistic focus on healthy integration of the self within the context of spiritual community. Are you ripe for surrendering to a holistic path of healing? It is time to stop being numb, shaming or destroying yourself. Shift from worrying about the future or regretting the past to choosing a rejuvenating lifestyle each day. Spend time in healing ways. Listen to the wisdom of your body and the messages it gives you about your emotional and physical health.

My healing takes many forms, including an engagement with beauty, nature, creativity, friendship, laughter, meditation, and exercise.

kyosaku (kyo-sah-koo)   Japanese
The bamboo stick used by a meditation master to discipline students.

Life is always offering surprises when we most need them. While sometimes unpleasant at the time, in retrospect they are often exactly what was required to wake us up, to get our attention. Pain is a great motivator, and while we may engage in change because we are drawn to a higher purpose, for most of us relative inertia is the dominant state. The *kyosaku* is used during sesshins, prolonged periods of extensive Zen meditation practice. When the master senses a student is drifting or falling asleep or in need of a dose of immediate mindfulness then the bamboo stick is utilized to deliver a swat to the back or shoulders. Like an unexpected splash of cold water or an unanticipated crash of thunder, the effect is startling rather than painful. If you catch yourself in a negative frame of mind, obsessing or worrying about something beyond your immediate capability to influence, then provide yourself a sudden flash of awakening, the mental equivalent of this powerful tool. Wake up! Summon the gifts of the present moment.

I keep my intentions clear and my attention on the present.

August 28

inua (EEN-oo-ah)   Yupik
The essence of a human that is always there in a mask.

A dancer or shaman who wears an animal mask in a ceremony is frequently believed to be possessed by the spirit inhabiting or represented by the mask. Because of the great power and concomitant danger of this communication, the *inua* reminds the wearer to eventually return to mankind, and not be swept away by the animal guide. Each of us must also protect the core of who we are, beneath the social disguises. Because of difficulties experienced, we all become expert mask makers, hiding from ourselves. It is a way of learning that helped you to survive. Now you need no longer be afraid of what you might find below the facade you have constructed. Such fears are allies, guiding and stretching you, marshalling resources you did not know existed. Your true nature calls, a reminder to take off the false face and to come home.

I will not lose myself in the illusions I show the outside world.

kak sazhe byela (kahk SAH-zhee bee-YEHL-ah)   Russian
As soot is white; awful!; a response to How are you?

We may have limited skills, but by adulthood most of us are very good at denial. Occasionally known to masquerade as inner peace, it is often a trick you play on yourself to convince you all is okay. Such disavowal wears many disguises: you minimize, analyze, trivialize, fantasize, narcotize and distract yourself so you don't fully experience pain. Why not just surrender and exclaim *kak sazhe byela!* No need to wallow in the details. Just acknowledge to the world that things are terrible. There is a kernel of humor and lightness contained in this remark, a subtle suggestion that this too shall pass. Press for the depths of your feelings. Allow the confusion they often bring, staying with them and not withdrawing. Rather than always trying to figure life out like a detached observer, live it and embrace the mysteries. Be a part of what you experience instead of apart from it. Your full whole-hearted generous participation carries humanity on your shoulders, and through you humankind also evolves.

Just another lousy day. No big deal!

August 30

mihrab (mih-rup)   Turkish
Prayer niche or ceremonial arch in a mosque.

Most of us have secret drawers or boxes that function like black holes for our special stuff. The distinctive shell found on a sunset walk snuggles next to a bolt of ceremonial cloth gifted by a friend. A small amulet is neighbor to a delicate family heirloom. The ebb and flow of such objects is astounding. As long as we imbue them with meaning, their presence is part of our awakening. At some point we bring them out of hiding and devise a special place to proclaim their unique contributions to our journey. Each laden with its own story, they find prominence on a shelf, desktop, or corner. A far cry from the elaborate and ornate *mihrab*, but the sentiment is the same. These inspiring alcoves where the spiritual vitality is palpable can serve as incentive for establishing a simple sacred site within our home. The act of developing an altar of meaningful objects that nourish our psyche carries the potent intent of consecration. As a place for meditation, prayer or quiet reflection, we consciously develop an interactive relationship with the part of ourselves that is eternal. A positive cycle develops wherein the good feelings we bring when before this simple structure are reflected back in an existent pervasive sense of tranquility and calm. We have transfigured a small space, and in so doing transformed ourselves.

My household shrine is a source of great comfort.

wulunda (woo-LOON-dah)   Ndembu
Special bond shared by those undergoing initiation together.

We experience many transitions in the course of our journey. Deep ties are often formed and alliances initiated through the commonality of shared hardships. The friendship that develops among those who have endured together a rite of passage in Zambia is known as *wulunda*. During their time of ritual seclusion, all food is shared equally, and no special favors are bestowed on anyone. Participants sleep together in clusters around fires and as part of the ceremonies become linked by special ties which last even into old age. This enables an individual to have a group of others from whom they can receive help and support throughout life. College buddies, veterans, sports teammates, or survivors of the difficulties of legal, medical or law enforcement training may create similar long term relationships. Friends offer the comfort of sitting in silence together. Their simple words can be touchstones that bring you out of confusion. Like a rock cairn, they help you recall the path and return to it. Since they have probably seen you at your best and worst, they are a reminder that, despite imperfections, you are accepted rather than abandoned.

I can strengthen contact with dear friends with whom I shared a special bond.

SEPTEMBER

I finally see
It is safe to let my heart
Lead my dancing mind

tufani pole (too-FAH-nee po-leh)   Kiswahili
Give me your sympathy, as I tell this tale of woe.

We are social creatures, born with the desire to communicate. We learn early that sharing our misery makes us feel better. Somehow a burden is lifted when we articulate the confused darkness within. In most cultures, one is not quite as straightforward about seeking assistance as certain Africans who have the simple injunction *tufani pole!* Asking for support can feel like a burden in itself, an obstacle we place in the way of our basic impulses. We are conflicted about taking another's time, sensitive to spreading around too much negativity. We also are aware that our current misfortune may seem insignificant to another whose suffering is perhaps greater. No one likes to hear bad news or a terrible story, which can stir up the psychic container of potential despair we all carry. Yet beyond these considerations is the reality that commiseration is a fundamental act of caring, available everyday, and reflects well on one's ability to uplift our shared human condition.

Both giving and receiving compassion is a gift.

September 2

gelassenheit (gay-LAAH-sen-height)   German
The letting go that is a solution to suffering.

When you have little else, there is still the nurturing source of
your beliefs in a higher power, whatever form that might take.
With *gelassenheit*, one invites a spiritual self surrender, a relaxing
into the embrace of the almighty's will. For the Amish, this is not
welcoming pain or sacrifice, but a desirable and attainable state of
mind. It is not an emotion or feeling, but rather the determination
to focus on personal actions that uplift the spirit. By letting go of
worldly concerns and turning one's life over to a higher power,
there is a freedom found that transcends immediate difficulties.
Such an attitude, even taken in small doses, can be a life saving
remedy when suffering is about to overwhelm you. This mindset
is not one of denial, but rather a cultivation of serene detachment
from your individual will power. This quality is sorely lacking in
our society, where letting go may be viewed as defeatist, passive
or unmanly, rather than the first step toward liberation.

I realize I am not always in control.

nakhes (NOKH-ess)   Yiddish
Pride from another's achievements.

Joy asks us to be excessive, nurtures our natural expansiveness. It arises from delight in the world, from the allure and bounty of our senses, from the great dance where simplicity joins infinite diversity. There is a special kind of happiness, a swelling of pleasure known as *nachas*. Watching loved ones, especially our children, succeed and contribute to the world in beautiful ways fills us with intense elation. You can just relax and revel in appreciation, knowing that their attainments reflect well on you as well. Sometimes it is the manifestation of a dream you or your parents were unable to achieve, a longing passed down through generations. We recognize past struggles that have made this present glory possible, which make it even more meaningful. If only for this moment, things are perfect, and complete satisfaction rules. Laughing wild amid severest woe is possible when you have beautiful inner pictures and memories such as these to draw upon. The unknown changing circumstances of your path always leave room for joy. The space between your suffering and your laughter can be filled with counted blessings.

I lavishly acknowledge loved ones for a job well done.

September 4

Kalachakra (KAHL-chah-kruh)   Sanskrit
The process of destroying a sand mandala.

A mandala welcomes every shape and form that arises in our collective unconscious, every mysterious link to all that we are as a species. It is another path by which we can set free the divine light that shines within each of us. A visual aid for the act of meditation, this magic diagram often unites polarities such as male and female, consciousness and form, heaven and earth, desire and asceticism. Mandalas appear in ancient cave drawings, Hindu and Buddhist rituals, Christian god images and Pueblo Indian sandpaintings. As a kind of sacred microcosm, these works of spiritual artistry represent both order and chaos. Within their circular borders they mirror both the turbulence of existence, and the restraint of disruptive forces of our world. The *Kalachakra* is the body of secret knowledge that reveals the language of these patterns. After hundreds of hours of constructing a pattern in a transformative trance like state, the monk destroys the surreal beautiful sand picture. This seemingly ruthless act highlights our impermanence, and is a stark reminder that our precious existence is gone in a flash, with a gentle sweep of the great hand of time. We must therefore make diligent use of our time in this life to increase our compassion for the benefit of all beings.

With each breath, I am aware of the fleeting nature of this life.

mizukakeron (me-zoo-kah-kay-rohn)   **Japanese**
Dispute without end.

Some relationships always seem to be in a state of war. An occasional truce may be called, but the basic underlying tone is one of antagonistic associations. When we hold onto anger, it tends to get stuck inside, feeding an escalating cycle of retaliation. We use our red stamp collection of resentments to justify our ongoing hostile actions. Most often, these difficult relationships develop between people who once loved one another. A succinct term for this common and unfortunate situation is *mizukakeron*. Like constantly dumping water on each other, these arguments have little point and serve only to disrupt and hassle. More about perceived power and the need to be right, they create much misery. How do you work out a loving relationship with a former partner with whom you are still jointly raising children? Is it possible to heal a family feud that has continued for generations? The way out of such conflict is to not hold onto the unresolved undirected anger that is forever on the verge of exploding forth. Embracing a path of forgiveness is hard work, and can only be successful if you express the underlying fear and pain that fuel resentments. Like an open festering wound that must mend from its depths up, you can only heal from the inside out.

When only one person changes their approach, the nature of a long-standing conflict can be altered.

September 6

gan (gahn)   Apache
Mountain spirit guardians of wildlife.

Being imbued with spirit is not just the purview of humans.
Many traditions honor the sacred that exists in all living things.
Our inner wold, or invisible reality, clearly influences our actions.
The same is believed to be true for those spirits that inhabit this
plane of existence, and live in certain places, as well as within
creatures. An appreciation of our kinship with everything that is
alive leads us naturally to honor the forces that make possible our
own survival. The *gan* are to be revered and offerings made so
that one's prayers may be heard. A hunter embarking on a journey does not give thanks for the game he will capture. Instead he
seeks to honor and value the natural world, through an expression of gratitude to the spirit world for what is right now. Such a
connection to the invisible cosmos exists for each of us, though in
some it may be faint due to lack of knowledge or exposure. You
can revitalize this bond and close the chasm that exists between
your seen and unseen universe. You can express thanks for all the
gifts received from a source larger than the self.

*I acknowledge the existence of wisdom beyond myself, and humbly
request assistance.*

tampak tanah (TAHM-pahk TAH-nuh)   **Bahasa Indonesia**
To be able to see the ground.

Emotional pain often clouds our conscious awareness. What threads might be necessary to create a tapestry of healing for ourselves? We need a safe environment, unconditional positive regard, empathy, respect, non judgmental support, and the absence of shaming attitudes. These are the attributes that promote rejuvenation. Whatever our struggle, relapse is a part of the process of change. Slipping from our goal is a necessary aspect of continual healing, another fragment in a series of turning points that move us steadily to recovery. One of the three phases of dawn is called *tampak tanah* by the Iban people of the island of Borneo. It is when there is just enough light that the details of where one is stepping can be discerned. Not fully dancing in the morning light, but beyond the despairing confusion of night. As you journey toward wholeness, and a reawakening of your essential beautiful being, you can accept the dark stumbling times, and fall forward rather than backward, until the next obvious step reveals itself. You advance adamantly in the deepening of your spiritual aliveness, which is the foundation for all sustained change.

When I can't perceive where to go next, I can wait until I can.

September 8

pensieroso (payn-SIE-roh-zoh)   **Italian**
Pensive and thoughtful.

The faculty of introspection is best when, like a river, it is sustained and continuous. The art of solitude is inspirational, and often clarifies what parts of your life need to be simplified. Contemplative time offers a liberty and silence that allows new possibilities to rise into awareness. Such a process cannot be forced by a demanding ego. It is its own potentiality, time that is your own time, not to be filled up but rather enjoyed for itself. To welcome being *pensieroso* is to slow dance with the big inquiries. It is to take an illuminating long walk with yourself. This secret isolated garden can be experienced no matter what the external surroundings, though to fully relish the encounter, quiet and seclusion are the preferred companions. Do you answer the mid night call to awakening, the hour of the wolf, to think or write and sift through the busyness to touch the clear light within? Some prefer the early morning, or just before retiring to engage in this relaxed yet active process of reflection; others create special time once a week or month for this pursuit. This particular state of awareness functions as a seedpod, where intentions are nurtured and clarified before being released. It is as essential as air and water.

I enjoy exploring the deeper questions behind the obvious answers.

uthsaha (oot-SAH-hah)   Sanskrit
Spiritual encouragement.

A person takes a walk after supper and looks for the connection to the divine they know is out there. They sense that there is more than the world created by our egos. Many of us rejected the religious teachings imparted to us as children. Some of the basic values may have stuck, but continued participation in the institution was not satisfying. The spiritual call is often vague and hesitant, though sometimes quite clear and compelling. It may appear when least expected, or arise in response to immediate need. More like a sense of direction than a road map, it will first appear on the fringe of awareness, a barely perceptible shift in feeling. Spirituality is your active relationship with a power greater than the self that gives a sense of meaning, purpose and significance to your life. We all need the presence of *uthsaha* in our lives. It can arise from many sources: an inspirational teacher, an enlightening book, a conversation with friends, a regular devotional practice. Both symbolic and practical, the divine can be awakened by continually acting upon the small still inner voice. As you experience the positive aspects of its guidance in your life, a stronger bridge will be built, based on increasing trust and unfolding delight.

I do not resist the truth that every moment is sacred.

September 10

un cinq a sept (ahn SAYNK ah SEHT)   French
A quick sexual exchange.

At times it seems that we are trapped in a secret jungle of expectations, restrictions and misconceptions, searching for the new position, plaything, practice, or partner that will penetrate into the cosmic chamber of sexual fulfillment. Just about every male has had days when he was obsessed with his sexual urges. Most women, encouraged to be a "good girl" and yet also expected to be ribald, are set up to not trust their own natural impulses, and to always equate sexual contact with intimacy. While there is much to heal in our sexual relations , there is also the challenge of keeping sexuality alive and exciting in a long term relationship The relaxed notion of *un cinq a sept* speaks of an intense form of sexual contact that can add a sense of surprise and adventure. The ability to quickly sink into ecstasy anywhere with a loved one is remarkable. How wonderful to know each other's bodies and spirits so well as to pleasure each other capably and effortlessly. On the other hand, such a practice is never a substitute for the long slow meandering rediscovery of sensual sharing. Both expressions of sexual vitality are gifts from creator!

I enjoy the different paces and spaces of lovemaking with an intimate partner.

tsanahwit (tsah-NAH-weet)   **Sahaptin Nez Perce**
Equal justice.

We all desire leaders who are not greedy, and whose motive for acquiring power, which is not misused, is service to others. Such humanism derives from an unshakable sense of responsibility, fairness, strong determination and a blending of human intelligence and heart. When *tsanahwit* is a guiding principle, all prosper. Implicit in this community organizing quality is obedience to the law, mediation, and fairness. There is an appreciation of natural consequences and the law of the harvest: what is sown shall be reaped. Forgiveness is more empowering than the futility of carrying a grudge. "Power over others," wherein dominant and subordinate groups are created, is minimized. This concept is not about achieving a perfect state of getting along, but speaks to the value of keeping these issues of fairness and justice at the forefront. What we have forgotten can be remembered again.

Without social justice true prosperity will always be elusive.

September 12

achya (ahch-yuh)   Bengali
An affirmative response to a question; the great yes!

Just for today follow only the yes. Dance with the affirmation of all the goodness in your being. Say yes to your talents, your kindness, your work and your play. Generously wear all the hats given to you: parent, lover, teacher, healer, driver, worker, son or daughter, neighbor, friend. Dwell in the realm of acceptance and welcome even the shadows, the sufferings, the physical and emotional hardships you usually shun but also endure. No need to fight them off or engage in the habitual struggle. The negative will wither of its own accord as you focus on the power of the simple yes. Utter it in as many languages as you know. *Achya!* Said with passion and exuberance, this response is a testimony to possibility. Let's get on with it, let it happen, make it happen, fully engaged. Say yes to your life, to love, to all the children everywhere. Join forces with the enormous yes of all of humanity to become a flowing stream of positive actions rising higher and higher for the benefit of all beings.

Make it so!

chidelglo (ch-EE-deel-DLO)   Navajo
A baby's first laugh.

Babies are born with an instinctual drive for social interaction. At about six weeks, the first smile acts as an automatic social reinforcer, washing away the parents' fatigue and intensity of the earlier time. Babies at this age soon begin to smile at anyone who smiles at them, since each person in their immediate environment may be important for future survival. Around four months cooing sounds erupt into a giggle. This is perceived by Navajo people to be such a special occurrence that it has its own name, *chidelglo*. It is a wise and rich culture that takes the time to honor this remarkable event, and views it as a cause for gift giving. The Navajo value humor which plays a significant role in many stories and tribal mythology. Laughter is prayer, for it helps us discern our own crazy patterns of living. Its lighthearted message constantly reminds you to not take yourself too seriously.

Nothing compares to the joy of hearing children's laughter.

September 14

Nubaigai (noo-BAY-gay)   **Lithuanian**
End of harvest festival.

Following Lithuanian tradition, corn, ears of wheat or rye, and wildflowers are carefully woven at this time of year to craft a wreath of celebration. A doll is also constructed of the final sheaf of grain, decorated with ribbons and flowers. Sometimes the farm worker who bound the last sheaf will be wrapped in the figure. Old songs are sung during the procession from the fields to the landlord's house, where feasting will take place. Part of the magic of *Nubaigai* is the bond forged with both previous and future crops. The rite weaves together thanks for past and present abundance with hopes for continued prosperity. This bounty is meant to be shared. Giving nourishes growth and uncovers new parts of yourself, just as each harvest produces new seeds. Now is the time to open up, and give without any expectations. Love yourself enough to harvest the goodness in your life.

The gifts of this season fill me with vitality.

Tsukimi (TSU-kee-me)   Japanese
Moon viewing as a mid-autumn activity.

Every culture has its moon mythology. From goddess lore to stories explaining the mysterious body's cyclical sky movements, this celestial object has been revered for thousands of years. Perhaps because its rhythms are so intimate with our lifeblood, there has never been a shortage of offerings or ceremonies in her honor. Mystery and magic, romance and fertility, prosperity wishes and seasonal timekeeping, all are evoked in customs like *Tsukimi*. On the fifteenth day of the eighth moon, or the full moon nearest September 15th, Asian communities all over the world celebrate a time of thanksgiving, family reunions, and gift giving. Making offerings to the lunar spirit and eating moon cakes, which symbolize family unity, are also traditional. On the eastern horizon, over mountain tops or across the enormous expanse of open water, the exceptionally bright full moon rises at the same instant that the sun sets. Voices from undiscovered gardens deep within wail at the harvest moon, asking that their songs be heard. The moon expresses the depth of life reaching for new manifestation, consciousness waxing and waning as the cycles of existence continue.

Doing anything by moonlight adds a dimension of enchantment.

September 16

hoa'ai waiu (ho-ah-'eye vie-oo)   Hawaiian
Companions at the breast who have a special life-long relationship.

Like the milk of other mammals, human breastmilk is a species specific, nutritionally balanced, complete survival food. The immunologic protection it offers is truly astounding. The colostrum or first milk is especially rich in protective cells and antibodies, to help the newborn through a very vulnerable time. Your mother was your earliest source of nurturing and comfort, and it is important to honor all the loving and courageous acts she did for you. Her very presence reduced your fear of what was new, and provided the assurance you needed to explore the world. She gave you sustenance through her own body, as well as all the benefits of her clarity, concern, insight and caring. Just two generations ago, if a mother could not breastfeed, then a female relative or close friend would. Sometimes a mother with a lot of milk would breastfeed her own baby and another as well. This sharing of the same life giving source was highly regarded and the two babies were called *hoa'ai waiu*. The closeness experienced in this way created a bond of love and caring that was never forgotten as their separate paths unfolded.

I honor those with whom I share a bond of nurturance.

ting (ting)   Chinese
To listen with the heart, eyes, ears and mind.

Choosing to listen and developing an ability to not talk is a critical skill. Listening with an intensity normally reserved for speaking opens the space for others to share deeply. When one feels truly heard, rather than judged, they will take more risks in expressing deeper feelings. Listening is an active process that lets the speaker know they are accepted. The complexity of good listening is clearly reflected in the practice of *ting*. The auditory equivalent of reading between the lines, attending carefully penetrates to the core of what is unsaid, and gently moves toward the most vulnerable place, to elucidate what lives on that edge. Rather than having a conversation with yourself about what to say next, engaging in the present moment with full attention on the other is transformative. By reflecting back what you have heard, and asking clarifying questions rather than giving opinions or analysis, you allow the release of what is bothering the other. When you also allow the space of silence, you open the dance of communication so that the fullness of your empathy and caring is evident..

I never underestimate the healing power of just listening.

September 18

salam alekum (as-sa-LAAM-u a-LAY-koom)   Arabic
Greeting meaning peace be upon you.

Our early spiritual experiences are often contained in our bodies: the smell of incense, the sight of lit candles, the taste of foods associated with holy days. In an early ritual, at 4 years, 4 months, and 4 days a Muslim boy gets dressed up and travels to the family Mosque where he recites his first verse of the Koran which is written in honey on a slate. After this demonstration of mastery of his first spiritual teaching, the honey is dissolved in water which the boy drinks. Notions of spiritual thirst and hunger cross many traditions. These concepts are so woven into the fabric of daily life that the simple greeting, *salam alekum*, awakens the deeper spiritual connection between individuals. Thankfulness and prayer increase our sense of belonging, acknowledge our interdependence and mutuality, and create a self reinforcing upward spiral of awareness. We long for the richness of the spiritual tapestry in all its physical and emotional forms.

The sweetness of communing spiritually is very satisfying.

soon (soon)   Burmese
Alms offered to monks.

Our secret self yearns for the apparent simplicity of the wandering mendicant. To have no possessions to deal with, and no apparent problems except those that appear to assist in forging a stronger spiritual path, it can seem the ideal life. The tradition of *soon*, still prevalent in many Eastern countries, sheds some light on the reality of the commitment involved in such a reclusive lifestyle. Becoming a monk is not about escaping from the turmoil of daily life, in order to benefit the small self. Through their thoughts, speech and actions, such dedicated individuals bear witness that a life of peace, wisdom, love and mindfulness is possible. Like springs of fresh water, they remind all of us, by their awakened presence, that the suffering, injustice and danger in the world can be influenced positively. Socially engaged religion seeks to help one become more selfless and less selfish, not by retreating but by actively helping where needed. The tradition of Mother Teresa represents a long lineage of brave souls who accomplish much through both inner and outer work. Their light inspires us all.

In whatever way I can, I support those who devote their lives to improving the human condition.

September 20

moyn (MOH-een)   Welsh
Deep longing.

Childhood experiences are the womb within which our adult life gestates. Gradually our emerging personalities begin to discover what activities contain the most allure and promise for our future. We are drawn to people and experiences that manifest what we yearn to become. Samples of our fate were often revealed in the early interests which commanded our attention. *Moyn* is a repository of energy and stamina that guides you, through desire, to your destiny. Acknowledge the deep restlessness that searches for experiences. It knows that routine can be a killer of spirit, and that there are times in life when you must get on the open road. Don't take too long getting ready. Don't die with a lot of unexplored potential. Life is not about waiting until everything is safe. *Carpe diem!* Seize the day! There is no growth without risk. Venture across safe boundaries, and explore new thoughts, behaviors and feelings.

My yearnings illuminate my journey toward wholeness.

pakikisama (pah-kee-kee-SAH-mah)   Tagalog
Going along with the group.

As two separate individuals grow in closeness, a third entity of awareness is created. It is alive and bigger than either person, a string of moments shared together, an evolving adventure shaped and sustained by love. When interacting with a group of people in either a family, social, or business setting, these principles of sharing are still operative. In Western culture there is so much emphasis on me and mine that we can get tunnel vision when participating with others. A quality worth emulating is *pakikisama*. When you set aside your wants to allow for the needs of the collective, the process of personal growth is actually strengthened. Seeking to create harmony within a group benefits all. Just as one takes individual responsibility for their own life, each member contributes to the life of the alliance through their open hearted, generous involvement. Instead of seeing the process of cooperation as giving in or giving up, one can view it as a conscious contribution to the whole.

Surrendering to the will of the group can be empowering.

September 22

pratibha (PRAH-tee-bhah)   Sanskrit
Poetic sensibility and glittering inventiveness.

Grace can always be summoned by accessing our creative center.
Like a series of predictable miracles, expressions of our intuitive
imagination are full of surprise and wonder. To open a channel to
this potent genius, we first acknowledge its existence, and feel
worthy of its gifts. *Pratibha* expands as we learn to touch its
source. Honing your creative senses takes place within any discipline, and loving the practice enhances a free spirit of exploration. Surrender to our generative capacity opens the gates for
the impulse to travel the inner depths to the outer world beyond
the self. Freed from normal restrictions, editing and judgements,
this vital flow can reshape your reality. Behold the world in unexpected ways and reach for an original form to reveal the inner
feelings engendered. Change your perspective, and open to ingenious possibilities. Second star to the right, then straight on till
morning.

My ability to create novel ideas and works continues to blossom.

halak (HAH-lahk)   Bahasa Indonesia
A dream guide.

The inner magician is guardian of the realm of deep imagery. He is the messenger who remembers dreams, and urges you to access their meaning by re-experiencing them, rather than interpreting them. He knows the central questions that allow you to dialogue emotionally with your dream content. Rather than leave dream inquiry to the individual, the Senoi people have made it an established social discourse specifically for this purpose. Each morning community members gather to talk about their dreams of the previous night. The *halak* encourages people to share the messages, warnings, and gifts discovered in their night wanderings. A piece of artwork, a song, or an action that would smooth social relations might have appeared. Imagine how enriching it would be to have a regular supportive forum for exploring this symbolic and intuitive way of relating to the world. More holistic solutions to daily dilemmas might reveal themselves effortlessly. As you become more receptive to this mode of guidance, your inner wisdom will respond, sharing information in unexpected ways through an image in a day or night dreamscape.

I can join and benefit from an ongoing dream group.

September 24

kai so (kay so)   English Creole
A shout of approval, like bravo.

We normally reserve applause for human endeavors. What if we slowly began an underground custom of wild clapping for a sunset, moonrise or a rainbow? Cloud formations might spontaneously generate huge crowds of cheering children. Stadiums would fill to listen to the latest songs of popular birds and the wail of crickets in the night. *Kai so!* would be heard throughout the land as people everywhere bestowed richly deserved approbation in appreciation for the gifts showered upon them each day by nature. Crusaders for better recognition of these myriad episodes of delight, we would tirelessly show up at meetings and conventions with flowers and invitations to come outside and enjoy the play of light on the mountains. Television sets and surfing the net might take a back seat as humans find sustenance in the night sky and gentle breezes. If we could slow down long enough to really let it all in, we might discover that we already have everything we need to feel satisfied.

I cherish our planet and voice my appreciation extravagantly.

patamou (pah-tah-MO-uu)   Yanomami
Elder harangue to create change.

An old person in a fairy tale often provides a needed magical talisman, some unlikely, unexpected and mysterious power to help others overcome a difficulty. The aged sage urges people to "sleep on it" when dealing with a dilemma, as a way to begin self reflection. In this way they serve as a visionary guide to what needs to be done. The wisdom of such an approach is embodied by the Yanomami tribe of Brazil, where community decisions are made by an informal council which includes older tribal members. The elderly, imbued with respect, manifest diplomatic and leadership qualities in their moral authority. Engaging in a *patamou* is a dramatic example of their responsibility. This public passionate speech attempts to convince others of the necessity of a decision involving support for those in need, or suggests rules of behavior for the younger people. Sometimes it is a way to just state an opinion to cause thought in community members. Without any real power of coercion, elders lead by word and by example.

I listen closely to the wisdom of elders and act on their advice.

Tanekert (tah-NEH-kert)   Tuareg
Return of the rains celebration.

By about 2500 BC, the cultivation of beans, squash and corn had been achieved by hunter gatherers around the globe. Life depended on these crops, known as the three sisters because of their complementary nutritional properties. Their cultivation could only be successful when there was sufficient water. Thus arose the ancient ceremonial pleas for rain and fertility at the beginning of the planting season. Dancers might use gourd rattles, mimicking the sound of pattering rain, and stamping motions to awaken the spirits of the earth. The swaying of the fringed sashes of the participants suggests torrents of moisture falling on the thirsty earth. Offerings were made to the rain cloud people. For the Tuareg, a nomadic group in North Africa, the time when such supplications are answered is honored by an event known as *Tanekert*. Some traveling hundreds of miles, they gather at a specific oasis, where dancing, singing and camel races take place. The simple joy of surviving another season with abundance soaks into the desert soil. Their love of life is like misty rain, coming softly yet flooding rivers.

I can stand in the rain and celebrate its power and gentleness.

Tashlich (TAHSCH-leej)   Yiddish
Casting one's sins symbolically into a stream or river.

The use of water for spiritual purification is as commonplace as it is ancient. Perhaps because it is so essential for sustaining life, and so useful for cleansing our bodies, water finds its way into many rituals and celebrations. With the solemn observance of *Tashlich*, supplicants of the Jewish faith throw crumbs into a moving body of water as atonement for past transgressions. This is a time of reconciliation for those who have done each other harm in the past year, and an opportunity to offer charity to those less fortunate. It is a clear request for absolution, in order to wash the slate clean and to begin again with renewed vigor. Forgiveness of self, life, and others softens you, dissolving bitterness and illusion, enlarging your perspective of humanity's shared flaws. Letting go of the past, and dropping the baggage of an earlier experience, opens the way to move beyond judging and accept responsibility for your actions. Flow with difficulties like a river, and become an open and expansive ocean of love.

I can find joy in accepting and releasing my imperfections.

September 28

daramulun (dah-rah-moo-loon)   **Arunta**
Master of thunder; the noise made by an instrument known as a bullroarer.

A rainmaker whirls a thin carved oval piece of bone or wood tied to the end of a cord. The noise that is produced by this marriage of invisible wind and palpable form throbs with vitality. Varying in tone and pitch depending on speed, and the size and shape of the oval pendant, the idiophone mirrors the varying moods of the wind. This early form of musical instrument played an important role in rainmaking ceremonies and in honoring the gods of wind in African and North and South American tribal societies. *Daramulun* is the Australian aboriginal equivalent of attracting the attention of a supreme being through haunting music. The sacred sounds produced by the whirling motion call forth the inner thunder which turns the world, and demand that you pay attention to what is most essential and life giving. It is a summons to live a passionate existence, a call to gather your strength and resolve, an invitation to enter a trance and discover a reservoir of visionary intelligence. The roar is a reminder that the voices on the wind whisper softly so you can wake up! The sudden silence when the supplicative sounds cease invokes the power of the space between thoughts through which the channel to the universal is opened.

Indigenous music is a form of powerful prayer, in which I can partake.

pivik (PEE-veek)   Inuktitut
A person who gets upset easily and is thus considered childish.

An "entitlement" view of the world holds that others and life itself should be giving you what you want. Combined with the stresses of daily life, this worldview sets the stage for your anger. Don't be a *pivik*! Anger is not good or bad, it just is. What you do with this energy is what is important. It exists along a continuum ranging from feeling peeved to being annoyed to ranting in rage, and for some the escalation of their anger meter is dramatic. Part of maturity is utilizing a coping strategy at the earliest indication of frustration, so the emotion can be released harmlessly before it explodes. Take a time out, get in touch with your breath, count to ten, or do something to improve your physiological state of imbalance. Let go of expectations. Choose to temporarily suspend communication when it is going down an injurious path. The destructive folly of this transient dance of insanity can be avoided.

Learning about the patterns of my anger and frustration is the first step in releasing them.

September 30

hetman (HEHT-mahn)   Ukrainian
Leader recognized by the people.

Whether looking for someone to take charge of a block party or to govern a state, we seek in our leaders an individual who makes requests of others while creating an environment where people want to contribute. We yearn for one who embodies excellence, admits mistakes, is committed to ongoing improvement, and shows a willingness to enter, explore, and confront the community's shadows. While forging a common dream, this visionary guide constantly acknowledges and appreciates human resources. Such are the qualities of a *hetman*. The main work of your inner chieftain is to empower. Authentic potency emerges when you align the highest part of yourself with your thoughts, emotions and actions. When the realm of your life holds meaning and purpose, and you are fully engaged in it, your dominion expands. Like a good king or queen, you anticipate needs and are proactive, yet also understand when it is better to wait. Call forth your leadership, realize your significance, and enter the circle of your own potential.

I am willing to lead in both my inner and outer worlds.

OCTOBER

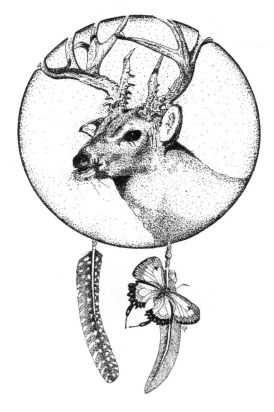

A gong sounds softly
Be happy for no reason
Dream of butterflys

naka ima (nah-kah ee-mah)   **Japanese**
The time and space between the past and the future where human life manifests.

To live fully in the unfolding reality of the present moment is to touch immortality. Our power exists only in the here and now, protected from the onslaught of past concerns and future worries. In order to encounter this state with any regularity, we must walk the path of interior mastery, quieting the wild horse of mind, and stabilizing the calm center that is relaxed yet alert. Expect nothing, be ready for anything. When we leave the realm of *naka ima*, we can never discover reality, but are mired in deception. We have all had the experience of being fully awake and aware, when everything seems sharp and crisp. In that reality we are not attached to our previous notions of what is, and phenomena are experienced as if for the first time. There is no desire to grasp onto anything, and we can let go into the truth of our existence. Daily living does require us to plan and consider tomorrow, and to reflect upon and examine yesterday. But our modern age has shifted you too much into this form of perception. To regularly practice returning to the present, through meditation or another discipline, is to find a better balance. You gradually enlarge your capacity for bliss, and abandon the illusion that you are separate from others.

Focusing on my breath returns me to the present moment.

October 2

satyagraha (saht-yah-GREH-hah)   Sanskrit
Unmasking injustice so truth is brought to light.

Your enemy can be your greatest teacher. Achievements gained through violence are not stable, and the temporary win leaves a seed of negative consequences. Punishing or destroying an oppressor initiates a new cycle of violence and suffering, liberating no one. Gandhi, an East Indian spiritual leader, coined the term *satyagraha* in the early twentieth century. This involves shedding clarity on what is not right, and holding on to that truth by non violent means. For this principle to carry moral weight sufficient to ensure success, there must be no hatred in the heart of the resistant against the opponent. In addition, the cause itself must be substantial and true, and those involved willing to commit till the end. The sword of non violent resistance is the unshakable firmness of love. Your spirituality is the only protection from the brutality of the destructive forces that you seek to bring into harmony.

None of us is free if one of us is chained.

karibu chakula (kah-RIH-boo chah-KOO-lah)   **Kiswahili**
Come and eat with us.

Myths of magic vessels that provide limitless quantities of food and drink were probably spun by our species' storytellers in order to assuage our great fears of hunger and deprivation. It is no wonder that gifts of food are part of many religious ceremonies, and an essential ingredient in fostering friendships among peoples. In an African community if either friend or stranger approaches a dwelling, the villager is prompted to utter *karibu chakula*. It is a generous and welcoming gesture, which immediately conveys that whatever there is will be shared. The phrase automatically invites participation on equal terms, and bears witness to our shared human status. The welcome reveals our interdependence, and an appreciation that we too can reciprocate the generosity when visitors come to our community. The simple comfort of this act is a portal to distant memories when the ancients finally learned that cooperating and sharing food was in everyone's best interest. Our consciousness is also raised realizing that one fifth of the world's population does not get enough to eat each day.

I contribute in some way to ending world hunger.

October 4

Ch'ung Yang (chung yang)   Chinese
Family remembrance day when one visits ancestors' graves.

Every death we witness is a harbinger of our own passing. Physical, emotional or mental injury represent little endings, minor variations on this same theme of mortality. When we think of those who have passed on, we are forced to confront and question the meaning and purpose of our lives. On the holiday of *Ch'ung Yang* it is customary for Chinese families to visit and tend gravesites, making food offerings which are later shared at a meal. Families fly kites to carry away misfortune into the heavens, where difficulties are rendered harmless. Like holding a mirror to your own heart, the act of contacting and addressing departed relations is illuminating. Many of your kin braved difficult situations, and yet managed to survive before the wheel of time prompted their passage to the next adventure. You might draw strength from this awareness, have a dialogue with a departed one, or seek advice about a current dilemma from those who are physically gone, but whose lifeforce you can still contact.

A special place in my home with family photos or mementos reminds me to honor those who came before.

turiya (tu-dee-yuh)   Sanskrit
Not waking, not sleeping, not dreaming.

In betwixt and between our usual states of awareness lie new frontiers of being. Like a primitive watercolor, they have a misty quality, portraying a sense of something already known and important wandering on the edge. With practice, the realm of *turiya* can be used to increase our creative capacity. As we drift asleep, daydream, roam while meditating, or awaken from the night, we might experiment with whatever we perceive. When we find ourselves in the midst of an extensive reverie or interior monologue, we can create a central focus around which the images can gather, such as a phrase or tone, and then place a conscious wish into the mix. More than just a fantasy stream of thoughts, these impressions are the inner workings of your own personal wish fulfillment process. They serve as rehearsals for future action, and allow you to try on what a given situation might be like.

Tuning into your own inner theater takes you down new paths of insight.

October 6

ruskaa (rus-kaah)   **Finnish**
Beautiful fall colors.

You took your essence, your seeds, and planted them. Then came the hard work of nurturing the growth and potential of your dream. Now is the season of manifestation, a time to harvest. Maybe you are reaping the rewards of physical bounty, or emotional wholeness. Perhaps you have created an abundance of useful knowledge, or spiritual connections. There is a freedom in the brisk autumn air, a sense of peace, a permission to lighten your load, to take time to watch the more rapid growth, development, and passing away of *ruskaa*. The brilliant blaze of forests responding in unison to the call of the season invites you to do the same. Enter the outdoors and revel in the glory of the goodness Nature offers you. Celebrate your continuing vitality and the spontaneous glory in everything that is alive.

I welcome the changes that this time of year brings.

mbuki mvuki (MM-bookie MM-vookie)   Zulu
To shuck off clothes in order to dance.

Dance is a living entity, vitally present in your body. Even new-borns move in synchronous rhythm to the speech patterns of their parents. When you enter the timeless place of such stirring, you touch the center of the universe, the heart of being. The surrender and abandonment involved in dancing is manifested in the urge to *mbuki mvuki*. More than just a simple foreplay, this sensuous release demonstrates a serious yet playful commitment to celebration. Unfettered by unnecessary garments, one can get down to the essentials. From the beginning motions you move through an increasing buildup of intensity, ultimately climaxing in the sounds of heavy breathing and the flow of sweaty bodies. The entire process embodies the perpetual creation destruction rhythm of all life: awakening, unfolding and cessation. To be lost in such powerful passionate rhythms elicits the awe and mystery of the untamed parts of who you are.

After a long day, I can strip down and dance spontaneously in my living room.

October 8

via negativa (VEE-ah NEH-gah-TEE-vah)   Latin
The exploration of what is not in order to understand what is.

We sometimes approach our journey too perplexed to even for-
mulate a query. Yet through our feelings of helplessness and powerlessness arises the beginning of wisdom. The first of the twelve
steps clearly invokes this state: "we admitted we were powerless." You have let go, accepted your limitations and realize that
your own willpower cannot get you through this difficult time.
The *via negativa* is a key process in this surrender. In an attempt
to discover and affirm your true spirituality, you must also examine what it is not, the ways it differs from religion or therapy.
Such observations deepen your appreciation of what is really
nourishing to your spirit. Your exploratory path is not about
judging or comparisons, but rather distinguishing and finding
the intrinsic value in each perspective. Wandering down seemingly divergent paths ultimately brings you closer to home. Like
being in the center of a healing vortex, what is needed will be
drawn to you. The universe is conspiring to help you.

I can relax and trust that I will find my way.

Tod kathin (toad kaht-heen)   Thai
Pilgrimage season; the time when monks receive new robes.

The concept of pilgrimage is ancient. Through the difficulties inherent in a long spiritual voyage, we develop inner strength, determination and courage to face problems. Many Buddhists travel to the Place of the Diamond Scepter in India, where Buddha gained enlightenment over one hundred human generations ago. Jews, Christians and Muslims visit the sacred sites of Jerusalem, reaffirming their spiritual connections. Hindus trek to the source of the Ganges, and many Muslims journey to Mecca at least once in their lifetime. Many Huichol Indians of Central Mexico return each year to Wirikuta, a high desert plateau hundreds of miles from their mountain homelands. *Tod kathin* refers to a wooden frame used in Thailand to stretch cloth scraps before sewing them into new robes for Buddhist monks, during a time when pilgrimages to temples are common, and visitors offer food and clothing to the monks in residence. Some say that if you can't discover meaning where you are standing, where do you expect to wander in search of it? Spiritual quests are not about escaping those parts of your life you do not want to face. They are not running away in denial. Their gift is that they can reconnect you with the natural world and your higher power. Going out into the world can be a way of bringing you closer to the true dwelling of your inner village.

I respond to the call of a special sojourn.

October 10

gemeinschaft (gay-MINE-shahft)   German
Society as a system of inter-related parts; community.

Many of us long for simpler times, when relationships had a more relaxed pace, and isolation and loneliness were less pervasive. Our extended family was close by and no matter how crazy they seemed, they were still a source of caring and support. Neighbors took the time to know one another and interact regularly for the benefit of all. Friends were more available, and not quite as scattered across the country as they seem to be at present. We yearn for the strengths of *gemeinschaft*, with its three pillars of kinship, neighborhood and friendship. On some level, we recognize that the personal safety nets have been cut, and replaced with complex bureaucracies trying to hold things together using mental health therapists, social workers, lawyers, probation officers, and other professionals. The more points of contact any constellation of people has, the more cohesive its bonds will be, and the more the community will flourish. We yearn to rub up against each other more frequently in meaningful ways. Create more Kodak moments in the community commons. Practice turning soft and lovely with everyone we encounter.

I choose to create more random acts of kindness.

nichevo (nee-chee-VOH)   Russian
Don't worry, doesn't matter, nothing to do about it.

Good morning. This is God speaking from these pages. I will be handling all of your problems today, without any assistance from you. I'll let you know if I require your input. So just relax and enjoy the day. This message is a gentle reminder to simply lighten up. We spend so much time resisting life, trying to command it, ignoring the basic reality that what we resist persists. Fatigue is largely a matter of resistance, which drains our energy. When someone is upset and anxious, gently speaking the word *nichevo* might remind them that their challenge at the moment is simply to not hold on so tightly. Clinging to what is not controllable is, in part, the source of their misery. Bouncing between blame and self pity only brings more suffering. When circumstances cannot be altered, you can always shift your attitude, the way you hold the situation. It is very empowering to view change as more prevalent than stability, and as a stimulant to growth rather than a threat to security. Curiosity and acceptance will get you through whatever highs and lows may be encountered in manifesting a goal, dream or vision. To yield with life solves what only appears at the moment to be insoluble.

I can relax and find the gift hidden in any hardship.

October 12

sz (SHH)   Chinese
Good wind of the first faint touch of autumn.

We are part of the pattern woven into the breath of Gaia, the rhythmic dance of planetary awareness. The turning of the seasons touches us at a deep cellular level. Our bodies respond invisibly to the barely palpable nuances of change, as days begin to shorten, evenings chill and final harvests are undertaken. We can almost taste the *sz*, the delicious stirring of treetops, the wispy sighs of autumn traveling clouds. How good it is to pause and appreciate this gentle breeze polishing our being. We can breathe in the teachings of this time, and exhale the tensions accumulated through hard work. Now it is time to relax, loosen the pace, and participate in the season's abundance. Proclaim the wonder of this period, and listen to the silence filled only by the voices of streams and forests. Part of the beauty of the harvest is in sharing it. Your generous, open hearted and welcoming nature knows that giving your time, energy and material resources helps create a better world. Giving nourishes your growth and teaches you about new parts of yourself, just as each harvest produces new seeds. Now is the time to open up, and give without any expectations.

The autumn breeze reminds me to love myself enough to experience gratification, to harvest and share the goodness in my life.

susto (SOOS-toh)   Spanish
Soul loss.

The notion that mind and body are separate has delayed our understanding of the true nature of illness. Our physical, mental, emotional and spiritual aspects are clearly interdependent and do not exist in isolation. Feeling upset or spiritually empty adversely affects the ability of our body to function. When we focus on healing an imbalance in any of our windows on the world, we positively influence the other openings. This more holistic view of dis-ease is shared by many peoples from diverse cultures. *Susto* is attributed to a frightening event that causes the soul to leave the body, resulting in unhappiness and illness. The impact is global, including somatic complaints of muscle aches and pains, along with appetite and sleep disturbances. Feelings of sadness, lack of self worth and motivation, and difficulty functioning in normal social roles intensify one's difficulties. Ritual healing focuses on calling the soul back to the body, followed by thorough cleansing of body and spirit to restore overall balance. As you struggle to heal the traumas of the past, it is essential to acknowledge that every element of your being was affected, and needs the nourishing gifts of your loving attention.

Creating a healing ceremony with loving friends helps me move beyond past hurt.

October 14

ototeman (oh-toh-the-mahn)   Ojibwa
The mystical connection between humans and other living creatures.

Indigenous peoples everywhere have various methods to open a channel to the teachings and powers of the animal kingdom. Many African clans, for example, have a totem which enriches their daily lives. When a stranger is encountered, one of the first questions may be "What do you dance?" meaning from what community do you come. The response may be "I dance the panther," which identifies the animal totem for my clan, and relates me to other clans that also have the same special animal. The general term in Ojibwa for this remarkable relationship of mutual respect between humans and animals is *ototeman*. But industrial societies have lost the link with wild four leggeds, substituting anthropromorphized cartoon characters and stuffed toys. When you begin anew to consciously open yourself to intimacy with animal brothers and sisters, you re-establish a link that is millennia old. A mask, a carved fetish, or even a picture of a favorite beast can stimulate the forgotten ties. Inward journeying to discover animal guides, or getting out enough to have contact with wildlife in their own habitat deepens your ability to receive the mystical gifts that are your birthright.

I listen to the messages brought to me by the creatures with whom I share this world.

Jilla (jee-llah)   Boran
Naming ceremony for a newborn child.

You were born helpless and dependent, unable to walk, talk or take care of basic physical needs. Who named you, and what is the story behind their choice? Traditional African tribal rituals for a newborn vary in both timing and complexity. Often there is a waiting period during which the young one has only a generic name, until after a week, a lunar cycle or the faling off of the umbilical cord. No matter the tribal origin, there is always some public honoring, blessing and naming of the new member. The baby is seen as a gift for the entire community, which also collectively shares the responsibility for its well being. The *Jilla* is a way the Boran people of Kenya have of strengthening this bond, expressing thanks to god and seeking continued blessings. Lighting a fire, feasting, singing, divination of the child's future, and special sacrifices occur over two days. Reflecting on the customs, hopes and wishes behind your own appellation allows memories long buried to surface. The struggles and joys your parents experienced at the time of your naming may parallel some of the difficulties and successes you now face as a parent, uncle or aunt. What might the newborn that we once were say to us now?

I can design a welcoming ritual for myself, as if newly arrived.

October 16

ginnungagap (gee-noongah-gahp)   Old Norse
The endless abyss at the edge of the world.

If you could read your life story, would you want to know how it ends? Wake up each morning refreshed by the thought of death. Carry it on your shoulder or in your pocket as a reminder of how you really want to live. This very moment all over the world many beings are passing on. Death is our most basic fear, so make it your friend. Because we have no direct knowledge of the event our concern is intense, much like trying to imagine the forbidden reaches of *ginnungagap*. In olden times the worst possible fate was to find yourself at this termination of the flat earth, an unknown realm replete with dire consequences. Cartographers who had mapped out all details within the scope of their knowledge and understanding would often inscribe along the edge of the parchment, "Beyond here be dragons." Everyone dies at the right time, and until then learning never ends. When death arrives it will no doubt provide both answers and more questions. Every act counts when we live with death as our eternal companion. Live or die! Each moment asks nothing more of us.

The unknown relentlessly beckons, even in our final moments.

pwe (pweh)   Burmese
All night theater festival.

Besides allowing for public enjoyment, feasts across cultures share many commonalities. They represent an intergenerational gathering, where contact with elders allows for the transmission of folk knowledge and lore to younger generations. Heritage is enriched through the sharing of special costumes and foods, and a bonding occurs that transcends personal concerns. Solar and lunar calendars and the cycle of seasons often determine the timing of these historic events. In Myanmar, the Land of Golden Pagodas, Buddhist culture and local animist rituals are brought together in *pwe*, a performance art combining religion, spectacle and entertainment. All levels of the society, from rice growing peasants to the business class, come together in long enlivening gatherings where folk opera and dance forms predominate. The plays are elegant yet light hearted, and full of educational allegories. You understand well the nostalgia and comfort of attending rituals over years. Although the form may change slightly, the underlying soothing balm persists. Such time is to be cherished and passed on.

I embrace the joys of my cultural heritage.

October 18

shanachie (SHAH-nah-hee)   Gaelic
Person fond of telling the old tales.

In ancient times, a tribe would often assign the maintenance of hot coals to certain individuals so that the next night's fire might be easily kindled. Storytellers are the keepers of a different sort of flame. They preserve a wealth of secrets cradling the verbal, spiritual, and material aspects of a culture. The light of the many faceted folktale survives through oral transmission, with constant variations influenced by memory and talent. The *shanachie* was a traditional Celtic entertainer, creative artist and sage. More than just protectors of idle quaint or romantic ramblings, these individuals were a powerful source of human learning for centuries. In this rich cornucopia of narrative imagination is a repository of truths that defines and inspires us with heros and heroines and mystery and magic. When you begin to tell a few stories, you are part of a long and important tradition. Take a class or drop by the local library for story hour to get the feel of how it is done. Or just turn everything off for an evening—no newspapers, magazines, phone, TV, VCRs, radio or surfing the net—and start spinning yarns of earlier times for your friends or family.

I hold within the seeds of a few recountings waiting to be told.

se do bheatha (SHEH DOH VEH-ah-thah) Celtic
Life to you.

Our planet began in the blaze of an exploding star. Like a sacred fire within, the process of living with and moving beyond the conflicting parts of ourselves is essential for personal evolution. Fire is destructive, purifying and transformative. Too much struggle burns us, and yet we must be close enough to feel the heat of change and growth. Just holding a question, breathing deeply and not forcing an answer, allows different possibilities to emerge. *Se do bheatha.* This is a greeting from the heart that offers an insightful reminder to lightly persevere. More a magical incantation than a simple exclamation, it penetrates to the core of how you view this precious existence. Your blessings are many. Be generative in your approach to difficulties. You have the ability to grant yourself freedom from struggle at any moment, to rest and gather energy, allowing time for the situation to clear. From a centered relaxed perspective, you can more effectively engage and resolve a dilemma. Be gentle with yourself. You possess the strength to strive for self improvement and simultaneously to joyfully welcome fallibility and imperfections. Accept the cleansing breath of your inner flame, and release yourself from strife.

Lighting my own life's candle, I see what before was hidden.

October 20

nith (neet-j)   **Inuktitut**
Song duel.

In relatively closed societies methods for settling disputes, regardless of cause, had to be powerful and effective. One unique way of dealing with ill will was the *nith* of the Inuit people. This forum was both simple and profound in its approach. In such contests, the offended and offending persons traded scathing yet funny songs with each other while an amused audience enjoyed the match. The reciprocal unpleasantries were exchanged within a safe space, and humor manifested in the situation, no matter how grave the circumstances. The festive playful yet serious context was a healing balm. A highly regarded song used metaphors alluding to accusations rather than exposing them in controversial detail, avoiding argument and self justification. Both singers took care not to escalate the quarrel, but sought to restore the social balance while dissipating discontent and resentment. Incorporating the essential elements of respect and humor in our own dealings takes patience and courage.

When in conflict with others, I can practice adding humor and letting go of being right.

sabat (sha-BAAT)   **Yiddish**
A break or rest of the heart.

Sometimes our assurance drops away. We lose all sense of direction and feel a heart weariness that seems ancient, primitive. "I've used up all my sick leave, so I'm calling in dead", says one bumpersticker. Softly at first, traveling the edges of our awareness, we realize somehow we must create time for regeneration. The path of our heart needs clearing, the well of our being seeks replenishment. Absorbed in the daily spinning of our lives, we find ourselves far from where we thought we might be. It is time for a spiritual romance with ourselves. We feel the pull, the call, the yearning of *sabat*. So how will you set about it, and approach this rest of the heart? If we gaze too far into the distance, we will only see tomorrow, tomorrow. Today is where we must find the strength and courage to truly rest and heal. By translating our sense of caring for ourselves into a sacred celebration, we honor this impulse towards wholeness. One often knows exactly what needs to be done to touch the power of healing renewal. And when we arrive, and come home to that place, we will wonder why we waited so long to visit.

I will find whatever I need this moment, this day, this week, this month, and this year to celebrate a rest of the heart.

October 22

bambai de (bahm-BYE duh)   Dutch Creole
Time is a great healer.

We spend much of our lives wanting unpleasantries to pass. Like desperados waiting for the train, we feed on hope and dreams in order to survive present suffering and despair. The someday isle beckons like a mirage, disappearing as we approach. At some point we may realize that these obstacles are the very fabric of our existence, rather than something else to be gotten through so our true life might begin. Locked in the dungeon of the past lie the scarred remains of unfulfilled desires. Enough of this wallowing! *Bambai de!* By and by things move forward. Common wisdom states that a tincture of time is all the medicine required for wounds to heal. Yet this is not at all certain. The passage of years may dull the pain, and allow only the better memories to surface. What really helps is what we choose to do with the time. You must enter into the darkness, grieve, vent and process, and then embrace the light of forgiveness, and rediscover that joy and ecstasy are possible. Your feelings of depression and hopelessness are not weakness, but rather the necessary seeds of resilience, that nurture your innate ability to bounce back from adversity.

I welcome the gifts of time and use them wisely for my own recovery and that of others.

nazarlik (nuh-ZUR-lick)   Turkish
Talismanic symbol on a tapestry to ward off the evil eye.

The concept of the evil eye is found throughout the world, but is especially prevalent in Mediterranean cultures. Children and young animals are the most susceptible to the curse, perhaps because they are so vulnerable and open to others. Once afflicted, they may suffer from a variety of symptoms, including fitful sleep, crying without apparent cause, fever and gastrointestinal complaints. Various forms of protection have been developed, including use of amulets with horns, moons or hands, or the wearing of sacred writings. A unique form of prophylaxis is the presence in the home of a *nazarlik*, which is meant to deflect the negative energy or to attract the malignant glance onto the talisman itself. Originally, the ability to injure or even kill with a look was thought to be involuntary, generated by intense feelings of envy. At times each of us falls under the spell of this emotion. A simple remedy is to think of the envied person, and say silently "may your successes be multiplied" whenever jealousy arises. The regular practice of this sympathetic joy enriches you, makes you feel good by shifting the focus away from bad feelings, and prevents the development of negativity that may hurt others in ways we do not fully understand or intend.

I have ways of protecting myself from destructive thoughts or actions.

October 24

teeka (TEE-kuh)   Hindi
A symbol of worship of the intellect and consciousness present in every person.

It is possible to move beyond the delusions of a separate struggling self. Through inner growth and development and outer right livelihood and actions in the world, we can strengthen a core of awakened wisdom. This serene yet vigilant awareness is large enough to hold both good and bad, pleasure and pain, oppression and freedom. The spiritual path is not a series of rote exercises, with a formula to imitate and follow. Rather it is the unique unfolding of our higher selves, as we give permission for the expression of the eternal parts of who we are. The red dot, or *teeka*, is an East Indian custom with many names and associated traditions. During the marriage ceremony, it is placed by the bridegroom on his bride's forehead. In other rituals it is also applied to men. Different sizes and shapes may denote marital status, childhood or adolescence. Seeing this marking on a person is a reminder to honor and be humble in the presence of the divinity and intellect of another being, who is also engaged in cutting through the veils of illusion.

I hold in great esteem the inner eye of understanding in others.

pusaka (poo-SAH-kuh)   Bahasa Indonesia
Sacred heirlooms passed down from generation to generation.

Some of the treasures we hold most dear were given to us by family members. Most of us have a secret cache for *pusaka*. We may love a piece of furniture or an aunt's frypan, but the most special are often small enough to be cradled in our hands, or hold close to our heart. Whether it is the memories they seem to carry or the innate beauty of something made long ago, such objects have survived the flux of material goods that pass in and out of our lives. They may not have significant monetary value, but their very lack of commerciality reinforces their bond, and they become consecrated through the power we imbue in them over time. Often they are something the loved one had worn close to their body, and that therefore impart some of their energy and life force. When you honor these items by occasionally wearing or admiring them, you also acknowledge all the intangible generational gifts of stories, songs and wisdom you have received.

A few simple inherited articles can feed my eyes and my spirit.

October 26

Szuret (SOO-rreht)   Hungarian
Grape gathering festival when many marriages take place.

The beauty of this time elicits a desire to join the creative pulse of nature, to mingle in the realm of gods and bring forth new life. As it was in ancient times, a huge bouquet of grapes leads the joyous procession that takes place during *Szuret*. Musicians and entertainers enliven the growing crowd. Garlands of flowers, feasting and dancing herald the celebration. Couples prepare to bond for life and to publicly declare their intended union. The fragrance of the grapes fills the air with the aroma of expectant love. We pick intimate partners whom we intuitively recognize will hold the most potential for helping us to heal. You can relate to your mate and really see them in their individual specialness, only when you have relieved them of the burden of carrying your projections and wounds. Take full responsibility for nurturing yourself through such internal work, and you will have more to bring to the relationship. Toast each other at this time of harvest, and honor the sweetness of the fruits you have gathered and continue to share.

I am grateful for times of revelry in loving relationships.

bungisngis (boong-ee-SEENG-ess)   Tagalog
Infectious ear to ear grin.

Smiling has been called mouth yoga. The activation of the thirty odd facial muscles alters our mood for the better. When in the midst of our worst uptight major malox moment, we can form the habit of cracking just the smallest beginning of a beaming expression. Invite an instant joy wave to suddenly overwhelm us and carry us to a new dimension. Why not invoke the beauty of a *bungisngis* as often as possible? This is the no holds barred, all out, out there bliss reflector variety in which your entire spirit radiates through the body. Eyes twinkle with delight, the limbs exude joy and the heart chakra shines like a sunrise. People may think you are either crazy or not too bright if you engage in this behavior too often, but they will also be drawn to the dynamism you create. We love to be around people who laugh and joke a lot. They generate something palpable, perhaps some undiscovered pheromone, that invites others into their glowing aura. Now is the moment to do this. Right now! Stretch the corners of your mouth to the heavens and feel the beat of ecstasy grow stronger.

Enlighten up!

October 28

aware (AH-wah-ray)   Japanese
The feelings engendered by indescribable beauty.

We suffer so many disappointments in love and life. Yet we are drawn again and again to whatever our spirits need to experience on our journey. At times hardships are suspended, as we are captured by a clear perception of wonder beyond thought and words. Wrapped in the embrace of the beauty of our existence, we feel connected to the larger ebb and flow of the life force. Our mortality may speak to us through the falling leaves, the turning of the wheel to another season, the beauty of a moonset that filled us with awe and then was gone. It is the fleeting aspect of astonishment that generates the richness of *aware*. Overcome with emotion, tears and laughter mingle in the bittersweet recognition that this too shall pass. Tasting brief interludes of perfection in an imperfect world sustains your hope and strengthens your will to survive. To live with such an open sensitivity to loveliness is to allow your heart to break open, and enlarge who you are.

Bliss can be discovered in the ordinary.

ho'oponopono (HO-OH-poh-no-poh-no)   Hawaiian
To come together in a problem solving process.

If the way to conquer hatred is by kindness, and the path to transform selfishness lies through charity, then why is it hard to achieve? It may be noble to work for the cause of peace and to reduce violence in human life, but many of us struggle just to get along with our teenagers, and deal with insensitive neighbors. We require practical instruments in our toolbox to deal more skillfully with the everyday conflicts that arise, such as active listening and the ability to stay centered rather than to be swept away emotionally. The social covenant to *ho'oponopono* carries teachings beyond dispute resolution. It is also a healing process that combines religious ceremony, counseling, community meeting and arbitration. Besides speaking to the willingness to engage until things are set right, this approach strengthens the collective ability of the entire culture to get along. Each success adds to the foundation for future peaceful resolution. When such techniques become part of the fabric of the culture and are institutionalized in societal process, we all benefit. It is the nature of relationships to occasionally get out of tune. You can join in the revolutionary activity of the slow and deep reorientation of hearts toward a more harmonious course.

Choosing to mediate and learning to listen well alter the destructiveness of my conflicts.

October 30

Los Angelitos (los ahn-he-LEE-tohs)   Spanish
Day devoted to children who have died.

Grandparent dies, parent dies, son or daughter dies. This is the natural order of things. Living after a loved one has died is never easy, and the task seems all but impossible when a child departs. We have a word for the spouse who has lost a mate, and for a young one who has lost parents, but none for people whose offspring have passed. Perhaps the hole of grief is too deep to even try and express. Descendants of the Mayan peoples of Mexico and Central America have a public forum for sharing this sadness in the feast of *Los Angelitos*. Families decorate doors with flowers, hold vigils, and prepare special foods for the little angels who will visit during the night. It is an opportunity for commemoration and release of some of the burden of anguish. You can't hold onto the grief of a tragedy forever. The slow recovery from such a loss is not an act of disloyalty. It is a sign of healing. The memories of departed children are yours to keep, and though the past will always travel with you, you will learn to survive and thrive one day at a time.

I treasure my loved ones each day, for they may not always be with me.

hejnal (HEY-nai)   Polish
A warning call from a high tower.

Imagine that we all carried an internal sensor similar to an airport metal detector. It would beep everytime we drifted from our true spiritual path. It might sound off when we begin to tell a lie or to withhold information from an intimate. The sensor, functioning also as a sort of spiritual strip search that peels away rationalizations, would take our moral inventory to keep our actions congruent with our truth and our values. The *hejnal* was a five note trumpet tune played in Medieval times from an elevated post to signal danger to the four corners of the world. It is still sounded in modern day Poland as a reminder of olden conquests and the struggle for freedom. We can use a similar simple warning signal to intercept the invading armies of negativity and hatred. More effort sometimes produces less results. Just pay attention and get out of your own way. Be mindful of those moments when you are not compassionate or are straying from your moral course, and heed the admonition by immediately shifting both mind and heart.

I can stay true to my higher aspirations.

NOVEMBER

Flickering candles
We're spiritual beings
On a human path

heyoka (hay-YO-kah)   Lakota
Sacred clown.

We sometimes have fantasies of being invisible for a day, free to observe the intricate foibles of our fellow human beings, and to make mischief. Dancing in and out of situations, we might point out that people are not as in control of their destinies as they think, and leave a few of the best laid plans languishing in the dust, sprinkled with a dose of healthy humor. As court jester and spirit world ambassador, the *heyoka* holds the keys to delight and to serve. Often wearing black and white makeup, with hair in two cornhusk horns, his pantomime and ribald antics both entertain and protect the people from enemies. In order to make a point, and hold up a mirror of self reflection, this spirit clown gently mocks tourists, neighboring Indians or anyone else who is cunning, predatory, greedy and without morals—including themselves. Are you taking life too seriously these days? Maybe you are trapped in a self destructing pattern because of your own self defeating behaviors that you refuse to acknowledge and change. Call upon the energy of the heyoka to illuminate your shortcomings, but in a light-hearted way.

I see the wisdom hidden in humorous situations.

November 2

kvel (kvel)   Yiddish
To feel the joy of things going well.

Happy people tend to like themselves, be optimistic and somewhat extroverted, and possess an internal locus of control that focuses on the cherries rather than the pits that life offers. Ethnicity, wealth, sex or lifestage are not good predictors of subjective well-being. Happiness is always transient, and its dictionary definition speaks of contentment, good fortune, prosperity and good luck. Joy is more effusive and expansive, spreading over the edge of normal expression. To *kvel* is to vibrate with delight, gladness, rejoicing, and the pleasure of feeling grace in your life. The day is filled with right timing, and unexpected surprising good news. The universe seems to hum a tune that harmonizes with our own actions. We feel the goodness and strengths of others, and everything seems more alive. Imagined failures are transformed into bountiful success. We do not need to grasp onto this magic, we simply allow for and appreciate what is.

Today my beaming grows even brighter.

makurakotoba (mah-KU-ra-ko-to-bah)   **Japanese**
Pillow talk.

Sex is dirty; save it for the one you love. Many of us were raised with significant confusion about our sexuality, executing distancing U turns under the sheets whenever confronted with an issue. As we grow and learn, this union becomes more the harmony of two spirits as well as the contact of two epidermal layers. Sexuality is a surrender to deep sensuality and sensitivity. Part of its bliss is that time ceases and we become egoless, a part of nature immersed into something greater, lost with the beloved into something else. The intimacy between you and the loved one opens the door for honest exposure through *makurakotoba*. This intimate sharing allows you to be vulnerable and to voice your fears and longings. It can create moments of exquisite closeness and allow for the release of buried feelings inexpressible anywhere else. The more you are aware of the ebb and flow of these affectionate energies, the easier it is to transform what causes you pain and difficulty in relationships. The notes of love's duet gone flat can be brought into harmony once again through careful attention to the dream like encounters preceeding and following the sexual embrace.

The whisperings before and after lovemaking are soft and lovely.

November 4

minototak (mee-no-TOE-tahk)   Algonquin
Ethical conduct.

We often lament the loss of values in our society. Many young people, we say, are developing in a character vacuum dominated by the words instant, now, me and money. They are floundering about, unanchored by a set of principles upon which to build their lives. Unable to agree on all values, the caring adults in their world often avoid discussing any of them. Values, such as *minototak*, are the voices of our hearts, cultivating attitudes of mind that in turn inspire standards of action. When we are willing to talk about our core value dilemmas, in which appropriate action is not immediately apparent, we teach children the importance of holding and examining the question against experience to know when it is acceptable to withhold a bit of truth, or stretch the rules. Since values are more often "caught" than taught directly, our model of action is what young people will absorb. Values shape and influence your responses to the choices and challenges presented to you. These ideals order your life, and are what counts in the long run.

My values help me discover what I am really after.

oonagamessok (oo-nah-gah-MAY-sok)   Abenakis
Spirit beings who presided over the creation of petroglyphs.

The earliest known art was produced on cave walls between 40,000 and 10,000 BC. From simple handprints outlined with colored earth to sensitive portraits of animals, geometric designs and an occasional human like figure, these drawings and carvings filled with wonder the hearts and minds of those who witnessed them. Symbolizing life in the afterworld, or depicting aspects of hunting or fertility, they were imbued with great magical power and played important roles in ancient rituals. Guided by *oonagamessok*, the artists expressed their deep connection to the universal in common appealing themes. Kokopelli, for example, a Southwestern Native American figure, first appeared in rock art around A.D. 600. He is portrayed with a hump on his back, perhaps reminiscent of the earliest farmers bringing in the harvest, or the packs of traders who moved northward from Mexico into what is now the southwestern United States. Legend says he often gave to young maidens babies, blankets or seeds from his pack. He also plays a flute and is always a joyous element, his music tender and sweet, uplifting and healing to all who hear it. Like other characters represented by this special form of artistry, Kokopelli's penetrating touch has traveled through the centuries to stir and excite the most primitive parts of our being.

In the cave of my mind live fanciful nourishing creative images.

November 6

mara (MAH-rrah)   Masai
Motley; one of thirty adjectives used to describe the cow.

Language shapes our thoughts and feelings and stretches consciousness. The more languages that enrich our lives, the greater the diversity of perceptions from which we can create possibilities. Various peoples often have a panoply of linguistic descriptors for appreciating the nuances of common natural elements. For example, Inuit and Eskimo natives have more than one hundred terms to describe types of snow and ice. Polynesians use multiple phrases for discussing the quality of waves and sky, and Australian Aboriginals use more than twenty words for sand. African tribes whose lives are deeply affected by cattle have many terms, such as *mara*, for cows. If you are a musician you live in a world enlivened by rondo, rubato, allegro and adagio. Lawyers, doctors, scientists and artists each have their own alphabet soup of jargon incomprehensible to those on the outside. Rather than lament these specialized forms of communication as systems that separate us from our common humanity, we can appreciate the rich diversity of human thought and expression.

Today a certain word will unlock a door I have never entered before.

holopis kuntul baris (hoh-LOH-pees KOON-tool BAH-rees)
Bahasa Indonesia
Phrase uttered to gain extra strength when carrying heavy objects.

The work of head, hands, and heart can sometimes be exhausting. Pushed beyond the ordinary into situations that challenge and tax every fiber of our being, we marshall a reserve of energy and commitment previously untapped. Breathlessly spoken, *holopis kuntul baris* becomes an invocation for additional stamina. Used by a group or an individual, it summons whatever is required to get the job done. The use of the voice to focus and direct physical prowess is an ancient practice. The chosen phrase becomes the portal to another dimension of possibility. More than a collective grunt, the words conjure assistance from the universal force. Astounding feats of strength are often reported by individuals in emergency situations when they enter a sort of trance like state that is capable of harnessing undreamed of power and ability. In the midst of actions from the mundane moving of a refrigerator to the heroics of saving a life, you can feel the nearby presence of a unique faculty waiting to be uncovered through a strong verbal summons. This wellspring of concentrated vitality becomes more palpable and trustworthy with practice.

I can use my voice as a source of strength in pushing limits.

November 8

wiltja (weelt-yah)   **Arunta**
Temporary bush shelter.

A culture's definition of itelf influences the social norms it creates. If the predominant images are of peace, cooperation, and connectedness to natural environs, then both the structure and function of the society will be different than if the perceptions are more aggressive, exploitative and xenophobic. The very existence of a *wiltja* evokes a way of life that regularly feels the heartbeat of its mother earth, and contains a minimal core of fear, because of the trusting mindset that life does provide. Somehow in any given day both food and shelter will become available. The debt one owes to the land for basic survival is paid by being grateful each day for all that is given. All living beings are regarded as having a close kinship with humans, and possessions are minimized. The more things you have, the greater your worry about losing them, and you begin to live your life mainly to both accumulate and protect these objects. The Australian Aboriginals prefer to focus on the value of relationships and connectedness. Their perspective is also an eloquent statement about the transitory nature of our existence. Both the newborn and the elder approaching death hear the same words from loved ones, as they enter and leave this life: we love you and support you on the journey.

I can let go of most of what I think I need.

nagashi (nah-gah-she)   Japanese
Flow referring to water, your life, and the use of utensils in the tea ceremony.

By entering into the flow of our lives, we create a timeless dimension in which anything becomes possible. We have all tasted moments of being fully engaged in the unfolding cascade of events in our lives. The slower-moving, deeper circumstances of our lives also progress forward like a river, whether or not we are aware of them. As we drift back and forth between the shores of pleasure and pain, we are carried onward into the unknown. Surrendering to this flow is not passive; rather it is an active yielding, a giving over of energy so it can be channeled elsewhere. Harmonizing with life's difficulties entails first accepting them, and then shifting our relationship to them. In that here and now moment of transformation of the relationship to our concerns we experience the profundity of *nagashi*. Approaching small acts of daily living with impeccable presence entrains the body, heart, and mind into a single flow of activity. From there you will be able to stretch out moments of inspiration into a continuous stream of ecstatic living.

I surrender easily to my life's flow.

November 10

bilita mpastshi (bee-LEE-tah mm-POT-she)   **Bantu**
Blissful dreams.

Recurring nightmares storm through our sleep like hungry tigers. Our worst imaginings take over our bodies and fill us with fear and anxiety. Running or breathing hard, we struggle to escape to a place where we might feel protected. Healing power comes in realizing what we must do in our waking lives to feel safe and whole. What a wonder to experience, even occasionally, the reassuring form of night visions, *bilita mpastshi*. The ones we never want to return from, where we can fly, make love, dance or sing in a complete state of joyous abandon. It is as if all the threads of transient blissful moments are woven into a prolonged tale of delight. Sometimes the focus is on a reunion with a loved one, or reliving a tragedy where all is forgiven and resolved favorably. These positive empowering images stay with us for days. Surely there must be some amazing archetypal energy that courses through us after dipping in this pool of collective unconscious rapture. In the request box of our brains, there must be a slot for wish fulfilling prophecies, somewhere we can put in a plea for reruns of our favorite night time fantasy shows.

I am willing to remember the delicious details of a beautiful dream.

kenosis (KEHN-oh-sihs)　　Greek
An emptying.

We are born of the spirit to undergo suffering in physical form. Pain is a great motivator, and our darkness and doubts lead the way to a spirituality of imperfection, a thirst for something greater than the small self. Reaching out to a higher power is an admission of our own powerlessness, and comes from hitting bottom, and realizing that by ourselves we are lost. The surrender of *kenosis* is extraordinarily scary and difficult, challenging us to face our own ultimate helplessness. When we feel so used up and spent, it is easy to blame ourselves rather than see the deeper truth that the human condition involves suffering. Often we will recreate difficult relationships mimicking those of our childhood in order to provoke healing. Our father was an alcoholic, or our parents divorced, or we were abandoned by one of them. So we find ourselves in very similar situations with a mate, triggering all the past hurt. When we sink down into any abyss, there is a turning point toward healing when awareness and resources appear in the outstretched hands of others who have moved beyond their own despair.

When there is nothing left to lose, I can find myself.

November 12

anam cara (AH-nam KAH-ra)   **Gaelic**
Soul friend.

Sometimes we find ourselves reacting very strongly to another, positively or negatively. When we wish to avoid someone, they probably have something very valuable to teach by reflecting back some aspect of ourselves not yet fully accepted. Communing with those to whom we feel deeply attracted is more appealing and often effortless. When we are very open, trusting and accepting with another person, the clouds of light surrounding our bodies mingle, and the two souls flow together in the special bond of *anam cara*. There is a reciprocal appreciation of the specialness and beauty present in each, and a longing for an even deeper exploration. Such a companion helps us to inhabit our eternal infinite side in daily life, and to see our wildness and passions as prayer. Joined in a union of mutual awakening, each assists the other in the mysterious discovery of life's fullness. In the light of such loving acceptance, self analysis can become self trusting as you tap into your capacity for intuitive guidance.

I acknowledge those soul mates with whom I share the journey home.

roulade (roo-LAHD)   French
An ornamental flourish.

Ta da! To do! We don't spend enough time in the space of ta da because we always have too much to do! There are a hundred ways each day to say yes to life, to embrace its gifts, and to engage in glorious appreciative excess through an explosion of little expressive acts. Instead of offering just a verbal thank you, how about sending some flowers too? Not just applause, but a resounding "Bravo!" Rather than a simple goodbye, offer an effusive outpouring of how good it was to see or talk with the person. Beyond a boring "good job on the test," how about a celebration of hugs and praises. We serve no one by thinking and acting small when it comes to emotional positivity. Bring on the uplifting energy of *roulade*. In the music we create in relationship, there is always room for an extra surprise, either a deliciously subtle movement or a grand expansive display of affection. Value the unexpected, for it is the most important guide you have in this world. Deepen your open warm hearted generosity of spirit. Practice unpredictable feats of random dramatic gestures.

Today I will generate the bliss of unanticipated expressions of appreciation.

November 14

dorje (dor-jeh)   Tibetan
The pure indestructible principle that contributes to awareness.

In Tibetan cosmology, a congealing of cosmic winds within the great void formed a gigantic spinning double dorje, a cross made from two diamond scepters whose ends at rest point to the four cardinal directions. This ancient symbol, variously translated as thunderbolt, holy stone, or adamantine diamond, signifies the pure indestructible distilled energy of the universe, that cuts through everything without being affected. The *dorje* represents the male principle which when combined with a tilbu, a handbell signifying female wisdom, produces awareness in the soul as the remedy for ignorance. Both images are frequently found in Tibetan art, often in the hands of a god or goddess, and are used by monks in Buddhist temple rituals. The presence of both the dorje and the tilbu emphasizes the union of opposites, yah-yum, similar in concept to yin yang or prajna-upaya, in order to produce the clear light of understanding. What confusion are you carrying that you most need to penetrate? Welcome the insight that arises from combining stillness with clear intention. Open to the vastness of your being.

I breathe in awareness and breathe out freedom.

hart ducha (heart DU-ha)   Polish
Self-mastery and dignity in the face of external forces.

Competition rules men's lives from a young age, as they are taught to perceive life as a contest with winners and losers. This sets up an inner dynamic within which males often think they are better than everyone else, yet at the same time they are afraid of everyone, simultaneously special and unworthy, superior and inferior, incessantly inflating or shaming themselves. *Hart ducha*, a stable principle of self respect, helps overcome this early destructive training. A term of honor and a form of worthiness and self control, this concept refers to a noble self respect exhibited in the face of demeaning circumstances or menial tasks. It is alive in the fierce independence of a poor peasant or a new immigrant, and in the persistent courage of a rebel fighting an oppressive regime. Some people seek protection against feelings of inferiority by becoming a master of disguise, using a variety of masks to hide insecurities. Others draw upon an inner reserve of discipline and capacity to persevere.

Humiliation or attacks on my rights simply strengthen my resolve.

November 16

ngon (nong)   **Vietnamese**
Putting loving energy into food.

The art of preparing, presenting and serving a meal delights and stimulates all who participate. Whether exchanging recipes, cooking up a feast for friends, having food fantasies when hungry, or browsing in a market, food often simmers in our consciousness. We all have memories of comfort foods, offered when we were ill or feeling sad. They often can still work their magic, evoking wonderful sensations of benevolent loved ones. The presence in our lives of someone who knows how to practice *ngon* is a blessing, for we are nourished through them both in body and spirit. From the moment of conception of the meal, patience, skill and loving kindness have been invoked as different ingredients are selected, washed, chopped, sliced, and heated. Even the arrangement of the table, and cleaning up afterwards are part of a seamless gift of caring. The warmth and generosity of the preparer manifest in the details of the dish, and linger on our palates and in our hearts.

I can infuse everyday meals with loving attention.

kutho (koo-tho)   Burmese
Merit or what one acquires through doing good deeds.

In Sanskrit, karma means action, the inescapable rhythm of cause and effect. As ye sow, so shall ye reap, in speech, deed and thought. It is a natural ecology of mind which understands that for every act there is a related reaction. Buddhists interpret karma in a personal way. The results of deeds performed in former existences can be transcended by proper use of the mind and will in this life. Proper altruistic motivation brings good thoughts and actions and beneficial results to all concerned. This is the nature of *kutho*. It is choosing at any given moment to embrace kindness and compassion rather than ignorance, attachment, hatred, pride and jealousy. Kutho is not spiritual bookkeeping. It is a generous outpouring of love and service, an attitude of heart as vast as the ocean, that in itself brings tremendous joy. Embracing such an approach each day strengthens the possibility that negative emotions will gradually wither through disuse.

Through right action I plant seeds of future happiness rather than suffering.

November 18

majie (MAH-jhee)   Chinese
To curse the street.

During the week, parents mostly disappear into offices or run a business, often bringing home more stress and irritability than teachings of love and patience at the end of a day. No success at work is worth failure at home. This is one reason a healthy transition from the workplace to the homefront is so important. Remember to say "stay" to all the unfinished piles on your desk as you leave the office! Peel off an imaginary wetsuit of troubles and toss it in the trash. Sing on the drive home. Before going into your home, enter deep relaxation for a few moments, or even exercise if possible. Greet those you love with huge hugs. Take a quick shower to wash away the difficulties of the day. You can also incorporate a regular release of tension by learning to *majie*. The ground, rather than loved ones, can absorb and neutralize all the swearing, muttering, bombastic verbal abuse and denouncing profanity you can muster. All that potential harm to others is quickly dispersed. The back yard, a favorite trail or even a quiet street corner can assist you in the important activity of lightening your load.

Anxiety and stress weigh me down. I don't need to give these burdens to others.

binag (BEE-nahg)   Tagalog
Practice of giving everyone nicknames.

We tend to introduce ourselves from the outside in. Starting with our name, we move on to what we do, and then speak of our relationship to others. Gradually time and trust may open and reveal the more secret passages of our hearts. Many of us have special nicknames reserved for use by family members and close friends. Enter the common process of *binag* ! What a wonderful way to enhance intimacy and foster unique bonds. Buried under the sands of the past are appellations bestowed long ago. Many of us have mixed memories of the terms of endearment we were given as youngsters. They may have lovingly referred to a physical or behavioral characteristic we would have preferred remained unnoticed. Sometimes you are still called by these labels. Perhaps you have acquired a new sobriquet by a lover or acquaintance. With these different names, do you remain the same or become another? You are like a wave which appears uniform, but is a continually shifting mass of water, a flame which is constant as it burns and yet always different, without any break in continuity. Each of your designations reflects a different strand of your true nature.

I can choose a spirit name that acknowledges the emerging blossoming of my true nature.

November 20

bubinzana (buu-beab-ZAH-nah)   Quechua
Chant that leads a vision.

Use of the voice to induce trance in an ancient practice among a variety of global cultures. In the Navajo tradition, for example, tension among relatives can be cured by the correct chant. A Singer may be called, and the appropriate ceremony performed. Navajo Singers may know as many as 35 major curing chants, each one containing some 500 songs which must be memorized. A special ceremony requires preparation, making arrangements to feed those who will come, gathering ritual materials, all of which involves the community cooperating with each other. In the Amazon the haunting sounds of a *bubinzana* mingle with the jungle night as the ayawaskha, a sacred drug, is prepared and shared among the people. This musical prayer sung by sorcerers in certain ceremonies guides the participants in a sacred journey. The intuitive wisdom that comes as a waking dream benefits the entire community. Gentle chanting can lift us out of our bodies and transport us to an altered state of awareness. Whatever the tradition—monastic, Native American or indigenous shamanism—the repetition of certain sounds serves as a communication vehicle for higher spiritual aspirations.

Chanting with others connects me to a higher consciousness.

kula (KOO-luh)   Melanesia
Exchange of goods to keep relationships smooth.

Warfare often arises from the competitive and acquisitive aspects of human nature. Many cultures sublimate aggression through ritualized displays of wealth. Fighting with property, instead of weapons, serves as a more peaceable mode of confrontation, and satisfies the need for displaying social prestige. This was one of the functions served by the *kula* or potlatch of ancient island societies. After successful harvest of the sea and land, months of leisure were left for making art and holding feasts. Public gatherings were common during the months of less intense survival activities. Through the practice of kula, individuals could display their virtue and value in a peaceful context that affirmed social standing. An insult could be wiped away, ill feelings reduced, and a community reunited after a tragedy or the death of a chief. The kula could also take place as part of a marriage, birth, or the taking of a new title by a member of the tribe, and might involve a special honoring of ancestral spirits with a rededication of their monuments. On a practical level, this get-together also provided for the refurbishing of some village homes, created a dynamic recirculation of resources, and improved trade. Guests invited to the festivities were given gifts, honored with songs and the retelling of myths, and plied with complimentary speeches.

I value the modern day potluck as a significant parallel to the ancient custom of kula.

November 22

alu (ah-loo)   Runic
Signifying protection.

From the oldest hieroglyphics to modern day graffiti, humans have been drawn to express inner abstractions in physical form. The earliest surviving Runic inscription is from the late second century A.D. Found throughout northern Europe, these mystical characters were part of an olden alphabet used by Germanic peoples. The characters were often carved on a stick or emblazoned on spearpoints, jewelry and stone monuments. Groupings or sequences beginning with *alu* served as both ritual identifiers of a clan and repositories of cryptic potency. They converted the objects they adorned into amulets, imbuing them with secret powers. In the area that is now Scandinavia, large blocks of limestone were also meticulously carved with graceful runic inscriptions and designs. These stones were a legacy of Viking exploits, memorializing heroes or special occasions. The runes evoke a primitive longing for mystical contact. In modern life we seek to rediscover what might have been lost, to imagine that certain faculties are still available to us as a safeguard against threatening forces we still do not comprehend.

I can find strength and refuge in ancient symbolic teachings.

ts'aa' (ts'-aah')   Navajo
Basket whose design reflects the beginning of the world.

Women of the Navajo, Paiute and Ute tribes have for many centuries gathered sumac strips and dyed them with mountain mahogany roots and juniper ashes to create circular containers of exquisite beauty. Their uses are many. They can be holders of ritual paraphernalia such as rattles and medicine bundles, serve as a food plate in certain ceremonials, or even become a drum when turned upside down and beaten with a yucca drumstick. The soft intricate patterns of the *ts'aa'* symbolize the emergence of the people from the underworld, their sacred mountains, the dawn, clouds, rainbows, and the sun's life giving rays. Such a generous cosmology reminds you that life is a mystery to be lived, not a problem to be solved. Try to break out of believing you know so much. Let go of your current plan. Empty yourself, like a bowl or a basket, and welcome possibility. You can move from breakdown to breakthrough only by spending more time with what you don't know. Guide yourself to experiencing new things in the old, and old in the new. The chaos both within and outside you will clear, and a new meaning and purpose will become evident.

When I really look, artistry inspires.

November 24

cargo (CAR-goh)   Spanish
A burden or sacrifice one makes for the sake of the community.

Too many people consistently choose violence and aggression over inner development. Such individuals know little about being loved and supported, or standing together shoulder to shoulder. They are not able to acknowledge their blind spot, the weak side that makes mistakes, and instead remain lost in the endless need to always be a winner, accept every challenge, or take every dare. Liberation from this mindtrap can come in the form of assuming *cargo*. In Mexican Zapotec communities the term refers to taking a position in a civil or religious hierarchy for the benefit of others, but its context can easily be expanded to encompass modern day community service projects in which students do work that benefits the neighborhood. Many troublemakers have been subjected to abuse in their own lives. Some of the most successful programs for these youthful offenders create opportunities for them to be softened by giving, and tempered by learning empathy, through caretaking the elderly or developmentally disabled. Appreciating youth as resource rather than problem, and helping them to feel needed rather than scorned, reaps benefits for all.

I can extend beyond myself by volunteering in the community commons.

andenken (AAHN-deng-ken)   German
Thankfulness rooted in the memory of being without.

There are so many forms of thanksgiving prayers. Most honor the creative force in the universe, and express gratefulness for abundance and bounty. Beneath the commercial glitz of holiday fanfare is a genuine impulse to create a state of appreciation. Many of our grandparents and parents experienced poverty and hunger, and many children today are hungry and homeless. *Andenken* is a natural state for those who have experienced deprivation. Their remembrance of being without intensifies their ability to express thankfulness for what they have in their lives. It is gratitude rooted in one's body and emotional depths. It is a vision of understanding that the flow of gifts can be interrupted at any time, a realization that makes the largesse of the moment all the more precious. We are blessedly touched not only by having the basics of food, shelter, warmth and safety, but by the sound of children laughing, the joys of loving friends, and a sense of inner contentment. To acknowledge that which has been freely given to us, strengthens both our ability to give, and receive, generously.

I remember and am thankful.

November 26

'ahlan wa sahlan (AH-laan wa SAH-laan)   **Arabic**
A form of welcome that indicates you are considered to be one of the family.

Generosity is fundamental to all spiritual paths. Like forgiveness or compassion, its energy is both boundless and transformative. When we bestow hospitality upon others and overflow with an expansive greeting, we envelop the encounter in sacred magic. By sharing our most basic personal comforts in our unique dwelling, we create a nurturing warmth that evokes the best qualities of humanity. The greeting *'ahlan wa sahlan* embraces our deep desire to be of service. It is a wish that our guests may walk in our home with a sense of relaxed openness and peace and prosperity. We are thankful for the very blessing of their presence. May the visitors find as many simple delights in this humble abode as they might on a walk in a meadow or open plain. Now is the time to offer the best that you have. This is true not just for sharing material possessions, but also applies to offering the gifts and talents with which you are endowed. Hiding and playing it safe is bondage. Freedom lies in being totally exposed, in opening up and pouring yourself into existence with the giving nature of your own heart.

Upon entering my home, my guests feel its light and warmth.

Wuwuchim (woo-WOO-cheem)   Hopi
A new year ceremony which celebrates the first dawn.

Many tribal peoples have a series of rituals to welcome the changing seasons. The opening festival of the Hopi ceremonial year is called *Wuwuchim*, from "wu" meaning to germinate and "chim" meaning to manifest. The festival celebrates the first light of Creation, giving thanks for the germination of all life on earth, including plants, animals and man. It occurs during the Hawk moon, the lunar month just prior to the winter solstice, and in certain years may include initiation rites. Since life began with fire, a flame is often considered mysterious and sacred. The first part of the ceremony involves elders building a new fire with flint and native cotton, fueled by coal from desert outcrops. Participants in dawn rituals enact the germination of seed, as they carry a torch lit by the first fire to three other ceremonial spaces or kivas. Just as the blaze of one candle is not diminished by lighting another and another, the bounty of your being can be shared. When you let your own light shine brightly you give permission to others to do the same. Let your brilliance sparkle like starlight gifts to hold at bay the darkness of late November.

I embrace the hope of a new day dawning.

November 28

takos (TAY-kos)   Chinook
A philosophy in which any decision should be considered in terms of its effects on seven generations.

From 1955 until 1998, the earth's population has consumed as much goods and services as humankind had, in its entire history, up to that era. Like insatiable hungry ghosts we ravage the soil, forests, air, oceans and all animal life to demonstrate our power. Poverty ignorance and greed continue to strengthen the foundation for present and future suffering. We are in the midst of a destructive out of control adolescent phase of our species' evolution. To survive we must strike a more mature balance. In this period of the religion of materialism and the glorification of excess, we have wandered far from the principles of *takos*. It seems that we can never get enough of what we don't really want. Seeking to fill the emptiness, we often choose more stuff rather than life enhancing time with community. The constant stream of addictive mass media junk is not the stuff of liberation. Putting a stop to this mental pollution is a positive step for ourselves and our families. Can you joyously and consciously begin to embrace the richness of desiring and consuming less?

Voluntary simplicity calls me to action.

khleeb (hkhlehb)   **Ukrainian**
Life-sustaining peasant bread.

Though our physical forms are but clothing for the spirit, they require good care to function properly. A healthy diet and regular exercise contribute to the quality of our lives, and paying attention to what and how we eat becomes another mindful practice. In the early 1970's at the Whitney Museum in New York City an exhibit of breads from around the world filled an entire room with simple and profound diversity. Like a visual culinary safari, the exploration yielded many delights, from popcorn sized nuggets to huge loaves, to the rich variety of sweet frybreads, to dark solid mounds of *khleeb*. When was the last time you made bread, and experienced the profound joy of sharing it with friends, while it was still warm and fresh from the oven? We can be very happy sitting at a table with people we love, smiling at each other, and partaking of a simple repast. Talking together or enjoying the food in silence, we can appreciate our bounty and see how fortunate we are, for so many lack the precious gifts of both food and companionship. With the first bite of any edible we can always be reminded of this and be filled with great compassion. We can discover joy and taste the whole universe in a morsel of bread.

I am grateful for the food on my table.

November 30

tonglen (tong-lehn)   Tibetan
Meditation in which the practitioner focuses on breathing in suffering, and breathing out joy.

In the meditative state voices on an empty wind call out to no one. The pain of the world is palpable in one's own being, and a single tear embraces all of humanity. As meditation practice deepens, overwhelming and yet familiar feelings of indescribable openness and connectedness arise. As you inhale the misery of the world, your exhalation can transform it into a pouring out of blessings. Breathe in all the negativity and darkness, and let it be absorbed by the heart. Breathe out all the joy and gratefulness that you have. To practice *tonglen* is to invite endless surrender. You surrender to the physical discomfort of sitting for long periods of time, to the crazy monkey mind of unfocused thoughts leaping about, to notions of escaping here and now. You work to give up looking into the future or referencing the past. You release again and again what the small "I" is expecting, and enter more fully into this moment, this eternity. The doors of compassion are flung open, first for yourself and then for all living beings.

I can bring to mind an image of a friend who is undergoing hardship, and simply say "may you be free from suffering."

DECEMBER

Enter the silence
Passionate, focused and clear
Like moonlight on snow

lo aleichem (low uh-LAY-hem)   **Yiddish**
May it not happen to you.

We love to talk about our misery. Bad news travels at light speed as people recount in detail whatever recent tragedy has touched them, even in the most indirect way. One can tune in to endless hours of televised disasters occurring around the globe. This sharing of grief is a collective catharsis, an attempt to make sense of all that seems out of control in this reality. We are so attached to our stories of suffering that we fail to distinguish them from the abundant reality of our lives. *Lo aleichem!* May you never be visited by such hardship. Yet we can appreciate that each difficulty carries its own tailored teachings. Life is not just a series of obstacles to overcome so that your real biography can begin. Clinging to past hurt, we often do not see the beauty of how we have changed, and are no longer who we once were. The penetrating truth of lo aleichem is a wish that misfortune not visit without some good coming from it, without a deepening of your wisdom and capacity for wholeness. Of course we desire easy living for both ourselves and those we love, yet each trying situation calls forth resources heretofore unappreciated or untapped.

May my worst enemy be free from suffering.

December 2

shibui (she-BOO-ee)   Japanese
The beauty of aging.

From the growth of moss on a rock to the patterns of wrinkles on a face, time bestows loveliness upon all that is alive. Maturity cannot be rushed. It is dependent on the everlasting cycle of development and decay. Whether referring to a mellowed tea, a landscape feature, or an aged room, *shibui* is a quality that speaks of persistence and sustained unfolding. It describes the deeper character and enchanting vitality that is molded by diverse experiences. So much history is contained in an individual's face, in which the aspects of personality reveal themselves more clearly through the years. In a culture which glorifies both youth and speed, this elusive sense of beauty may be hard to grasp. Yet it helps us to redefine how we embrace everything from old growth forests to revered sacred sites to the old people living next door. When we are able to appreciate the gifts that only the passage of a lifetime can manifest, all of existence seems more precious. In one face we perceive all the olden features that have ever been. Within a single ancient oak lie the forms of all the trees yet to come.

I gaze at my aging face in the mirror with delight.

wayamou (wah-yah-MO-uu)   Yanomami
Ceremonial dialogue as a method of releasing anger and frustrations.

When tension arises between distant neighboring groups, some Amazonian people turn to a process that combines the function of de-escalating quarrels and a mechanism for the exchange of goods. The notion is to first move through differences, and then trade and enjoy each other's company to solidify the bonds. On the occasion of a visit or a feast when the groups might already be coming together, a *wayamou* may be held. This ritual format enables grievances to be exposed rather than continuing to fester. One host and one guest face each other at a time, with replacements occurring throughout the night. The speaker can say anything, and often accuses, insults, intimidates, threatens and challenges the listener, who listens meekly without speaking until it is his turn. Each individual accompanies his own words by rhythmically striking his own body with his hands, in varying intensity and tempo. By raising the images of potential hostility, this process restores peace. By expressing feelings in all openness, those involved calm down, and their anger subsides. This is a community based form of conflict resolution, in which both young and old participate. All learn well the practice of intense listening, and the art of eloquent, witty and powerful rhetoric, both essential tools for any lasting peace.

I can hone my ability to resolve disputes through win-win methods.

December 4

wulgis (WUULT-gees)   Arunta
Spirits of dead medicine men who transform an individual
who is exhibiting psychic talent.

How can we enter into the full realization of our talents and abilities without the assistance and guidance of our elders? The modern day lack of contact with the elderly creates a schism in our psyche that contributes to our confusion about the purpose and meaning of our lives. The belief in the presence of *wulgis* enables support from the olden ones to occur in a profound way. These spiritual helpers exist as part of the underlying structure of the tribe, and are located at an elemental level of social organization, with intricate connections to tribal mythology and cosmology. The ability to have potent and nourishing relationships with the group's ancestors encourages individuals to risk the full discovery of hidden capabilities. Sometimes an individual's severe illness or bizarre behavior is viewed as a sign of wulgis intervention, which offers the opportunity of a healing passage into a new vision of self. Aboriginal cultures revere and encourage psychic qualities as affirmations of a continuing linkage with the universal force, and as gifts stimulated by the powerful presence of a deceased elder.

I am open to receiving guidance in some form from those who have passed on.

entschlossenheit (ant-SHLAW-sen-height)   German
The resolve to make of oneself what one wants.

It is said that there are three great mysteries: air to birds, water to fish, and human beings unto themselves. The journey inward to discover a driving force for being is fraught with obstacles and confusion. Once we have touched and clarified the essence of what we might contribute, we begin the struggle to manifest it. Somehow we must find the inner well of *entschlossenheit*, and drink deeply from its source. More than cultivating desire or will power, this concept is a symbol of unlocking what anxiety & self seclusion have imprisoned. It is the exploration of what needs to drop away in the dance, as well as what must be held onto. You become what you think about. Whatever the mind conceives it can achieve. You currently act as you currently believe. The "should be," the "ought to be" is not something you find; you create it. This quality of entschlossenheit embodies the courage to seek the truth, to be involved, to reject cynicism and assume responsibility. It is a lifelong song of persistence and service.

I stand in my truth and act upon it.

December 6

marime (mah-REE-meh)   Romany
Impurity of both body and spirit.

In many societies proper social attitudes and actions may be seen
as more important contributors to well-being than nutrition, exercise or other touted preventive measures. A holistic approach to
health embraces everything that affects the intimate mind body
spirit continuum, and dramatizes the importance of addressing
all concerns in a curative process. The condition of *marime* indicates a state of pollution, that could lead to group rejection. It is a
defining term for a variety of social taboos such as contact with
unclean food or lower body secretions, or inappropriate sexual
behavior. This exposure to impurity can be remedied in various
ways, including ritual treatments. An understanding of marime
can illuminate and expand Western medical viewpoints. Someone
who has been raped, for example, may require a healing ceremony to feel cleansed. An individual who could not save a friend
from drowning may need a special ritual to overcome shame. A
child who has witnessed violence may find relief from nightmares and stomach aches through an art based grief process.

I can attend to all aspects of healing.

orita (o-REE-tah)   Yoruba
Term for the crossroads that attract spirits.

The Yoruba of West Africa believe in the existence of a special intersection, where this world and the spirit universe meet. The path to this spiritual locus is learned over time by exposure to the two things that invite spirits to this mystical junction: music and stories. When the people of this tribe make a drum, they draw an eye on the part of the finished instrument that will face the player. It is to this focal point that one may offer sounds or stories to the drum's spirit to call forth ancestors, guides and beneficent helpers from the other realm. The *orita* can be a powerful reservoir, and exposure to its energy is not taken lightly. Creating drums often involves rituals in the selection of wood and the carving process. Drummers require special initiation in order to be able to handle the spirit or voice emanating from the drum. Imagine the joy that might be summoned in your life if you associated singing, spinning yarns or making music with prayer. Everytime you sang it was with the knowledge that Creator is listening, waiting to be fed with a tale or the sounds of lilting rhythms.

There are many ways to praise the everlasting.

December 8

meiyou (may-you)   **Chinese**
Forget it!

When a door slams in our face, we may react with disappointment, anger, or feelings of unworthiness. When we seek something and are told that it is not possible, we have the opportunity to reflect on our reactions, and notice our internal conversation. Is our dialogue empowering or are we looking to blame ourselves or someone else? The "if only" cycle of regrets usually just prolongs our unhappiness with sulking and resentment. No one enjoys hearing *meiyou!* Not possible! No way! So sorry but you must be crazy! We have been raised on a diet of platitudes that nourish hope with the "where there is a will there is a way" mentality. Surrender often feels like a defeat, rather than a blending with the situation so that something else might emerge. When we are too attached to a specific outcome, the universe has little room to maneuver and come to our assistance. When we simply notice our reactions to the blocked path, rather than getting attached to them as well, we liberate possibility. Synchronicity has an opportunity to breathe, and serendipity can come out to play.

Each obstacle is an invitation to let go and discover a different way.

**mamihlapinatapei (mah-meeh-lap-een-ah-ta-pay) Tierra del Fuegan
A meaningful look shared by two people expressing mutually
unstated feelings.**

From across the room their eyes are drawn to each other like
hummingbirds to red flowers. The sexual tension is palpable.
During a business meeting, a gaze from the CEO to a colleague
signals that the proposal will never take off. The darting visual
exchange between two teens about where they supposedly were
the night before reveals all to the discerning parent. Two men
stand toe to toe their eyes locked in an aggressive stance. These
are all examples of *mamihlapinatapei* in action. So much of our
communication is nonverbal. In matters where the tension of conflict or love is high, a certain glance can better express what is
desired, but not yet acted upon. When two people stare at each
other intensely it is as if the two are engaged in a sort of telepathy,
seeking verification and agreement through the windows of their
eyes that their intentions are similar. These encounters are precious
for they remind us of the vastness of human communication.

*Using my eyes to speak, I discover I can convey remarkable depths of
feeling.*

December 10

shilditee (sheel-DEE-tee)   Apache
Getting cussed out.

Interacting with people who really annoy us is wonderful practice in patience and compassion. Since such people are relatively few, they must be appreciated and treasured. Sometimes it is hard to do because people can be very nasty and cranky or even overtly aggressive, or refuse to live up to what we expect of them. Usually whatever is most bothersome in others is simply a reflection of something we have not yet fully recognized or accepted in ourselves. What is a skillful response to the unpleasantness of *shilditee* ? In Apache culture angry energy is always met with silence, in recognition of the fact that the other person has simply forgotten who they are. Rather than join the dance of temporary insanity, the person being verbally attacked waits for the angry one to again find within, their true calm nature. When you mindfully deflect anger in yourself or from others, your practice progresses quickly like water flash flowing down a dry riverbed.

I can shift my irritation into gratitude for the chance to explore patience.

likomeng (lee-KO-mengh)   Sotho
The pattern when divinatory bones are thrown that indicates "the whisper."

The dingaka are Lesotho specialists who intercede between the forces of the invisible world and the everyday affairs of the visible. Mediators with the spirit realm, they try and keep the peace and maintain equilibrium through divination practices that reveal what remedies might be necessary to restore harmony. One of their tools is a set of special tablets of horn, bone, wood or ivory, carved with traditional designs. When thrown, these magical dice delineate patterns of relationships and social roles, offering possible choices for actions or answers to apparent dilemmas. Those involved can then act in concert with the spirits to assure the best possible outcome. A particular configuration known as *likomeng* is viewed as very positive. The components are said to be smiling or walking and they represent the voice of those who know the secret songs. People who fit this pattern have a highly refined intution, and can coax hidden knowledge from a situation because they are capable of seeing what others cannot. They have a special sensitivity based on years of insightful involvement in a given field of inquiry. The best artists, scientists, entrepreneurs, healers, and teachers embody this quality.

When the voice of intuition whispers, I listen well.

December 12

sipapu (see-PAH-pooh)   Keris
Hole in the ceremonial room or kiva symbolizing the center of the universe.

According to the Hopi, we are currrently living in the fourth level of existence, a time where we are experiencing humanity's ruthless materialism and imperialistic will. Hopi cosmology stories tell of our species' rise through seven successive worlds, each representing a psychophysical center of consciousness. Life began with fire. That universe was destroyed and mankind mounted to the second stage where our ability to survive was severly tested. A dangerous ascent led us to the third world of the kiva, a structure built partially underground where initiates gather and various ceremonies are still performed. Among all the Pueblo peoples, as well as the Hopi, the kiva traditionally contains a *sipapu*, an opening in the floor where spirits can emerge. It is a sort of spiritual womb, from which rebirth into higher consciousness can occur. Like a magical portal, it is a symbol of transformation, of your aspirations for greater development and evolution. The ladder which traditionally leads up and out from the kiva represents the passage from the underworld of the first people onto earth. In this way the history of creation is relived with every ritual performed in this sacred space.

You too now have an opportunity for continuing to rise in awareness on your life journey, to come forth from the darkness of your difficulties and step clearly into the light.

quipu (qee-pooh)   Quechua
Device for counting and recording events.

Individually as well as collectively, we engage in the hunting and gathering of significant memories, storing them in photograph albums, audio and video recordings, and family stories. The quipu stimulates us to recall another way of honoring the past. This tool of the ancient Quechua people consisted of a main cord with smaller cords of different colors knotted at varying distances from each other for the purpose of counting and recording episodes of consequence. It was essentially a mnemonic device for transmitting oral chronicles of olden times. Although the *quipu* was used primarily for recording communal tribal affairs, we might imagine creating a rope representing our own cycles. Births, deaths, graduations, marriage, and other transitions would call out through the years with their tales of joy and woe. With a single strand of fiber we see the completeness of our lives, the dance of light and shadow over time, and the profound joy of still being around to remember.

I can delight in recollecting various turning points that I have lived through.

December 14

ojala (oh-hah-LAH)   Spanish
Would to God; wishful thinking.

Grief is welcome here. Profound sadness is bliss itself, the face of God we have kept away because we were looking elsewhere. The regrets of the past languish on the shores of our mistakes like vultures at a fresh kill. How long can we deny the simple purification of surrender and acceptance? The only response to the question do you want to be healed is a resounding yes. Our rejuvenation occurs whenever we turn toward the light of new possibilities. The sounds of *ojala* rise upward, spiraling into the vast sky. This is a form of "praise be to the all powerful, your will is my command." It is also part supplication, a humbling expression of the need for assistance. Suddenly hope is no longer missing in action. Like a phoenix, it arises from the ashes of complacency or despair, born again into a new day. Said immediately after a desire or wish has been expressed, it seals the intention with a prayer.

What small piece of pain can I release today?

omommomo (O-mo-MO-mo)   Ainu
To omit tedious details.

People can go on and on, filling your head with the endless details of their stories and dramas. Sometimes the urge to flee is intense when encountering a talkative individual who seems insensitive to normal social nonverbal cues. Imprisoned by the grasp of their ramblings, remaining in their presence is challenging. Throughout the twistings and turnings of their tales you wonder when they will finally get to the point. Or perhaps the shroud of negativity that persists through the boring recounting is what demands escape. This is when you wish the person had developed the skill to *omommomo*. This term is traditionally used during the telling of long, chanting ancient Ainu narratives, and honors the audience by sparing them the plethora of particulars with which they are already familiar. Passing over these elements of the story actually enhances the overall effect. Good advice, for a succinct retelling often conveys a more powerful, penetrating message. "To make a long story short.." invites the listener to pay more attention, to open their hearts and listen between the phrases for the essence of the sharing.

Editing myself can deepen a communication exchange.

December 16

koi-si (koy-see)   Kung
Kind and generous person.

We are the recipients of much benevolence every day. Most human beings are engaged in helpful and amicable rather than hurting and destroying activities. Within our collective experience, there are certainly those who are caught in their own cycle of suffering and violence. Yet we are more likely to be exposed to a *koi-si*. Koi refers to the human race, and this language root suggests the inherently beneficent nature of humanity. Our willingness to help is part of who we are as a species. Heroism is ordinary people empowering themselves to make a difference. You are surrounded by valor, people exhibiting their decency every day, and allowing their goodness to manifest. You may lose your way on the journey but your integrity will bring you back to the path of living your values, the principles that order your life. You define your daily reality by living what you know to be true. Being genuine and admitting failures contributes to greatness. Heroes act as if what they do matters. There is much to admire and respect in you as well. You can be no one else. Relax, for the universe needs you as you are.

My thoughtfulness flows from within, fed by all of humanity's good deeds.

drala (d-dah-luh)   Sanskrit
What occurs when the wisdom of your being is linked with the power of things as they are.

In the Tibetan Shambhala tradition, all sense perceptions are regarded as sacred. They connect us with the phenomenal world, and are thus a source of wisdom and goodness. *Drala* is a term used to denote the primordial insight inherent in the nowness of this moment, where harmony and chaos co-exist, and you allow the vastness of life to touch you. Just as the sun is always in the sky and rain always falls from a storm cloud, the original ground of cosmic wisdom is always there, whether we relate to it or not. Drala is an energy invoked when you are fully present, greeting everything with awareness and openness, without judging. The universe is contained and reflected within you, just as every part of a holograph contains the whole picture. When you fully embrace the expansiveness of the universe in a moment of nowness, everything seems connected and harmonized. You then travel the eighth step on the Buddhist path, Samma Samadhi, which is a trance, psychic ecstasy, awareness of the still center of the turning world.

I can use all my senses to contact greater understanding.

December 18

samideano (sah-mee-day-AH-noh)   **Esperanto**
One who shares the same idea of a friendly world speaking the same language.

A youngster passes by a playground and waves to a group of ethnically diverse friends. A baby is passed around a community event cradled by young and old, dark and light skinned individuals. A *samideano* embraces cultural diversity and envisions a planet at peace with a one world family, united by a commonly shared second language. This vision is not about creating a homogenized version of humanity, but represents an awareness that cross cultural communication is possible despite many difficulties. The major reason children grow up fearing people unlike themselves is lack of prior contact. Having no familiarity with people vastly different from themselves in customs and language, young people may develop judgments based on inaccurate media portrayals as well as anxiety provoking gossip. Breaking through our assumptions and getting to know people different from ourselves, we begin building bridges of trust. At the same time, our stereotyped perceptions of groups are replaced by real perceptions of individuals.

I speak out whenever I hear or see racist comments or actions.

la cafard (lah cah-FAR)   **French**
The blues.

There is no escape from the cold and dark of late December. In the paucity of light arises a deepening desire to just crawl into bed and wait for spring. In the morass of our melancholy is all the unfinished business of the emotional storms of the past year. The accumulation of difficult questions weighs us down as the season turns once again. We may sense the edges of depression, with difficulties in sleeping, eating or sexual expression. Perhaps activities that usually give pleasure now look pale and weak. In short, we are filled with *la cafard*. We may carry on and go through the motions, but the castle of our being feels deserted and cold. What saves us is the familiar knowing that we have been here before, and trusting that this oppressive despair will soon lift. It is a good time to reach out in small ways, to shift the center of our attention from ourselves. In attempting to alleviate the suffering of others, we may find relief from our own.

I acknowledge the hardships of this time of year.

December 20

puskita (poos-KEE-tah)   Muskogean
Fasting in a ceremonial way.

We have many ways to increase our capacity for an illuminated mind and an awakened heart. Willingly inviting a hardship such as fasting in order to increase our attention and connection to the great mystery is an act of grace. Great purification is possible when practicing *puskita*. Besides the natural cleansing that benefits the body, it also assists us in strengthening our foundation of compassion. Realizing that the temporary ache we feel in our bellies is an almost permanent condition for much of the planet, we feel the injustice and suffering of hunger in a world of abundance. The sweetness of taking only water speaks to an elegant simplicity and economy of scale. All our senses become sharp and focused, as we are lifted into deeper clarity. Food fantasies come and go, like so many other desires. Somehow we find the resolve to see it through and offer this gift of self denial for all of humanity. The first tastes of food, even after only a single day of fasting, become a meditation in appreciation and gratitude.

I join many others in fasting once a month in order to be reminded of world hunger.

samprajanya (sahm-pdah-jahn-yuh)   **Sanskrit**
The power of introspection.

External distractions easily sway us from contact with the source. How long will you wander in search of that which you already have? We access truth directly through our own experience. We may also arrive at its door through our capacity to reason. Both of these modes are relative, dependent on many factors. We may also choose the path of direct spiritual knowing beyond words, descriptions or rationalizations. Stare into the fire for hours. Journey into the adventure of your journal. Light candles and create a trance encounter with inner wisdom. Commence a rendezvous with *samprajanya*. Enter the void where all possibilities live. Change the channel of your awareness to the receptive mode. Listen deeply to whatever is revealed from the fountainhead of insight contained in the secret chambers of your being. Abide at the center of your essence. Hold the questions like flower petals raining down on snow, precious and beautiful offerings on the altar of existence.

Gradually I can live into the answers I already possess.

December 22

sooch (suj)   **Kafir Kalash**
Be pure!

We begin to enter into a more nourishing and dynamic harmony with ourselves when we relinquish the need to be perfect. *Sooch!* The words are whispered as part of the ritual purification during a December festival in northern Pakistan. Bathing, incense, special foods and ceremony combine in events around the world to encourage right living. Beyond simple moral compunction, sooch reveals more significant paradoxical realities. Strive to better yourself and simultaneously accept yourself. Welcome into your life those who can be confrontative and supportive at the same time, gently pointing out discrepancies between your actions and your words. The more you relinquish control of your spiritual destiny, the greater freedom you will experience. The embracing of your unique shadows allow the brilliance of your light to shine forth.

I welcome the wholeness of my imperfections.

tibu (TEE-bo)   Hopi
Painted representation of a Kachina, or god-like figure, on cottonwood, given to children.

You were once a master of play, a living stream of imagination and creativity, fueled by endless curiosity. Play offers the freedom of exploration and invention for its own sake. Children at play improvise, combine concepts and ideas, and act out the language and signals of their culture. A *tibu* is a Hopi toy of made of natural materials. The object represents Kachinas: living spirits of the dead and mysterious forces of nature, demons, animals, birds, and even clowns. When we choose sexist or violent war toys for our youth, we transmit these same values, encouraging a limited stereotypic worldview. A child can't do much with a plastic AK 47 except mimic destruction. A Barbie doll whose purpose in life is to be dressed up and to look pretty is not a model of reflective intelligence. Creative playthings bring out the best of the human spirit in our children, encouraging them to move into the unknown with joy and caring.

I conscientiously choose toys that support my beliefs.

December 24

koledarka (ko-leh-DAR-kah)   **Bulgarian**
Long elaborately carved oak stick.

The ritual singing of Christmas carols takes place at this time of the year in Bulgaria. Groups move from house to house, wishing people prosperity, good health, and continued blessings. The customs vary slightly in different regions. For exampe in some places the event occurs nearer to New Year's and carolers tap on the shoulder of those visited with a decorated twig while requesting good fortune for the family. A *koledarka* is often carried by the singers as a symbol of connection to the life-giving earth. There is something magical about the feel of a walking stick. A treasured companion over years, it brings forth the twin sensations of stability and adventure. It is a repository for memories of special places visited, and longings for others yet to come. Once held, you can hear its call to be carried into the wild. Let your spirit respond to the call.

At this season, I enjoy the simple pleasures of walking and visiting loved ones.

zamba (ZAHM-bah) **English Creole**
A small wooden cot or homemade bed.

On this special day, Christians around the world celebrate the birth of their savior, who entered the world with humble beginnings in a stable. Surrounded by animals, dirt and straw, the coming heralded a new era of teachings about peace and forgiveness, while supporting the intimate connection with the beauty of all creation. The newborn's bed was a simple and easily constructed *zamba*. Such an unadorned entry into the world reminds us to act with generosity as much as we invite prosperity, to embrace appreciation as often as we partake of the riches of our planet. It seems that many have made money their god, flocking to the hallowed chambers of malls, and buying products as if shopping were a form of prayer. Like anything else in our lives, our relationship to finances is a reflection of our beliefs and emotions. The empty cycle of consuming more and enjoying it less is ultimately destructive both individually and collectively. All religions emphasize the same essential practices: forgiveness, service and compassion. When kept at the forefront of our awareness, their guiding light benefits all. Let peace begin with me.

May I learn to live simply so others may simply live.

December 26

terima kasih (tuh-REE-muh KAH-see)   Bahasa Indonesia
This is given and accepted with love; a form of thank you.

Where have you sought God, the Buddha, or truth, and what did
you find there? So many different people are cajoling us passion-
ately in different ways "I have what you need." The truths of life
and love are bigger than individual small mind, which can never
entirely capture their secrets. Like the inflow and out release of
breath, the endless cycle of giving and receiving kindness is the
portal to the greater appreciation of spiritual mysteries. Uttering
terima kasih is a manifestation of enlightened wisdom. To be able
to offer and to accept the blessings of love, and infuse all of our
daily encounters with that awareness is to participate in the most
basic energy of life itself. Said with a smile, and a sparkle in the
eyes, this simple expression acknowledges the most essential
aspect of our lives. It reminds us that we are luminous beings of
goodness. Each moment of our relatedness is part of a sacred
dance whose rhythms we will never fully comprehend, but
whose music we can effortlessly enjoy. What we seek healing for
is already whole, already free and alive in the core of our being.

Today the many blessings raining down have my name on them.

ochemata (oh-heh-MAH-tah)   Greek
Soul sheaths connected to the visible body.

How are we connected to a stone, a sea urchin, a quark? The notion of panpsychism—that to some degree we share consciousness with all other creatures and everything that exists in the universe—conveys the image of a great continuity of being. The notion of *ochemata* is that we each possess a body of light which establishes and sustains our union with everything that exists. This concept is supported by varied cultural beliefs in phantom figures, subtle bodies and the spirit-matter of extraphysical domains. Both modern-day alien experiences and angelic visitations fall into this same category and are resoundingly rejected by the scientific establishment. The existence of an individual, imperishable, eternal, transcendental, luminous body might explain the healing power of prayer for another, as well as shamanic visionary journeys, widespread reports of collective visions, and the common pathway of near death experiences. High frequency sounds, and ultraviolent portions of the visible spectrum escape our attention because they are not easily perceived. By limiting our sensorium to our current ways of seeing, we are perhaps apprehending only a sliver of the universe we inhabit.

I am open to exploring multidimensional modes of being.

December 28

lung gom (luhng gohm)   Tibetan
Flowing meditative walking.

Karakoram is a magical Asian mountain system that stretches for 300 miles, and holds 19 mountain peaks that each exceed 25,000 feet. Deep within its majesty is a culture that practices *lung gom*, which literally means wind, or life force, concentration. This Tantric discipline allows a person to glide along a path with swiftness and certainty, even at night. While reciting the appropriate mantra the arjopa, or "adept" controls the weight of the body, so as to hardly touch the earth in passing. Matter flows as if it were pure energy, oblivious to weight and gravity. Normal consciousness is suspended, though the practitioner is still aware enough to avoid obstacles, even while moving across terrain at high speed. The discipline requires fixing concentration on a distant single object, without talking nor looking side to side. There are times when your journey captures such a relaxed yet focused quality. More often there is confusion, rather than flow. When you are feeling lost and muddled, remember that all roads lead to home, though there may be mirages and false summits along the way.

I travel lightly today.

zanshin (ZAHN-sheen)   Japanese
The awareness that is maintained even after an action is completed.

Expect nothing. Be ready for anything. The qualities of readiness and relaxed alertness that are essential for a warrior are also mandatory for anyone wanting to live life fully. Our potency lives in the present moment, oblivious to how something happened before, or how something might develop in the future. Being present throughout an experience is the dynamic quality of *zanchin*. To do this, each and every encounter must be held as if it were the first and last of our life. Just as it is, not how we suppose or want it to be. When a danger has apparently passed is often a perilous time. Stay awake! When we think we have come through the difficulty—a tense moment in sports, driving through a storm, hiking a steep slope—is when we most need to stay focused and present. When we engage the practice of zanchin in little ways we create the foundation for self-realization throughout our lifetime. Clearing the mind and paying full attention to our surroundings, over and over, we develop the capacity for seamless preparation and action.

As I prepare to transition to a new year, what needs to be noticed, is; what must be done is immediately taken care of.

December 30

**cacoethes scribendi (kah-ko-AY-tehs skree-BEHN-dee)   Latin
The urge to write.**

The Sufi masters said it well: "To become that which you were before you were, with the memory and understanding of what you had become." As we grow, it is natural to begin to contemplate our legacy, to examine the life we have created. You begin to pay attention to what you will leave for your family and the world. Those afflicted or blessed with *cacoethes scribendi* know these reflections well. We might point to the lingering considerations of material goods, work and family successes, or community contributions. But the essence of scribing our personal history lies in the free and creative expression of being yourself, and of setting the details down in ink for all to appreciate. The story must be told, in whatever form required. What lies inside must find its way out, transformed, fresh and compelling. The call of the wolf in the middle of the night needs to be answered. Don't go back to your dreams. Enter the chamber of your heart, and the infinity of a blank journal page. Your passions await you, and your imagination is a trusty guide. The adventure begins anew. Explore on! Rave on! Write on!

Why do you want to write? one asks. Why do you want to live? is the only possible reply.

kuumba (koo-OOM-bah)   Kiswahili
Creativity used to improve the community; one of the principles of Kwanzaa

Kwanzaa is an African American holiday celebrated from December 26 to January 1st which honors Black people and their history. For each of seven days, a different core value or principle of living is examined, guided by the perspective of past struggles and future visions. Today, *kuumba* reminds us to do whatever we can with our creative talents to leave our community more beautiful and healthy than when we inherited it. Personal inventiveness is seen as a gift to be used for the benefit of community. And in thinking of ways to make our community better, we also receive the joys of a deeper creative exploration of ourselves. This is truly something to celebrate! Kuumba adds an enriched perspective to those generous acts of turning a vacant lot into a community garden, sharing our talents at the local elementary school, or working collectively to support young people in the pursuit of their own original dreams.

I will use my creativity to think of new ways to benefit my community.

Reference Bibliography

Most of the words in this book were obtained through direct contact with native speakers of the language. However, a number of references were very valuable in expanding the storehouse of concepts. These include:

Drumming at the Edge of Magic by Mickey Hart. 1990, HarperCollins, New York.

Et Cetera Et Cetera, Notes of a Word Watcher by Lewis Thomas. 1990, Penguin Books, New York.

Free Play, The Power of Improvisation in Life and the Arts by Stephen Nachmanovitch. 1990, Jeremy P. Tarcher/Putnam Books, New York.

Heaven's Breath, A Natural History of the Wind by Lyall Watson. 1984, William Morrow & Company, New York.

Holidays, Festivals and Celebrations of the World Dictionary compiled by Sue Ellen Thompson and Barbara W. Carlson. 1994, Onmigraphics Inc., Detroit, Michigan.

Jambo Means Hello by Muriel Feelings. 1974, Dial Books for Young Readers, New York.

More Street French by David Burke. 1990, John Wiley & Sons Inc., New York

Phillipines Handbook by Peter Harper and Laurie Fullerton. 1993, Moon Publications Inc., Chico, California.

Talking Your Way Around The World by Pario Pei. 1971, Harper and Row, New York

The Anthropology of Peace and Nonviolence edited by Leslie E. Sponsel and Thomas Gregor. 1994, Lynne Reinner Pub. Inc., Covent Garden, England.

The Asian Journal of Thomas Merton edited by Naomi Burton et al. 1975, New Directions Publishing, New York.

The Grand Panjandrum by J. N. Hook. 1980, Macmillan Publishing, New York.

The Jewish Word Book by Sidney Jacobs. 1982, Jonathan David Publishing, New York.

The Spirituality of Imperfection by Ernest Kurtz and Kathering Ketcham. 1992, Bantam Books, New York.

The World of the American Indian edited by Jules B. Billard, National Geographic Society. 1979, Washington D.C.

They Have A Word For It by Howard Rheingold. 1988, Jeremy Tarcher Inc., Los Angeles, California.

What a Pistarckle by Lito Valls. 1981, St. John, US Virgin Islands

Word Dance: The Language of North American Culture by Carol Waldman. 1994, Facts on File Inc., New York.

A variety of Fodor, Lonely Planet and APA Insight travel guides.

Worldwords

a piacere (Italian) At your pleasure; whatever tempo you wish. 6/10

a solare (Italian) To sit in the sun doing nothing. 8/8

abigezunt (Yiddish) As long as one is healthy nothing else matters. 1/8

achya (Bengali) An affirmative response to a question; the great yes! 9/12

affectus (Latin) Openness in which we are vulnerable to the world around us. 2/29

ahimsa (Sanskrit) The purifying inward force of non violence. 8/10

'ahlan wa sahlan (Arabic) A form of welcome that indicates you are considered to be one of the family. 11/26

ai (Chinese) The slow unfolding of a heart relationship. 5/20

aji (Japanese) An energy imparted over time through the loving handling or wearing of an object. 3/1

allemansratt (Swedish) A law guaranteeing public access to the countryside. 4/14

aloha 'aina (Hawaiian) Love of the land, one of the three essential principles of the Hawaiian culture. 6/19

Alpaufzug (Swiss German) Ascent to the mountains festival. 5/26

alu (Runic) Signifying protection. 11/22

ama sua, ama llula, ama qella (Quechua) Do not be a thief, do not be a liar, do not be lazy. 1/25

anam cara (Gaelic) Soul friend. 11/12

andenken (German) Thankfulness rooted in the memory of being without. 11/25

angiqsarait (Inuktitut) Ready to accommodate.1/12

asbestos gelos (Greek) Unquenchable, inextinguishable laughter. 6/9

aubade (French) Morning music. 1/19

aura (Greek) First breath of air at dawn. 8/2

aware (Japanese) The feelings engendered by indescribable beauty. 10/28

Awoojoh (Yoruba) Thanksgiving feast honoring the spirits of the dead in which all family disputes are settled. 1/21

ayuqnaq (Inuktitut 5/12) Life is like that; it can't be helped.

ba whgii ya' (Navajo) Being in a state of wisdom that requires us to act in new ways. 4/25

bambai de (Dutch Creole) Time is a great healer. 10/22

banjar (Indonesian) Cooperative groups of neighbors bound to assist each other. 6/22

bas bas (Urdu) Enough! Refers to crowds, tea, anything! 4/14

ben detto (Italian) Well said! 2/17

biga peula (New Guinea Kiriwina) Hard words; potentially disruptive true statements. 6/20

bihtere gelechtr (Yiddish) Laughter through tears; bitter laughter. 2/1

bilibong (Arunta) Waterhole from which our spirits emerge at birth and return to at death. 7/31

bilita mpastshi (Bantu) Blissful dreams. 11/10

binag (Tagalog) Practice of giving everyone nicknames. 11/19

birkie (Gaelic) Lively intelligent clean cut person. 2/28

bith'haa (Tohono O'odham) Making decisions as if cooking with a clay pot. 2/2

blajini (Romanian) Kind magical beings who live on the banks of a river. 4/18

bodhisattva (Pali) One who has attained enlightenment but remains to help others attain salvation. 7/8

bricolage (French) Making do with the material at hand; expanding apparent limits. 3/29

buba (Sango) messed up; refers to anything not working right, including people. 8/19

bubinzana (Quechua) Chant that leads a vision. 11/20

bungisngis (Tagalog) Infectious ear to ear grin. 10/27

cacoethes scribendi (Latin) The urge to write. 12/30

cargo (Spanish) A burden or sacrifice one makes for the sake of the community. 11/24

chidelglo (Navajo) A baby's first laugh. 9/13

Ch'ung Yang (Chinese) Family remembrance day when one visits ancestors' graves. 10/4

chwarae teg (Welsh) Fair play; what is right and just. 7/15

conscientizacao (Portuguese) Learning to perceive social, political and economic inequities. 3/19

conte jondo (Spanish) Deep brooding fatalistic song. 5/4

cosi cosi (Italian) Life is so-so. 4/11

craic (Gaelic) The art of conversational banter. 3/16

csardas (Hungarian) A dance with sudden alterations of tempo. 5/25

cuchument (English Creole) Odds and ends; paraphernalia. 5/9

Worldwords

dak (Urdu) A stopping point or resthouse for long distance travelers. 6/28

dana (Pali) Generosity of giving, as in the form of Buddhist teachings, which are offered freely because they are considered priceless. 3/12

Danonal (Korean) Cold water shampoo day. 6/8

daramulun (Arunta) Master of thunder; the noise made by an instrument known as a bullroarer. 9/28

dephase (French) To feel out of it. 1/11

deptak (Polish) Central pedestrian promenade where the life of the town concentrates. 3/13

diyan lang (Tagalog) Wandering around; response to Where are you going? 6/15

do do (English Creole) To take a nap. 3/5

dorje (Tibetan) The pure indestructible principle that contributes to awareness. 11/14

drala (Sanskrit) What occurs when the wisdom of your being is linked with the power of things as they are. 12/17

dukka (Pali) Suffering, misery, unhappiness. 4/16

Ekeko (Aymara) God of prosperity. 1/10

elke (Algonquin) An expression of joy; great! wonderful! 2/27

eneenin'kujit (Masai) A cathedral of seven old trees where the grass sheaves are tied. 1/29

enlaki (Kayapo) "I'm another you"; greeting used when another is heard nearby in the rainforest. 7/24

entschlossenheit (German) The resolve to make of oneself what one wants. 12/5

fado (Portuguese) A haunting blues style music rooted in African slave songs. 6/29

favela (Portuguese) Impoverished sprawling hillside town. 1/15

felt (Yiddish) Something wanting; that which is missing and thereby preventing a feeling of wholeness. 3/25

ffreg (Welsh) Chatter or gossip. 5/17

funktionslust (German) The pleasure of doing, of producing an effect. 7/1

gambaru (Japanese) To strive against the odds. 4/27

gamzu l'tova (Hebrew) Even though this is unpleasant, it is for the best. 8/7

gan (Apache) Mountain spirit guardians of wildlife. 9/6

gatha (Sanskrit) A phrase to bring one's awareness to the present. 8/4

geduld (Yiddish) Both patience and temper. 5/13

gelassenheit (German) The letting go that is a solution to suffering. 9/2

gemeinschaft (German) Society as a system of inter-related parts;community. 10/10

ginnungagap (Old Norse) The endless abyss at the edge of the world. 10/16

goadnil (Saami) The quiet part of a river, free of current, near the bank or beside a rock. 3/2

granzevolk (German) Visionary people who live on the fringes of society. 1/14

gule gule (Turkish) Go smiling; form of Goodbye. 6/27

gunik (Semai) Benevolent spirits that appear in a dream and teach the dreamer a song. 3/11

hadai (Navajo) The special relationship between a boy and his maternal uncle. 6/30

halak (Bahasa Indonesia) A dream guide. 9/23

halus (Bahasa Indonesia) Describing the highest standards of behavior, performance and art. 8/23

hamam (Turkish) Bath. 7/27

hanare (Japanese) The moment when an arrow is released of its own accord. 8/16

hanbleceyapi (Sioux) Vision quest. 7/16

hart ducha (Polish) Self-mastery and dignity in the face of external forces. 11/15

hejnal (Polish) A warning call from a high tower. 10/31

hetman (Ukrainian) Leader recognized by the people. 9/30

heyoka (Lakota) Sacred clown. 11/1

hii' (Malaysian Semai) The band; all of us here together. 5/28

hiya (Tagalog) Trying to avoid shame or loss of face. 8/13

hoa'ai waiu (Hawaiian) Companions at the breast who have a special life-long relationship. 9/16

hoka hey (Sioux) Hold fast, there is more. 3/23

holopis kuntul baris (Bahasa Indonesia) Phrase uttered to gain extra strength when carrying heavy objects. 11/7

honami (Japanese) Study of the way in which different plants wave in the wind. 6/3

hoo ha (Yiddish) Expression of surprise, astonishment and admiration. 7/2

Worldwords

hoomaikai (Hawaiian) Grateful. 7/18

ho'oponopono (Hawaiian) To come together in a problem solving process. 10/29

hozhooji nitsihakees (Navajo) To think about and honor our differences in good ways. 5/22

huskanaw (Algonquin) Male rite of passage. 5/14

hyggelig (Danish) Warm hospitality. 3/22

hwan gap (Korean) The celebration of one's sixtieth birthday. 8/11

hytter (Norwegian) Cottage that is close to nature. 7/17

ibota (Nigerian Bini) A family gathering time for stories. 8/1

ichimyaku tsujiru (Japanese) To have something in common. 5/27

ikomeng (SothoThe pattern when divinatory bones are thrown that indicates "the whisper."12/11

inallaaduwi (Palaihnihan) Seemingly not connected to anything, meaning the destructive aspects of the white man. 1/24

intelleto (Latin) Visionary intelligence. 7/4

inua (Yupik 8/28) The essence of a human that is always there in a mask.

istiqara (Arabic) A request for spiritual or practical assistance in the form of a dream. 8/21

isumaqsayuq (Inuktitut) To cause thought; a conscious method of instruction. 2/8

jam karet (Bahasa Indonesia) Rubber time. 3/8

jihad (Arabic) A righteous struggle. 7/21

Jilla (Boran) Naming ceremony for a newborn child. 10/15

kaas (Yiddish) Anger, wrath and sorrow. 7/10

kai so (English Creole) A shout of approval, like bravo. 9/24

ka'imi loa (Hawaiian) The way culture helps in the personal search to find purpose and meaning. 4/30

kairos (Greek) Right timing. 1/2

kak sazhe byela (Russian) As soot is white; awful!; a response to How are you? 8/29

Kalachakra (Sanskrit) The process of destroying a sand mandala. 9/4

Kalevala (Finnish) A long narrative epic poem. 4/13

kamayan (Tagalog) Eating with the hands. 8/18

karibu chakula (Kiswahili) Come and eat with us. 10/3

kasa (Korean) Lyrical form of poetry expressing attachment to the beauty of nature. 7/13

kashim (Kodiac Island Russian dialect) Ceremonial house. 7/26

kesho (Kiswahili) Relaxed pace of life. 6/6

ketepepei (Xingu) Outgoing and sociable; aesthetically pleasing objects. 4/28

khleeb (Ukrainian) Life-sustaining peasant bread. 11/29

kilesa (Pali) Torments of mind. 6/12

Kinaalda (Navajo) Puberty rite of passage for young women. 8/17

kenosis (Greek) An emptying. 11/11

kirpan (Punjabi) A knife that is always carried to remind one that there are things worth defending. 4/19

kismet (Arabic) Fate or destiny. 6/21

koinonia (Greek) A community discovered through a shared story or other commonality. 7/9

koi-si (!Kung) Kind and generous person. 12/16

koledarka (Bulgarian) Long elaborately carved oak stick. 12/24

kopiec (Polish) Earthen mounds erected in honor of great people. 1/22

koyaanisqatsi (Hopi) Life out of balance 4/1

kubembeleza (Kiswahili) To caress. 4/3

kuden (Japanese) Gems of secret guidance passed on orally by mentors. 2/6

Kukulkan (Mayan) The god of wind, symbolizing light, water and motion. 7/7

kula (Melanesia) Exchange of goods to keep relationships smooth. 11/21

Kumbh Mela (Hindi) Festival to wash away sins of past lives. 2/18

kumsitz (Yiddish) Come sit, let's enjoy the cool of the evening after work. 5/2

kutho (Burmese) Merit or what one acquires through doing good deeds. 11/17

kuumba (Kiswahili) Creativity used to improve the community; one of the principles of Kwaanza 12/31

kvel (Yiddish) To feel the joy of things going well. 11/2

kyosaku (Japanese) The bamboo stick used by a meditation master to discipline students. 8/27

Worldwords

la cafard (French) The blues. 12/19

la couler douce (French) To flow sweetly through life. 7/14

la perruque (French) What you do for yourself while apparently working for another. 6/11

lagniappe (French Creole) An unexpected gift to a stranger or customer. 4/20

lammas (Old English) The time in-between summer solstice and fall equinox. 8/12

lila (Sanskrit) All of nature seen as the creative activity of the divine; the sportive, playful, free willing God. 3/4

lo aleichem (Yiddish) May it not happen to you. 12/1

Los Angelitos (Spanish) Day devoted to children who have died. 10/30

lung gom (Tibetan) Flowing meditative walking. 12/28

ma (Japanese) Empty space, the huge meaning carried by small silences. 6/17

ma ta la shol (Mayan) How is your heart ? 3/7

mai pen rai (Thai) Let it go; not worth hassling about; get off it. 3/16

majie (Chinese) To curse the street. 11/18

maka (Lakota) The womb of mother earth, which nourishes all life. 4/2

makurakotoba (Japanese) Pillow talk. 11/3

malama (Hawaiian) Mutual caring. 4/7

mamihlapinatapei (Tierra del Fuegan) A meaningful look shared by two people expressing mutually unstated feelings. 12/9

mammalucco (Italian) Dope, jerk. 3/26

mano po lolo (Tagalog) As a sign of respect for an old man or woman (lola), taking the right hand and touching it lightly to your forehead. 5/3

mara (Masai) Motley; one of thirty adjectives used to describe the cow. 11/6

marime (Romany) Impurity of both body and spirit. 12/6

Martenitzas (Bulgarian) Two tassels of thread symbolizing health and happiness. 4/10

mauvaise foi (French) Deception. 5/6

mbuki mvuki (Zulu) To shuck off clothes in order to dance. 10/7

meiyou (Chinese) Forget it! 12/8

meldado (Ladino) A gathering that focuses on reading spiritual literature together. 2/5

melmastia (Pashto) Hospitality to all visitors without expectation of reward. 1/30

mide (Algonquin) Mystically powerful. 8/3

mihrab (Turkish) Prayer niche or ceremonial arch in a mosque. 8/30

minototak (Algonquin) Ethical conduct. 11/4

miratio (Latin) Amazement; miracle; the wonder of the unique. 3/15

mitakuye oyasin (Lakota) We are all related to everyone and everything around us, above us, below us. 1/3

mithuna (Hindi) Statues of amorous couples. 7/12

mizukakeron (Japanese) Dispute without end. 9/5

mollo mollo (French) Easy does it; carefully, cautiously, sweetly.3/18

moyn (Welsh) Deep longing. 9/20

muatupu (Uto-Aztecan) An elder. 2/16

mujo (Japanese) A romantic sense of life's impermanence. 5/7

mulata (Portuguese) Revered beautiful female of mixed blood. 4/26

munkumbole (Arunta) Shamans who specialize in clairvoyance. 7/20

mushairah (Urdu) Open air recital of poetry dealing with devotional or erotic love. 7/28

mushin (Japanese) Empty mind, free of worldly thought. 1/4

nagashi (Japanese) Flow referring to water, your life, and the use of utensils in the tea ceremony. 11/9

naka ima (Japanese) The time and space between the past and the future where human life manifests. 10/1

nakhes (Yiddish) Pride from another's achievements. 9/3

nallik (Inuktitut) To be helpful obliging and considerate. 4/23

namaste (Hindi) A greeting that honors the part of you that is the same as me. 5/24

nanwatai (Pashto) Formal submission of the vanquished to the victor. 7/30

narahati (Farsi) Experiencing a wide range of negative emotions.2/10

nasha hozho (Navajo) To walk in the beauty way in one's life and actions. 1/1

nasim (Arabic) Whispering wind across the desert at dusk. 4/12

natchnienie (Polish) A moment of soulful inspiration. 5/31

nazarlik (Turkish) Talismanic symbol on a tapestry to ward off the evil eye. 10/23

ng'ambo (Kiswahili) The opposite bank of the stream from where you are standing. 5/8

ngon (Vietnamese) Putting loving energy into food. 11/16

nichevo (Russian) Don't worry, doesn't matter, nothing to do about it. 10/11

Worldwords

nimewisha kabisa (Kiswahili) I'm beat, done for, exhausted. 7/11

nisse (Norway) Good luck trolls. 5/30

nith (Inuktitut) Song duel. 10/20

nngoma (Kiswahili) Both drum and dance. 8/5

nona gathe (Sinhalese) The few hours between the old and astrologically determined new year. 4/22

nowa ochiamou (Yanomami) To ask to be invited in times of scarcity. 2/21

Nubaigai (Lithuanian) End of harvest festival. 9/14

nyambinyambi (Bantu) Rain calling ceremony in spring. 3/20

Nyambutan (Balinese) Ceremony when a baby is first allowed to touch the ground. 1/23

nyaweh gowah (Iroquoian) Great thanks. 8/6

Nyepi (Balinese) Day of silence. 3/21

oc ye nechca (Nahuatl) This is a true story. 2/12

ochemata (Greek) Soul sheaths connected to the visible body. 12/27

ocurrencia (Spanish) Sudden bright idea. 4/5

ojala (Spanish) Would to God; wishful thinking. 12/14

oleg (Bahasa Indonesia) The swaying of the dancer in a flirting dance. 2/11

oloiboni (Masai) Ritual expert. 2/19

omommomo (Ainu) To omit tedious details. 12/15

oonagamessok (Abenakis) Spirit beings who presided over the creation of petroglyphs. 11/5

orita (Yoruba 12/7) Term for the crossroads that attract spirits.

ototeman (Ojibwa) The mystical connection between humans and other living creatures. 10/14

pacha kuti (Nahuatl) The rising and falling of a great event. 5/5

pagdiwata (Tagbanua) The feeling that one belongs to the land rather than owns it. 4/30

pagodes (Portuguese) A samba center where musicians gather to jam. 5/29

paho (Hopi) Prayer stick. 6/4

pakikisama (Tagalog) Going along with the group. 9/21

Worldwords

pampero (Spanish) A wind that makes all the noises of man in various states of excitement. 1/16

p'ansori (Korean) Narrative song contest. 5/15

pasalubong (Tagalog) Gift of food one brings back after travelling. 7/6

passeggiata (Italian) Community ritual of strolling back and forth down the street. 7/22

patamou (Yanomami) Elder harangue to create change. 9/25

pega (Portuguese) Display of bravery when confronting a tired and enraged bull. 2/20

pensieroso (Italian) Pensive and thoughtful. 9/8

per cento anni (Italian) A toast; may you live your bliss for a hundred years. 1/31

peras (Greek) A space cleared out and made free; a boundary from which something begins its essence. 3/6

perchten (German) Old masks passed from generation to generation. 1/6

petana (Keres) Cornmeal, which is considered sacred and often used as an offering. 7/5

pi say (Burmese) Traditional protective tattooing. 2/4

pingnguaq (Inuktitut) Playful and not taking things seriously. 7/25

piropo (Spanish) Flowery spoken compliment. 2/22

pistarckle (English Creole) Confusion; a group gone out of control. 7/23

pivik (Inuktitut) A person who gets upset easily and is thus considered childish. 9/29

po (Hawaiian) The finishing process of making a lei; the final details of an offering. 3/31

pomana (Romany) Death feast. 4/29

pratibha (Sanskrit) Poetic sensibility and glittering inventiveness. 9/22

pregierz (Polish) Punishment post; site of Medieval flogging. 2/24

primum non nocere (Latin) First of all do no harm. 4/4

priya (Sanskrit) The beloved. 2/14

pusaka (Bahasa Indonesia) Sacred heirlooms passed down from generation to generation. 10/25

puskita (Muskogean) Fasting in a ceremonial way. 12/20

pwe (Burmese) All night theater festival. 10/17

pysanky (Ukrainian) Intricately designed Easter eggs. 4/8

qaqayuq (Inuktitut) One who likes being the center of attention and shows off. 6/26

qawwali (Urdu) Improvisational singer whose goal is to induce devotional ecstasy.

Worldwords

quipu (Quechua) Device for counting and recording events. 12/13

ranz des vaches (Swiss French) Yodels and other tunes sung as cattle calls. 8/9
rasa (Sanskrit) The essential flavor of deep artistic experience. 1/17
ravda (Romany) Strength that comes from being emotional. 6/24
rebbilib (Marshallese) Navigational aids based on the feel of the waves and swell patterns. 7/19
Repotini (Romanian) Festival in which the women are masters. 5/10
roogoodoo (English Creole) Noisy disturbance. 2/13
roulade (French) An ornamental flourish. 11/13
ruskaa (Finnish) Beautiful fall colors. 10/6

sabat (Yiddish) A break or rest of the heart. 10/21
sabsung (Thai) To satisfy an emotional or spiritual thirst. 1/26
saka na (Tagalog) Anytime later, maybe next year. 3/14
salam alekum (Arabic) Greeting meaning peace be upon you. 9/18
salat (Arabic) Repeated prostrations as part of the call to prayer. 2/25
sama (Persian) Whirling dance as a conduit for abandoning oneself to god. 3/27
samadhi (Sanskrit) Selfless absolute concentration. 5/16
samideano (Esperanto) One who shares the same idea of a friendly world speaking the same language. 12/18
samprajanya (Sanskrit) The power of introspection.12/21
sangha (Sanskrit) A supportive community for spiritual growth. 8/14
sanuk (Thai) Healthy fun and enjoyment with friends. 5/11
satyagraha (Sanskrit) Unmasking injustice so truth is brought to light. 10/2
se do bheatha (Celtic) Life to you. 10/19
senge (Sango) Naked, nothing; A response to How are you? 6/18
shanachie (Gaelic) Person fond of telling the old tales. 10/18
shibui (Japanese) The beauty of aging. 12/2
shilditee (Apache) Getting cussed out. 12/10
Shiva (Yiddish) Period of mourning between the death and burial of a relative. 4/9
shoshit (Albanian) To discuss a problem as if sifting flour. 2/9
simpatico (Spanish) Instinctively attuned to the moods and wishes of another. 6/16
sipapu (Keris) Hole in the ceremonial room or kiva symbolizing the center of the uni-

verse. 12/12

sisu (Finnish) Self-reliance. 2/26

skansen (Swedish) Open air museum. 5/21

sooch (Kafir Kalash) Be pure! 12/22

soon (Burmese) Alms offered to monks. 9/19

summum bonum (Latin) The greatest good. 8/20

susto (Spanish) Soul loss. 10/13

susu (English Creole) Be quiet; often said to a child in a soft way. 1/18

sz (Chinese) Good wind of the first faint touch of autumn. 10/12

Szuret (Hungarian) Grape gathering festival when many marriages take place. 10/26

t'aeguk (Korean) Yin Yang circle in the center of the Korean flag. 3/10

takos (Chinook) A philosophy in which any decision should be considered in terms of its effects on seven generations. 11/28

takuan (Chinese) To have seen through life and thus to take things lightly. 6/13

takwatsi (Huichol) A basket used to hold shamanic power objects 6/25

talanoa (Hindi) Small talk as social glue. 1/20

talelo (Tamil) The refrain in a lullaby that put the Hindu god Krishna to sleep as a baby. 5/19

tampak tanah (Bahasa Indonesia) To be able to see the ground. 9/7

Tanekert (Tuareg) Return of the rains celebration. 9/26

tasadimos (Romany) Pregnant with tears. 1/27

Tashlich (Yiddish) Casting one's sins symbolically into a stream or river. 9/27

teeka (Hindi) A symbol of worship of the intellect and consciousness present in every person. 10/24

teleios (Greek) Fully complete. 2/15

temenos (Greek) A magical circle in which extraordinary events are free to occur. 5/23

terima kasih (Bahasa Indonesia) This is given and accepted with love; a form of thank you. 12/26

terroni (Italian) People of the earth. 5/18

tibu (Hopi) Painted representation of a Kachina, or god-like figure, on cottonwood, given to children. 12/23

tiep (Vietnamese) To be in touch with oneself. 6/14

Worldwords

ting (Chinese) To listen with the heart, eyes, ears and mind. 9/17
ting ting (English Creole) Introductory phrase for a folktale. 4/6
tiwalla (Tagalog) Deep sense of trust. 2/23
tjotjog (Javanese) Harmonious congruence in human affairs. 4/24
tki'o tjuiks (Tohono O'odham) It looks like it may be going to rain on us. 6/7
tocayo (Spanish) One who shares the same name. 8/24
Tod kathin (Thai) Pilgrimage season; the time when monks receive new robes. 10/9
tonglen (Tibetan) Meditation in which the practitioner focuses on breathing in suffering, and breathing out joy. 11/30
ts'aa' (Navajo) Basket whose design reflects the beginning of the world. 11/23
tsanahwit (Sahaptin Nez Perce) Equal justice. 9/11
Tsukimi (Japanese) Moon viewing as a mid-autumn activity. 9/15
tufani pole (Kiswahili) Give me your sympathy, as I tell this tale of woe. 9/1
turiya (Sanskrit) Not waking, not sleeping, not dreaming. 10/5

ufffda (Swedish) A word of sympathy used when someone else is struggling in pain. 3/9
ujamma (Kiswahili) A tree carving representing the story of a Makonde family. 4/21
un cinq a sept (French) A quick sexual exchange. 9/10
utang na loob (Tagalog) A debt of the heart. 1/5
uthsaha (Sanskrit) Spiritual encouragement. 9/9

vade mecum (Latin) Go with me; a book for ready reference. 1/7
via negativa (Latin) The exploration of what is not in order to understand what is. 10/8

wa (Japanese) Sense of harmony and well-being. 7/3
wakanta logony (Osage) The great mystery is good 6/1
waka (Xingu) Ceremonial messengers. 8/25
wana (Yekuana) Twin ceremonial flutes. 1/9
wayamou (Yanomami) Ceremonial dialogue as a method of releasing anger and frustrations. 12/3
wewepahtli iktzeilwitl (Nahuatl) Greatest medicine; natural healing powers. 8/26
wiitokuchumpunkuruganiyugwivantumu (Uto-Aztecan) They who are going to sit

and cut up with a knife a black female buffalo. 6/5

wiltja (Arunta) Temporary bush shelter. 11/8

Windigos (Cree) Monsters or demons. 1/28

wokowi (Huichol) Peyote. 4/17

wu wei (Chinese) Continuous letting go of expectations. 2/3

wulgis (Arunta) Spirits of dead medicine men who transform an individual who is exhibiting psychic talent. 12/4

wulunda (Ndembu) Special bond shared by those undergoing initiation together. 8/31

Wuwuchim (Hopi) A new year ceremony which celebrates the first dawn. 11/27

ya'biiltiih (Navajo) A dying person's words, which might not otherwise be spoken. 3/28

yah ah tay (Navajo) A form of greeting meaning it is good. 2/7

yawari (Xingu) Ritual insults that follow certain rules and are spoken in the presence of bystanders. 6/23

yong (Chinese) Eternal; permanent; the oneness seen in water as it moves. 3/24

zamba (English Creole) A small wooden cot or homemade bed. 12/25

zanshin (Japanese) The awareness that is maintained even after an action is completed. 12/29

zayats (Burmese) Rest places around a pagoda. 8/15

zerrissenheit (German) A torn to pieces-hood, the state of being divided, fractured; pulled in a dozen directions. 3/3

ziji (Tibetan) The shining out and rejoicing that is attendant to confidence. 3/30

ziku (Choiseulese) Peacemaking procedures of exchanging valuables to settle a conflict. 8/22

zou ma guan hua (Chinese) Too much in a hurry; trying to observe flowers while galloping on horseback. 7/29

Victor La Cerva, MD, has been actively working in Violence prevention for more than twelve years. He is currently medical director of the Family Health Bureau of the New Mexico Department of Health and holds a clinical faculty appointment with the Department of Pediatrics at the University of New Mexico Medical School.

In 1984 Victor co-created the New Mexico Men's Wellness movement to promote an exploration of the physical, emotional, mental, and spiritual needs of men in our society. As a result, years before the national men's movement became known, annual gatherings, hundreds of small support groups, a statewide newsletter, and support groups for young men were activated in New Mexico. In 1989 he organized four statewide workshops on violence, in collaboration with the New Mexico Public Health Association.

His first book, *Let Peace Begin With Us*, was released in 1990 and updated in 1993 and 1996, highlighting levels of homicide, suicide, child and elder abuse, domestic violence, and sexual assault on a county-by-county basis. Both editions have served as catalysts for community involvement. Victor continued to "build the movement" as the New Mexico co-chair for the September 1994 and 1996 Silent Marches on gun violence in Washington DC, and the establishment of the New Mexico "Not Even One Team: Not One Gun Death in Any Young Person." He was recently interviewed by Bill Moyers as part of the "Solutions to Violence" series that was broadcast nationally.

Pathways to Peace: Forty Steps to a Less Violent America was published in 1996. Its immediate popularity as a source of practical useful information helped propel Victor to national prominence as a widely acclaimed speaker and trainer. He is available to help your group, conference, or community move forward with a clear, research-based agenda for peacemaking.

Victor is an avid practitioner of Aikido, a Japanese martial art that accepts and then redirects aggressive energy so that neither the defender nor the attacker is injured. The father of two daughters, he cares deeply about preventing violence in America. He believes that solutions emerge in the process of strengthening all that is good within ourselves, our families, our communities, and our diverse cultures.

Humans
Everywhere
Allied in
Love

HEAL

"The mission of the HEAL Foundation is to promote positive change and progress in understanding and improving human relationships through educational and peacemaking information, materials, and programs, in the hope of establishing a more common ground for all people to interact in peace and prosperity."

Stephan McLaughlin, Jr.
HEAL Foundation
Executive Director

FOUNDATION GOALS

HEAL is an organization of people, who care about people, and who are committed to:

- Exploring fundamental elements and dynamics of human relationships;
- Identifying tools and techniques for encouraging healthier, happier relationships between individuals and themselves, their families, their friends, and their communities;
- Promoting healthier relationships by increasing people's awareness and use of these tools and techniques;
- Creating positive change by utilizing knowledge and understanding of relationships to assist in conflict resolution, community building, and addressing social issues and problems.

We believe all humans have the desire to increase their own health and happiness and to decrease their suffering. HEAL seeks to affirm and stimulate each individual's capacity to live in healthy relationships. Our work is based on the assumption that human relationships have similar dynamics and commonalities. People's lack of loving and nurturing relationship skills is at the heart of many pressing and disturbing problems that trouble our society.

We hold the belief that an improved understanding of our basic human characteristics and relationships are essential ingredients in understanding and dealing with many of the problems and challenges faced by individuals, families, societies, and even nations in the world community.

It is not our goal to present some form of ultimate truth. It is our hope that our work will help identify certain aspects of the human family that can be used to increase positive, harmonious human interaction while reducing negative, harmful human interaction.

Relationship formation and maintenance play major roles in defining us as people. In fact, a vast majority of our time is spent interacting in an incredible number and variety of relationships. Failure to form and sustain healthy relationships frequently leads to abusive relationships, which pose fundamental challenges to our individual and communal health.

Relationships are part of all aspects of our lives. We are involved in them at home, on the job, in the car, in our spiritual groups, even when we are alone. Looking at these activities and seeking to understand them better could open a new approach to living life, to connecting and communicating with people, to loving and nurturing those we care about, and to reducing and resolving conflicts with others.

Your interest and support of HEAL and its efforts are greatly appreciated. For more information, or to tell us about your important work in this area, please contact us at:

HEAL Foundation
Stephan McLaughlin Jr., Executive Director
3181 Poplar Avenue
Suite 315
Memphis, TN 38111
(901) 320-9179
or visit our web site: www.healfoundation.org

Order Form
Materials Available from the Author

ITEM	COST	QUANTITY
Worldwords: Global Reflections to Awaken the Spirit (1999)	$15	————
Pathways to Peace: Forty Steps to a Les Violent America (1996)	$15	————
Way of the Peacemaker: Parenting in the 1990s Great for parents, teachers and parenting classes. Live audience video (90 minutes)	$30	————
Way of the Peacemaker: Parenting in the 1990s Audiotape (90 minutes)	$15	————
World Peace Begins at Home Discussion of domestic violence issues, including adverse effects on children who witness, resiliency, and advice from battered women on how the helping professions can be of assistance. Double audiotape set.	$15	————
Brain Wisdom Summary of the latest brain research and its relevance to our lives in terms of education, parenting, stress reduction and peacemaking. Audiotape (90 minutes)	$15	————

No shipping charges if prepaid. Otherwise add $1.25 per item.
Call for quantity discounts/ship charges on more than 10 items: ————

To order more Worldwords or   **Enclosed:**
view other offerings,
please visit
myheartsongs.org

Please PRINT your address and include your phone number.